LOGIC
COURSE

The
LOGIC
COURSE

second edition

Steven DeHaven

broadview press

Canadian Cataloguing in Publication Data

DeHaven, Steven Lee, 1943-
    The logic course

2nd ed.

Includes index.
ISBN 1-55111-204-3

1. Logic. I. Title.

DC71.D4J 1998   160   C98-931291-7

Broadview Press Ltd. is an independent, international publishing house, incorporated in 1985.

North America:
P.O. Box 1243, Peterborough, Ontario, Canada K9H 7H5
3576 California Road, Orchard Park, NY, USA 14127
TEL: (705) 743-8990; FAX: (705) 743-8353; E-MAIL: 75322.44@compuserve.com

United Kingdom:
Turpin Distribution Services Ltd., Blackhorse Rd., Letchworth, Hertfordshire SG6 3HN
TEL: (1462) 672555; FAX (1462) 480947; E-MAIL: turpin@rsc.org

Australia:
St. Clair Press, P.O. Box 287, Rozelle, NSW 2039
TEL: (02) 818 1942; FAX: (02) 418 1923

www.broadviewpress.com

PRINTED IN CANADA

Contents

Preface to the Second Edition

This edition has been considerably expanded, extended, and rearranged. It now includes, in the introductory Chapter 1, a technique for diagramming arguments as well as an initial account of some basic concepts. The next three chapters cover analogy arguments, various kinds of statistical syllogisms, and miscellaneous fallacious arguments. These chapters and chapters 11 through 14 could be used for courses in which one did not wish to cover symbolic logic. Chapter 11 discusses probability, and Chapter 12 polling and other uses of samples. A number of elementary discussions of such statistical concepts as variance and standard deviations are also introduced in these chapters. Chapter 13 considers hypotheses and discusses some ways to evaluate them. Chapter 14 includes a discussion of games as well as decision-making.

The symbolic sequence begins in Chapter 5 with an informal presentation of such familiar rules as modus ponens. Chapter 6 introduces truth tables and symbolizing. Chapter 7 presents a natural deduction system for sentential logic. Chapter 8 discusses categorical logic and Venn diagrams. Chapter 9 introduces quantification theory, and Chapter 10 provides a natural deduction system. The discussion of derivations in quantification theory uses a system that is, we hope, a significant improvement on the one in the first edition.

The text is now backed up by software that can be used over the Internet or local area networks. A standalone version is also available. Both this software and the text are supported at **www.tmpst.com.**

I wish particularly to thank Eileen Eckert for her patient and professional editing job. All remaining errors are, of course, my fault — without her efforts there would be many, many more.

CHAPTER 1

Some Basic Concepts

All of us are familiar with reasoning; it is something in which we engage, for better or worse, throughout our lives. *The Logic Course* is primarily concerned with reasoning, and in particular with distinguishing between good and bad reasoning. This is part and parcel of learning how to think critically. In this chapter we shall introduce some of the basic concepts that will be used throughout the course.

1 / Recognizing and Identifying Arguments

1.1 / Arguments: Some Initial Considerations

Throughout much of the course we shall take as our primary, though not our sole, focus what we shall call "arguments". If someone says that people are arguing we tend to think of loud voices, of disagreement, of disputes. Our use of the term "argument", although not unrelated to this, does differ in a significant way. We shall take as an *argument* any sequence of statements that includes statements put forward as supporting another statement and the statement to which this support is given. Here is one example of an argument. Suppose that I say that purchases of goods will decline because taxes have been increased. I am here claiming that the fact that there has been a tax increase gives one reason to believe (supports the claim that) purchases of goods will decline. The statement to which we are giving support is the one we shall call the *conclusion* of the argument. In this case, that is the statement that purchases of goods will decline. Those statements (in this case there was only the one: that taxes have been increased) that are taken as identifying the support are the ones that we shall call the *premises* of the argument. Here is another argument:

> **If the team continues to lose, then attendance will drop even further.**
> **The team will continue to lose.**
> **So, attendance will drop even further.**

This argument has two premises and the conclusion that attendance will drop even further.

The kind of sentences or statements with which arguments are concerned are those that are either true or false. Typically, we utilize declarative sentences such as "The birds are now flying south" to make statements that are either true or false. We mean nothing special or mysterious when we speak of "truth" and "falsity". For example, the statement "my pet bird is now flying around" is a true statement if and only if my pet bird is now flying around. And it is a false statement if and only if my pet bird is not now flying around.

With some distortion (though not a great deal) we may say that our primary concern will be to develop the ability to determine whether and to what degree the premises of an argument do support the conclusion of that argument. As we shall see, this involves developing a number of other skills, for example, the ability to distinguish arguments from non-arguments and the ability to determine what kind of argument one is considering. Nonetheless, we are primarily concerned with distinguishing good from bad arguments. A good argument presents a case of good reasoning; a bad argument presents a case of faulty reasoning. As we shall see below, a number of factors are involved in determining whether or not an argument is a good one.

To speak of arguments as involving statements or sentences might suggest that we are in some sense concerned with merely verbal matters. What of evidence? What of experiments? What of scientific studies? Well, we are concerned with these. I point to the fingerprints of Jones on the murder weapon and note that they provide evidence that Jones indeed committed the crime in question. Do they? Is this good evidence? One way in which we shall concern ourselves with these sorts of questions is by way of asking whether the argument:

The fingerprints of Jones are on the murder weapon.
Therefore, Jones likely committed the crime.

is a good argument. We shall ask how much support the premise that Jones's fingerprints are on the murder weapon provides for the conclusion that he committed the crime. Think of the position of a juror. A juror is presented with testimony. The juror's task is then to assess the testimony, to determine what conclusion can legitimately be drawn from the testimony with which she is presented. We must, of course, consider certain other questions. If we are to determine whether or not a particular study shows that

Joe Camel encouraged smoking by kids we must have some idea as to what is required for the study to be a good one. Similarly, we will be in a better position to assess experimental evidence if we have some idea as to what makes for a well-designed experiment.

Do you believe in God? If you do, you will likely have reasons for this belief. Present these reasons as a list of statements. This list will function, in effect, as a list of premises. Present the statement that God exists as the conclusion drawn from this list of premises. Clearly, part of what is involved in your belief being a reasonable one is that the argument is a good one in at least the sense that the premises do actually support the conclusion. But the same point applies equally to more mundane beliefs. I believe it will not rain today. Why? Well, I look outside and see that there are no clouds of the sort I associate with rain. So I don't bother wearing my rain jacket to the university. I am viewing the argument that since there are no rain clouds there will be no rain as a good one. Our concern with arguments is a concern with matters that can range from the most abstract to the most practical.

Arguments can be assessed in a variety of ways. One obvious question we can ask is whether the premises of the argument are in fact true. Another question we can ask is whether the conclusion we put forward is true. Though we shall not completely ignore these questions, our concern will be primarily to develop techniques for determining the kind of support that premises provide for a conclusion. As we shall have ample occasion to see, the ability to assess the goodness of an argument is a significant part of what is involved in the search for truth. And presumably, most of us would prefer to have true beliefs rather than false ones.

If we lived in an ideal world, persuasiveness might well dovetail with the goodness of arguments. That is, people might accept only those claims that are supported by good arguments. We do not live in such a world, but we can hope that the ability to distinguish good from bad arguments will help us to avoid holding unfounded beliefs. It will also help us to avoid being duped, that is, to avoid being taken in by what appears to be a good argument but is not.

We shall look at many of these questions in more detail later; for the moment, we shall take a look at certain passages with an eye to determining whether or not they contain arguments. Again recall that we have an argument on our hands if certain statements are put forward as providing support for (providing reason to believe in the truth of) another statement that is identifiable as the conclusion.

One word of warning: a premise or a conclusion may be embedded in a larger context. Consider the following example:

I was walking down the street and noticed that there were paw marks in the mud. So, a dog must have passed by here recently.

This passage does contain an argument. The conclusion is that a dog must have passed by here recently. But the whole first sentence does *not* function as a premise. That I was walking down the street sets the stage, as it were, for the argument; it is not itself used to support the claim that a dog has passed by here recently. The working premise in the argument is that there were paw marks in the mud. So the argument itself might be presented as follows:

There were paw marks in the mud
So, a dog must have passed by here recently.

Keep this point in mind when you are asked to identify the premises and conclusion of an argument. There is a further point to keep in mind. In saying that a passage contains an argument, we are not saying that the author of the passage is necessarily committed to accepting the argument, that is, to accepting the truth of either the premises or the conclusion. Consider the following passage:

You know what happened in class today? The professor claimed that abortion is sometimes permissible, since it is sometimes a case of self-defense and self-defense is always permissible.

The argument of the professor is, as we shall say, contained in the passage. The student is presenting us with the argument, but is not endorsing it. The argument that the professor stated may be formulated as follows:

Abortion is sometimes a case of self-defense.
Self-defense is always permissible.
So, abortion is sometimes permissible.

And sometimes arguments are put forward as merely hypothetical, or as arguments to be considered. Here is an example:

I was trying to decide how to vote and was wondering what would happen if the left-wingers came into power.

> **I thought that someone might claim the following. If they came into power they would indulge in their free-spending habits. If they did freely spend, there would be a great increase in the deficit. So, if the left-wingers came into power, there would be a great increase in the deficit.**

Notice that the person speaking is merely taking note of an argument that someone might put forward. The imaginary someone is taken to be supporting the conclusion that if the left-wingers came into power, there would be a great increase in the deficit. The person speaking is not herself endorsing either the argument or the conclusion.

As you proceed, then, keep the following points in mind. In an argument certain statements, the premises, are put forward as supporting a conclusion. The goal of argumentation is then to provide premises that actually provide support for the conclusion. In many oral or written passages the author is herself endorsing the arguments presented, but in some she is not. The author of the passage may be reporting someone else's argument, or simply putting it forward for consideration without herself endorsing it. But in all these cases we shall say that the passage contains an argument. And you should always remember that even if a passage contains an argument, not everything said in the passage need function as either a premise or a conclusion. Before continuing our study of arguments we shall look at some of the other functions of language.

1.2 / Non-argumentative Functions of Language

Actual discourse, actual passages, may be complex and difficult to analyze. There are many kinds of complexity and kinds of difficulty that we may encounter. For example, a passage need not contain an argument at all, or at the very least it may be difficult to determine whether it does contain an argument. In this section we shall attempt to give a brief (and necessarily incomplete) survey of some of the more obvious non-argumentative functions of discourse. Recall that in speaking of these as non-argumentative, we are saying that they do not involve putting forward a statement or group of statements as providing support for another.

1.2.1 / Description

Consider the following passage:

> He and his wife, the old lady who had received me, looked
> at each other in a frightened sort of way. He mumbled out
> that the money had been sent in a letter, and that was all
> he knew. When I asked him if he knew Count Dracula, and
> could tell me anything of his castle, both he and his wife
> crossed themselves, and, saying that they knew nothing at
> all, simply refused to speak further. It was so near the time
> of starting that I had no time to ask anyone else, for it was
> all very mysterious and not by any means comforting.
> — Bram Stoker, *Dracula*

This passage clearly does *not* contain any argument. It is a part of a narration and is of the sort that we shall call *description*. There are passages that are more difficult to analyze:

> Contemporary society suffers from many defects. The
> economy is growing, but not in a way which helps the
> poor. There are still far too many single-parent families,
> and the incidence of teen-age pregnancy is still far too
> high. While crime in general may be decreasing, teen-age
> and even earlier crime is increasing.

This passage includes a number of claims. Some may well be controversial; some may well be false. They no doubt need defense. But the author is not in this case providing that defense. The author is listing what she takes to be defects. You might think that she is wrong. Not everyone, for example, considers that having a great number of single-parent families is a "defect". She and you might go on to argue about whether it is a defect, and you might ask her to support the claim that there are far too many single-parent families. But, again, in this passage she is simply making the various claims, not arguing for them. So this passage is one that we will count as a description.

In order to better understand this, consider the following passage that, you will note, is very similar to the preceding one:

> Contemporary society is defective. You don't believe it?
> Consider the following facts. The economy is growing, but
> not in a way which helps the poor. There are still far too
> many single-parent families, and the incidence of teen-age
> pregnancy is still far too high. While crime in general may
> be decreasing, teen-age and even earlier crime is increasing.

We would count this passage as an argument. The "facts" are cited as providing support — evidence — for the claim that contemporary society is defective. This claim is the conclusion of the argument. The "facts" function as premises in this passage. But in the previous passage they were functioning as illustrations.

1.2.2 / Explanation

Often we are concerned neither with providing evidence that something happened nor with giving a description of what happened, but instead with explaining why something happened. My air conditioner goes off. I look around and notice that the plug has come out. I say to myself:

> **The air conditioner went off because it no longer has any power.**

I am not trying to cite evidence for the claim that the air conditioner went off. I already know that. I am instead explaining why that happened. So this passage is one which contains what we call an *explanation*. Suppose my television set is unplugged. I see someone heading for the set intending, I know, to turn it on. I say to that person:

> **Don't bother. It won't come on. It is unplugged.**

Here, I suggest, we would best view the passage as an argument. I am providing that person with evidence for the claim that the set won't come on. Our classification is context-dependent. Suppose instead that the person had gotten to the television set and pushed the on switch. It fails to come on. The person, somewhat annoyed, stands staring at the set. I say to him:

> **Don't worry. It's not broken. It's unplugged.**

Here I am providing the person with an explanation of the failure of the set to come on. Now consider the following more extended passage:

> **Steven went to the store very early this morning and bought some milk. That is not nearly so odd as you might think. He woke up early and desperately wanted some coffee. He had the coffee but noticed that he was out of milk. You know, of course, that he intensely dislikes coffee without milk.**

This passage is in part a description. But it also contains an explanation — namely that he went to the store because he wanted milk for his coffee. We are not here trying to *defend* the claim that he went to the store. Contrast this passage with the following one:

> **Hmm, I wonder where Steven is. Oh, I bet he went to the store. I see that we are out of milk, and he always wants milk with his morning coffee.**

Here the speaker is providing evidence for the claim that Steven has gone to the store. So we would classify this passage as one containing an argument.

It is not always easy to determine whether something is an argument or an explanation. Consider the following remarks:

> **Sex without condoms is unsafe. Physical contact can transmit AIDS.**

Without further information about the context in which this is said, we are unable to decide whether to classify this as an argument or as an explanation. Let us consider some possible contexts. Suppose you encounter someone who you know indulges in sex without condoms. You are quite amazed by this, so you say the above. In this sort of case it would, I think, be best to classify the remarks as an argument. You are providing that person with evidence that the practice is unsafe. Suppose instead that a person had walked up to you and said that while he understands that sex without condoms is unsafe, he really doesn't see what difference a thin layer of latex makes. In response you replied with the above remarks. In this case it would, I think, be best to classify the remarks as an explanation. That sex without condoms is unsafe is being taken for granted — it is not in this context being taken as a statement needing support. You are trying to explain why it is unsafe, why the thin latex might make a difference.

Finally, suppose that we are in a Grade Five sex education class. One of the fifth graders says that he doesn't see why thin layers of latex matter at all. In response the teacher says:

> **Sex without condoms is unsafe. Physical contact can transmit AIDS.**

Here it might be appropriate to view the teacher's remarks as both an argument and an explanation. That is, he might be trying to support the claim that sex without condoms is unsafe — the second statement is meant to support that claim — but the support he offers might also be intended to give his students an account of why it is unsafe, and the second statement also does that.

Our distinction between arguments and explanations does not precisely coincide with some of the ways in which the terms are used. A critical point is that we speak of an argument in those cases where one is providing evidence or support for a claim, or when one is defending a claim. Suppose you ask a salesperson why a particular computer is a good one. She states that it has a high speed CPU, a large hard drive, and so on. We might well ordinarily characterize the salesperson as explaining why the computer is a good one. But we will *not* classify this as an explanation; instead we will classify it as an argument. In this context, the salesperson is giving us reasons to accept the claim that the computer is a good one: she is defending that claim. Similarly, consider a situation in which you are considering who to hire. Someone might say that Garcia is clearly the best candidate, since she has the most experience of any of the candidates. Here again, we might say that the person is explaining why Garcia is the best candidate. But we will *not* classify this as an explanation, but rather as an argument. The person is defending the claim that Garcia is the best candidate. Given that the statement provides a defense, given that a case is being made, we shall classify this as an argument.

Our notion of an explanation is closely related to the notion of specifying causes. Consider the following passage:

> **Her driver must have been drinking because alcohol was found in his bloodstream.**

Here, we should be able to see that we have an argument rather than an explanation. Drinking does bring it about that the drinker will have alcohol in his or her bloodstream. But, typically, the presence of alcohol in a person's bloodstream does not bring it about that he or she had been drinking. So here we have an argument: the alcohol in the bloodstream is evidence that the person had been drinking. But typically:

> **There is alcohol in his blood because he was drinking.**

would be an explanation.

1.2.3 / Advice

Consider the following:

> **Your tires are very bald. If I were you, I would get some new ones.**

The speaker is suggesting that the listener do something. We shall classify this as a case of giving *advice* or a recommendation. Advice is intimately related to argumentation. That is, when one gives advice one is typically prepared to present an argument including reasons that would provide a ground for the advice and that would indicate why the advice is reasonable advice. In this example, the argument would involve noting that bald tires are subject to blow-outs and decrease one's ability to control the car. These, of course, put the driver and passengers at risk. The risk would be the ground for the advice, since, typically, advice is oriented toward what the speaker views as being in the interest of the person to whom the advice is given. In our example the speaker has not actually presented any argument, though typically he would be prepared to do so if asked. That is why we classify this passage as only a case of advice.

Consider the following passage:

> **There are lots of clouds in the west. So it will probably snow.**
> **I think you should postpone your trip**

This passage contains an argument and some advice. The argument is that it will likely snow since there are lots of clouds in the west. The advice is that you should postpone your trip. The ground for this advice would most likely be the dangers inherent in snow-covered roads.

1.2.4 / Command

Suppose you are a soldier. Your commanding officer says:

> **Do twenty push-ups.**

The officer is indeed trying to get you to do something. But he is not merely advising or recommending that you do the push-ups. He is issuing an order, or as we shall say, a *command*. He certainly is not presenting an argument. Commands are issued in contexts wherein the person giving the command has some sort of right or authority to do so. As the author of this book I can certainly advise you to read it carefully and to practice a fair amount. But I have no authority over you and consequently am not in a position to command or to order you to do so. Consider the position of an instructor. Sometimes, in class, students talk rather loudly among themselves. The instructor typically has the authority to tell them to shut up. This is not to say, as I know from experience, that they will do so, but the instructor can issue the order. But what the instructor tells you about studying and the like typically counts as advice. Sometimes we speak of "doctor's orders" such as, to me, "quit smoking". However, since my doctor does not have authority over me, he can only give me advice. By contrast, in a hospital, a doctor is typically in a position to give orders to a nurse.

1.2.5 / Request

What we shall call a *request* differs from a command in that the person making the request either does not have the authority to command you or is not at the point in question exercising that authority. Another way in which a typical request differs from typical advice is that what one requests of another need not be supposed to be for the benefit of the person to whom the request is directed. In the preceding section we considered the case of the instructor who ordered the disruptive students to shut up. Personally I do this as a last resort. Initially I might say:

Please stop talking.

Here I am simply requesting the students to stop talking. I am not here invoking any authority I have to order them to stop talking. If you ask someone for a favor, that is a case of a request.

1.2.6 / Exhortation

Consider the following passages:

Do you want to be saved? Turn to the Lord. Do you want to be saved? Trust in the Lord.

Don't be left out. Order now. This fantastic offer will end today.

In cases of this sort the speaker is endeavoring to get you to do or accept something. In this respect these cases are similar to cases of advice, commands, and requests. How, then, do they differ from these? They are not commands since there is no invocation of authority over you. They differ from advice and requests in that they are attempts, as we shall put it, to *move* you to do or accept something by way of the use of some psychological device. For example, the second attempts to appeal to the desire, which many people have, not to be left out, not to miss out. The first may be spoken by a skilled speaker who has the ability to get his audience completely involved in the situation. In either case the persons who are speaking might have arguments but they are not presented, and the appeals are not efforts at persuasion by way of argumentation. They are presenting what we call *ex-hortations*.

Many advertisements are cases of exhortation. These are designed to move or persuade us to buy a product without providing us with any arguments defending the claim that we should do so. Think of, for example, so-called lifestyle ads. In some beer commercials one sees attractive people having a wonderful time while swilling Brand X. It is clear that such ads do not function by way of persuading us by the presentation of evidence. To understand the theory behind advertisements, to understand how and why they are meant to move us, is an interesting study, but one that lies beyond the scope of this text. Do note, however, that we cannot automatically label every "sales pitch" an exhortation. We are in some cases presented with an argument as to why we should purchase a product. In a previous example a computer sales person was defending the claim that the computer in question was a good one.

Some situations involve a mix of requests, commands, and exhortation. One familiar example arises in conversations between parents and children. Parents do have some right to tell their children what to do, but often, when the child is being rather stubborn, the parent will mix requests, commands, and exhortations.

1.2.7 / Other

As noted at the outset, it is not our intent to attempt anything like a complete survey of the uses to which language can be put. For example, if I promise to do something, I am not arguing, nor am I saying anything that falls into any of the previous categories. Our category of *other* is just a "none of the above" answer. When we come to look at actual passages, we may often be in a position to explain precisely what is going on. (In this case, we might simply note that the person is making a promise.) We shall not, then, introduce any more labels, but instead rely upon our ability to characterize what is going on in a given passage.

1.3 / Clues to the Presence of an Argument

Many languages, including English, provide us with words and phrases that provide clues to both the presence and the structure of an argument. We shall call these words ***indicators***. Some indicators typically introduce a premise and others typically introduce a conclusion. However, as we shall see, we must exercise some care, since these words and phrases do not invariably play those roles.

Consider the following arguments:

> **The government will call an election soon, since they are riding high in the polls and their time is running out.**
> [In parliamentary systems like those of Canada and Great Britain, elections are not held on a fixed schedule. There is a maximum time, but the government can call an election at any point during that period.]

> **The incumbent will lose in the election, since her approval rating is so low.**

In both of these cases that which follows the word "since" is functioning as a premise. "Since" is one of the words that typically indicates that what follows is functioning as a premise. We shall call such words ***premise indicators***.

However, consider the following claim:

> **The score has changed since you last looked at the game.**

Pretty clearly we don't here have an argument. Rather, the word "since" is indicating a temporal order. The claim has the same meaning as:

> **The score changed after you last looked at the game.**

Now consider the following case:

> **I went to the store since I needed some bread.**

Here we do not have an argument, but an explanation. I am not attempting to establish that I went to the store or provide evidence that I did. The word "since" is introducing information meant to explain why I went to the store. It will sometimes be a bit difficult to decide whether "since" is introducing a premise or an explanatory factor. Consider the following:

> **The liquid turned the litmus paper pink since it is an acid and acids turn litmus paper pink.**

The problem here is one that was discussed above when we introduced our category of explanation. We would classify this "since" as a premise indicator, if, in the context in which these statements are made, the speaker were trying to support the claim that the liquid did turn the litmus paper pink. But imagine that someone is staring at the litmus paper, clearly wondering why it is turning pink. In this case the speaker would be giving an account of why that is happening. And, recalling our discussion of the Grade Five sex education class, we can likely construct cases in which it would be appropriate to say that the "since" is functioning to introduce both premises and explanatory factors.

All that we can do is to try to determine whether what follows the "since" is meant to be evidence for something, to give one reason to believe something, or not. If, in the context in question, what precedes the "since" is being taken for granted or is not something that one is trying to establish, then we do not have an argument. There may well be cases that are tough to decide, but usually a bit of common sense and a bit of thought will suffice to enable us to determine what is going on. Of course, as we noted in the preceding paragraph, more than one thing may be going on.

The word "because" is like the word "since" in that it sometimes introduces a premise, sometimes an explanatory factor, and sometimes both. Again, there is no magic means by which to say for sure what is going on. We must use a bit of common sense and thought. And we must recognize that there may be cases that are genuinely indeterminate. Nonetheless, the presence of words like "since" and "because" does inform us that we have a passage with structure, a passage which is more than a set of claims.

We have seen that "since" and "because" frequently introduce premises. Here is a more complete list of the words and phrases that typically do so as well:

Premise Indicators

as, as shown by, as indicated by, given that, for,
for the reason that, assuming that,
on the assumption that, can be inferred from,
is implied by, since, because

Again, though, we cannot simply be mechanical. While these words and phrases typically signal the presence of a premise, they do not invariably do so. And of course this list can make no claim to completeness.

There is a further point to be kept in mind. Consider the following passage:

The test will be given on Monday. I should do pretty well on it, since I am always at my best on Mondays.

The conclusion of this argument is that I should do pretty well on the test. That I am always at my best on Mondays is indeed one of the premises. But that the test will be given on Monday is a premise as well. An argument may contain, in addition to those premises introduced by an indicator, other statements that function as premises. How can one tell which other statements are functioning as premises? Well, we decide in our ordinary way. We ask ourselves whether they are put forward as providing support for the claim that we have identified as the conclusion.

We have just looked at some premise indicators. As you might expect, there are conclusion indicators as well. Here is a list of some common words and phrases that often are used to introduce a conclusion:

Conclusion Indicators

therefore, so, hence, consequently, it follows that, in conclusion, accordingly, entails that, implies that, thus, leads one to believe that, demonstrates that, shows that

---

But care must be exercised in connection with these. Consider:

I tell you that God is in his heaven and all is well. In conclusion, I can only say that the life of faith is a joyous one.

Pretty obviously, the speaker is not here arguing. The "in conclusion" does not indicate the conclusion of any argument; it merely indicates that the speaker is closing her remarks. But common sense should typically enable us to determine whether a word or phrase is, in any particular case, indicating the conclusion of an argument. But do not suppose either that our list is complete or that it is one that can be applied in a mechanical fashion.

1.4 / More Complex Structures

Our approach hitherto has, in a variety of ways, drastically oversimplified the task of identifying the argument or arguments present in a given passage. In this section we shall attempt to point out some of the ways in which it has been oversimplified. And we will introduce the strategy that will be utilized to "pull" the arguments out of passages as well as a diagramming technique that we can use to represent the structure of arguments.

1.4.1 / Extraneous Material

Consider the following passage:

> **The ambassador is coming to the party. I think you have met him before. At any rate, whenever he comes the party is a great success. So, the party will be a great success.**

This passage clearly contains an argument. That the party will be a great success is the conclusion of the argument. But what are the premises? If you consider the passage, you should see that the second sentence is *not* playing the role of a premise. It is serving as a reminder to the person being addressed, not as evidence that the party will be a success. Even if a passage does contain an argument, not all that is contained in the passage will necessarily be either a premise or a conclusion. How does one tell what is what? As we have noted before, the basic consideration (assuming that one has picked out the conclusion) is whether it is at all plausible to suppose that a given statement is being put forward as providing support for the conclusion in question. It may be possible to decide by leaving the statement out of the passage and seeing whether what remains is a candidate for being a good argument. Let's try that with this argument:

> **The ambassador is coming to the party. At any rate, whenever he comes the party is a great success. So, the party will be a great success.**

As you should see, we have here a good argument even though we have left out the second statement. It does not provide any additional support for the conclusion.

But we are again in a situation where there are no magic rules. We must in the end rely upon common sense and thought.

1.4.2 / How Many Conclusions? Some Initial Cases

When we examine a passage, we must, of course, decide whether it contains any arguments at all. But, supposing that it does, we must then determine whether or not the passage has one "overall" conclusion. Let us consider this in more detail, as there are various situations that can arise.

Consider the following case:

> **The lights just went off. The television won't come on. The circuit breaker must have tripped.**

Here we have a straightforward argument, albeit not necessarily a good one. There is a single conclusion and two premises. We will represent such an argument with the following diagram:

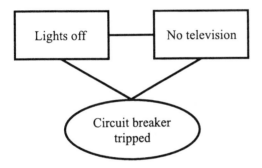

Here we enter the premises into rectangular boxes and conclusions into ovals. The connecting lines indicate that we have one argument with two premises.

But now consider the following case.

> **The leaves are changing color. It must be fall. Oh, and there is that characteristic chill in the air.**

Here the conclusion is that it must be fall. But here the arguer might seem to be presenting two simple arguments for that conclusion. One is that it must be fall since the leaves are changing color. The other is that it must be fall because there is that characteristic chill in the air. We might diagram such arguments as follows:

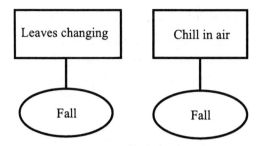

But instead we will typically present the arguments of this sort as follows:

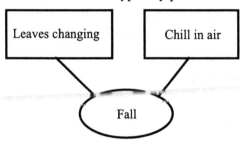

Here the absence of a line connecting the two premise boxes indicates that they are being taken as individually supporting the conclusion. So this single diagram indicates that we have two arguments. While the wording in the passage is compatible with our supposing that we have two arguments for the claim that it is fall, it is also compatible with our deciding that we have only one argument with two premises. Here we are viewing the speaker as stating his second premise in an afterthought. In this case the argument would be diagrammed as follows:

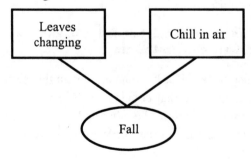

Note that in this diagram we have drawn lines connecting the premises, thereby indicating that we have one argument with two premises.

How do we tell whether to treat a passage as containing a number of arguments for a given conclusion or as containing a single argument with a number of premises? We are, unfortunately, in another one of those situations where there is no magical rule. Here are some guidelines that are of some use. If we find that we have at least a candidate for a good argument when we treat the passage as containing a single argument with multiple premises but a set of obviously bad arguments if we treat it otherwise, then it is best to treat it as containing a single argument. In general we try to be as charitable as we can to the person presenting the argument. That is, we try to construe the passage as containing the best argument or arguments that it can plausibly be supposed to contain. In this case it would seem that construing the passage as containing one argument with two premises gives the most credit to the speaker. But there may be cases (perhaps this is one) where there is no way of deciding how best to construe the passage.

A passage may contain more than one conclusion. Here is one simple case:

Mehul likely will not be in town on the day of the party.
He will probably be taking care of his father, who is ill.
However, Sarah will come. At least she said that she would.

We have two distinct arguments, with separate premises for both. So two diagrams would represent this passage.

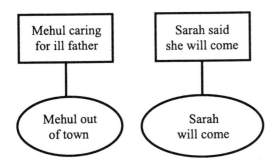

Consider now a very simplified murder case. The prosecution states the following:

The accused had the motive. The accused had the opportunity. So there is a good chance that she did it.

Here it seems clear that we have one argument with two premises. So this argument would be represented as follows:

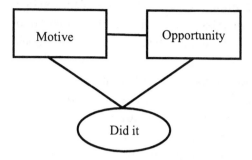

Contrast this with the following case:

You will not do well in the class. It meets early, and you have always done poorly in those. It is also a math class, and you have always done poorly in those.

The conclusion here is clearly that you will not do well in the class. But here it would seem that the best reconstruction is to view this passage as containing two distinct arguments for that conclusion:

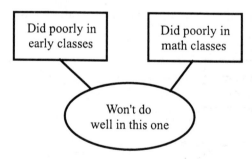

I decided to treat this as two distinct arguments since each premise does on its own provide decent support for the conclusion. But if you look back, the same might well be said of the passage above in which the leaves were changing color and there was a nip in the air. That we treated as one argument. For now we can only suggest that you reconstruct using your best judgment as to what the arguer is attempting and that you be prepared to defend your answer. We shall return to this sort of problem at various points in later chapters and, briefly, in the examples that follow.

At this point we may stop for a moment to consider the question of how we shall count premises. To see what this means, consider the following two arguments:

> **The bird is flying around the room. The turtle is walking on the floor of that room. Therefore, there are at least two animals in the room.**

> **The bird is flying around the room and the turtle is walking on the floor of that room. Therefore, there are at least two animals in the room.**

Clearly, these arguments are much the same. But they differ in one respect: we shall count the first as having two premises, and the second as having a single premise. To be sure, the statement that is the premise in the second is a complex one, but it is nonetheless a single statement. In reconstructing an argument we shall try to stay as close as possible to the way in which the person presents the argument. The first argument is diagrammed as:

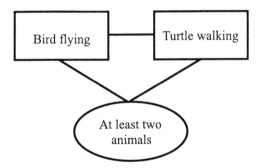

The second argument is diagrammed as:

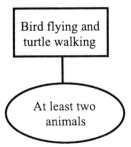

Let us look again at the first argument here, keeping in mind the question discussed previously as to how we decide whether we have single arguments with a number of premises or a number of arguments with the same conclusion. Note that in this case it would be unreasonable to assume that the author of the passage supposes that one can argue, for example, that the premise that there is a turtle walking in the room leads by itself to the conclusion that there are at least two animals in the room. So here we clearly have a single argument with two premises.

1.4.3 / How Many Conclusions? Some More Complex Cases

In many cases the argumentative structure of passages is much more complex than the structure of the passages we have been examining. Consider the following passage:

> Since the ambassador is coming to the party, it will be a great success. But if a party is a success, then people will eat and drink a lot. So people will be eating and drinking a lot.

This passage has what we will call an overall conclusion, namely that people will be eating and drinking a lot. But there are two arguments present. The first can be diagrammed as follows:

The second argument has as its conclusion what we spoke of as the overall conclusion, that people will eat and drink a lot. One premise for this argument is that if a party is a success, then people will eat and drink a lot. But the other premise for this argument is the statement that the party will be a great success — the statement that is the conclusion for the first argument. Viewing this second argument on its own we could diagram it as:

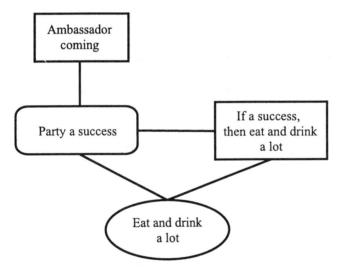

But presenting the passage in this way does not give us a good "picture" of the structure of this passage. So we will now extend our diagramming techniques and diagram the arguments as follows:

Notice that the statement that the party will be a success has been placed in a rounded rectangle. We shall utilize these in those cases where a given statement is functioning as both a premise and a conclusion. It is a conclusion from the premise that the ambassador is coming. It is then used as one of the two premises which lead to the overall conclusion that people will be eating and drinking a lot. Notice that the statement that the ambassador is coming is *not* itself a premise for the conclusion that people will eat and drink a lot. It is only a premise for the conclusion that the party will be a success. That statement, as we just noted, *is* a premise for the conclusion that people will eat and drink a lot. In terms of the diagrams we will stipulate that any premise "above" a particular rounded rectangle is not a premise for any conclusion "below" that particular rounded rectangle.

We spoke above of an "overall" conclusion. This notion remains in need of some explanation. We count a conclusion in a passage as an overall conclusion just in case it does not also function as a premise in that passage. Note that this allows that a passage may have more than one overall conclusion. But this should engender no confusion so long as you remember that overall conclusions are simply ones that do not also serve as premises.

As you can probably guess, passages can contain any number of arguments of any degree of complexity. Let us look at some more examples to get some feel for the varieties of structures we may encounter. Consider the following.

> **The watershed will be endangered since they will use clear-cut logging. Since they will use clear-cut logging, much of the animal life will cease to exist. If the watershed is endangered and if much of the animal life has ceased to exist, then we will not benefit economically. So, we will not benefit economically.**

Here the overall conclusion is that we will not benefit economically.

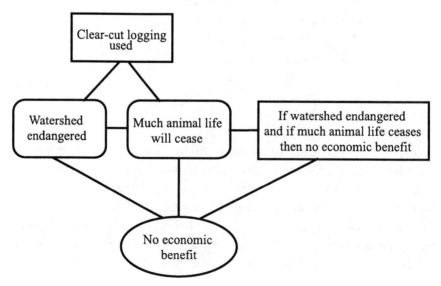

That clear-cut logging will be used functions as a premise for the conclusion that the watershed will be endangered and as a premise for the conclusion that much animal life will cease. These two statements also function as premises for the argument that has the overall conclusion that there will be no economic benefit. This argument also includes the claim in the rectangle on the right as a premise.

Identifying the structure of arguments in complex passages is not an easy task. As we proceed in the text, we will on many further occasions work on developing this skill.

1.5 / Missing Premises and Missing Conclusions

When we speak or write we don't typically say all that could be said. The same often happens when arguments are presented. Consider the following:

I have to go to Ottawa. So, I will be in Canada.

This short argument exhibits a feature shared by many arguments: one of its premises is unstated. Such arguments have come to be known as "enthymemes", but we shall not continue to use this term. Instead we will speak of arguments with missing premises, or of *incomplete arguments*. In this particular case it is clear that the argument has a premise that has not been stated: that Ottawa is in Canada. Other cases, as we shall see, are a bit more difficult.

There are various reasons why a premise may be omitted. One fairly common one, manifest in the preceding example, is that the presenter of the argument may take the premise to be so obvious to his audience that it is not worth stating. Less commonly, it may be that the premise is dubious and the arguer hopes that those she is addressing will overlook the fact that the argument does need the dubious claim. We will be looking at examples of these, but you might be wondering how we determine that there is a missing premise and how we identify it. One principle is that we decide what *kind* of argument the argument is meant to be. We shall later on be looking at various kinds of arguments, and will see how we can, once we have classified an argument, often identify missing premises. Another principle, albeit one that provides only a rough and ready guide, is that we look for something that will give an incomplete argument enough plausibility to make it worth assessing. We may view ourselves as asking how the arguer might plausibly be supposed to have gotten to the conclusion. All of this is to say that the identification of missing premises presupposes that we have some sense of what kinds of arguments there are and what makes arguments good and bad.

Consider the following argument:

> **Since there is a cat in the house, your bird will be safe only if it is in its cage.**

Clearly, several things are being taken for granted. Let us focus on one of them. The premise mentions that there is a cat in the house. Why? We might note that the following argument seems a bit peculiar:

> **Since there is a snail in the house, your bird will be safe only if it is in its cage.**

Noticing how peculiar this argument is should help us to identify one premise in the original argument: that cats pose a danger to birds. There seems to be no similar claim that could be made regarding snails. The second argument seems peculiar because we cannot easily imagine how a snail could endanger a bird. Surely, though, the missing premise is not that all cats always attack birds — this just isn't a very plausible claim. When we are trying to reconstruct arguments we should try to identify as missing premises claims that are as plausible as possible. (It won't always be possible to identify a plausible missing premise. People do sometimes hold silly views and do sometimes present silly arguments. I suppose it is conceivable that there is someone who believes in vicious mutant snails that delight in munching on birds. I doubt this, but many people do hold equally bizarre beliefs.) In the case of the initial argument a plausible missing premise is that cats pose some threat to birds that are not in their cages. So we could reconstruct the argument as follows:

> **There is a cat in the house.**
> **Cats pose some threat to birds that are not in their cages.**
> **So, your bird will be safe only if it is in its cage.**

Sometimes we will encounter arguments in which the conclusion is unstated. Such incomplete arguments are not so common as those with missing premises, but they do occur. Consider the following:

> **No one should cast the first stone unless that person is without sin. You are not without sin.**

It is clear that here the unstated conclusion is that you should not cast the first stone.

2 / Classifying and Assessing Arguments

One of the primary concerns in this course is to develop techniques for the assessment of arguments, that is, to develop techniques whereby we can distinguish between good and bad reasoning. In order to do this we shall develop a classification scheme. This section is concerned with some of the basic distinctions, with certain broad classifications of arguments that relate directly to the way in which arguments should be assessed.

2.1 / Deductive Logic

Consider the following argument:

> **All students who are enrolled in this class will be required to attend tutorials. You are enrolled in this class. So, you will be required to attend tutorials.**

This is an example of the sort of argument that we are concerned with when we study *deductive logic*. It is one in which the premises at least purport to provide conclusive support for the conclusion. In deductive logic we study the conditions in which the premises of an argument do provide conclusive support for the conclusion. We shall call arguments in which the conclusion is put forward as following from the premises, in which the premises at least purport to provide conclusive support for the conclusion, *would-be deductive arguments*. Here is another argument:

> **If he speaks French, then he is a good student. If he speaks English, then he is a good student. He is a good student. So he speaks either French or English.**

This is also a would-be deductive argument. Its premises purport to provide conclusive support for the conclusion.

We will assess would-be deductive arguments as *valid* or *invalid*. A *valid argument* is an argument in which the premises *do* provide conclusive support for the conclusion. The first argument above, which concerned enrolled students, is a valid argument. It is of critical importance to note that in speaking of conclusive support, in speaking of an argument as valid, we are *not* claiming that the premises of our argument are in fact true. What we are claiming is that *if* the premises were all true, then the conclusion would have to be true. Equivalently, we are claiming that there is no possibility that all the premises are true while the conclusion is false. Or, also equivalently, we are claiming that the conclusion follows from the premises. Our second argument, the one that concerned the good student, is, as we saw, a would-be deductive argument. But it is *not* a valid argument. We shall speak of would-be deductive arguments that are *not* valid as ***invalid arguments***. Invalid arguments are those would-be deductive arguments in which the premises do *not* conclusively support the conclusion; the premises could all be true while the conclusion was false.

Let us consider some more cases. First consider the following:

> **Only the good die young. Phil is good, so he will of course die young.**

This is an invalid argument. I doubt that the first premise is true, but that is *not* the basis for my claim that it is invalid. My claim is based upon my judgment, one that we will later learn how to defend, that the conclusion does not follow from those premises. Consider next:

> **All who are good die young. Phil is good, so he will of course die young.**

This argument *is* valid. I doubt here, as in the case of the first argument, that the initial premise is true. Some good people (I think of myself as one) do not die young. But this doubt is irrelevant to the assessment of the argument as a valid one. It is valid because the premises do provide conclusive support for the conclusion — were they all true the conclusion would have to be true as well.

So, two stages are involved initially. We first determine whether an argument is a would-be deductive one. That is, we determine whether it is one in which the premises at least purport to provide conclusive support for the conclusion. In the preceding example the presence of the phrase "of course" was the clue that the argument was to be classified as such. Given that the argument is a would-be deductive one, we then proceed to attempt to determine whether it is valid or invalid.

We will add one more concept to our current repertoire. A would-be deductive argument is ***sound*** if and only if it is valid and has true premises. If such argument is ***unsound***, then either it is invalid or it has at least one false premise.

A more detailed study of arguments of this sort will be undertaken in later chapters, but even at this point we can give some account of why the concept of validity is important. Why is it that we don't just ask whether a claim is true or false and leave it at that? Consider the following argument:

> **If there were a perfect being who created the universe, then the universe would contain no useless suffering. The universe does contain useless suffering. Therefore, it is not the case that there is a perfect being who created the universe.**

This argument *is* a valid one. Given that it is valid, any further discussion of it must proceed in a particular way. If, for example, we hold the conclusion to be false, we are thereby committed to the view that one or both of the premises are false. Since it is valid, the conclusion would have to be true were both the premises to be true. If we hold that it is sound, that is, both valid and having true premises, we would, if challenged, proceed by way of trying to show (assuming our challenger knows the argument to be valid) that the premises are indeed true.

Contrast the preceding case with this one:

> **Whenever interest rates decrease the dollar declines. Look at the news. The dollar is declining. So interest rates are no doubt decreasing.**

Here again we have an argument in which the premises purport to provide conclusive support for the conclusion. The use of "no doubt" is one indication that the speaker is claiming that the conclusion follows from the premises. But this argument is *invalid*. These premises, even if true, do not support the conclusion. The conclusion might be true, indeed at the time of writing this it was true. But that is neither here nor there. When we are assessing such arguments we are initially concerned with the question of whether the premises give the claimed support to the conclusion. Here the premises of the argument do not, even if all true, give you any reason to believe that the conclusion is true. Were you to be presented with this argument you would be completely justified in pointing out to the person who presented it that there is little point in discussing the question of whether the premises are true or false. There is little point in doing that because, given that the argument is invalid, we already know that the conclusion might be false even if the premises are true. In any case in which you are presented with an invalid argument it is legitimate to ask the person presenting the invalid argument to go back to the drawing board and present you with a valid argument. If a valid argument were presented, then a discussion of whether the premises are true would have some point.

We may summarize what has been discussed in this section as follows. If a would-be deductive argument is valid, then we have three possible situations:

Possibilities If an Argument is Valid

(1) The premises are all true and the conclusion is true.
(2) Not all the premises are true (that is, one or more of the premises are false) and the conclusion is true.
(3) Not all the premises are true (that is, one or more of the premises are false) and the conclusion is false.

Hence, if an argument is valid we are in either situation (1) or (2) or (3). What we know for sure is that if an argument is valid, we are *not* in the situation in which all the premises are true and the conclusion is false. If an argument is sound, it both is valid and has true premises. Consequently, if an argument is sound we must be in situation (1). If, on the other hand, an argument is invalid we have four possible situations:

Possibilities If an Argument is Invalid

(1) The premises are all true and the conclusion is true.
(2) Not all the premises are true (that is, one or more of the premises is false) and the conclusion is true.
(3) Not all the premises are true (that is, one or more of the premises is false) and the conclusion is false.
(4) The premises are all true and the conclusion is false.

Note that even if we know that the premises of an invalid argument are true we still do not know whether we are in situation (1) or situation (4). That is why we need pay no attention to invalid arguments save to note that they are invalid.

2.2 / Inductive (Non-deductive) Reasoning

Consider the following excerpt from a Sherlock Holmes story. The initial speaker is Doctor Watson:

> **"I wonder what that fellow is looking for?"** I asked, pointing to a stalwart, plainly-dressed individual who was walking slowly down the other side of the street, looking anxiously at the numbers. He had a large blue envelope in his hand, and was evidently the bearer of a message.
>
> **"You mean the retired sergeant of Marines,"** said Sherlock Holmes.
>
> **"Brag and bounce!"** thought I to myself. "He knows that I cannot verify his guess."
>
> The thought had hardly passed through my mind when the man whom we were watching caught sight of the number on our door, and ran rapidly across the roadway. We heard a loud knock, a deep voice below, and heavy steps ascending the stair.
>
> **"For Mr. Sherlock Holmes,"** he said, stepping into the room and handing my friend the letter.
>
> Here was an opportunity of taking the conceit out of him. He little thought of this when he made that random shot.
>
> **"May I ask, my lad,"** I said, in the blandest voice, "what your trade may be?"
>
> **"Commissionaire, sir,"** he said, gruffly. "Uniform away for repairs."
>
> **"And you were?"** I asked, with a slightly malicious glance at my companion.
>
> **"A sergeant, sir, Royal Marine Light Infantry, sir. ..."** He clicked his heels together, raised his hand in a salute, and was gone....
>
> **"How in the world did you deduce that?"** I asked.
>
> **"Deduce what?"** said he, petulantly.
>
> **"Why, that he was a retired sergeant of Marines."**
>
> **"I have no time for trifles,"** he answered, brusquely; then with a smile, "Excuse my rudeness. You broke the thread of my thoughts; but perhaps it is as well. So you actually were not able to see that that man was a sergeant of Marines?"
>
> **"No, indeed."**
>
> **"It was easier to know it than to explain why I knew it.**

> **... Even across the street I could see a great blue anchor tattooed on the back of the fellow's hand. That smacked of the sea. He had a military carriage, however, and regulation side whiskers. There we have the marine. He was a man with some amount of self-importance and a certain air of command. You must have observed the way in which he held his head and swung his cane. A steady, respectable, middle-aged man, too, on the face of him — all facts which led me to believe that he had been a sergeant."**
>
> **— Arthur Conan Doyle: *A Study in Scarlet***

Notice that Holmes's argument, presented in the last paragraph of the excerpt, is indeed a very good argument. Watson and Holmes typically characterize such arguments as deductions. In 2.1 we provided the account of "deductions" that we will be using. If you examine that account you should see that Holmes's argument is not a would-be deductive argument in our sense. The premises do not purport to provide *conclusive* support for the conclusion. Holmes is presenting an argument of a different sort. We will refer to these arguments as ***inductive arguments***. These arguments differ from the arguments discussed in the previous section in that their premises purport only to provide *some*, but *not* conclusive, support for the conclusion. Note that when we speak of some support we allow for support that might well, practically speaking, be overwhelming. Holmes, perhaps a bit over-optimistically, certainly views his argument as being like that. But his argument is not, as he himself knows, one in which the conclusion follows from the premises. So we should not ask ourselves whether it is valid or invalid. Instead we should attempt to determine how much support his evidence provides for his conclusion.

Let us look at a more ordinary example:

> **The downtown is not usually very busy on Thursday evenings.**
> **Today is Thursday.**
> **So, the downtown will not be busy tonight.**

This is an acceptable argument in that the premises do give us *some* reason to believe the conclusion. But it should be apparent here that the evidence is not and does not purport to be conclusive. The speaker certainly knows that even though the downtown is not *usually* busy on Thursday, it could, through some quirk of fate, be busy this Thursday evening. We do *not* use the vocabulary of validity and invalidity in connection with inductive arguments. Rather we will, for example, assess inductive arguments as **strong** or **weak**. Roughly, we shall count inductive arguments as stronger to the extent that the premises provide stronger support for the conclusion. But, as we shall see, the assessment of inductive arguments is much trickier than the assessment of deductive arguments. For now all you need to keep in mind is that inductive arguments are those that purport to provide some support for the conclusion, but do *not* purport to provide conclusive support. An inductive argument may then be strong and have true premises but a false conclusion. As we noted, the downtown could be busy even though it typically is not.

2.3 / Fallacies

There are a variety of reasons why an argument may fail to be a good one. The most obvious way in which an argument can fail is, of course, by having premises that are not all true. But, as we have indicated, the assessment of the truth or falsity of the premises of an argument is not typically one of our primary concerns. What does concern us is those cases where an argument is one in which it is purported that the premises give a certain kind of support to the conclusion, but do not in fact give such support. We shall speak of such arguments as *fallacious*. We will not, save in certain special cases, speak of an argument as fallacious simply because it has false premises. It is typically better, in such a case, to point out the false premises rather than attempting to apply some label. We will typically speak of an argument as fallacious when the premises of the argument do not give support to the conclusion, or do not give the kind of support that they purport to give.

If we reconsider our account of would-be deductive arguments we can see that *any* invalid argument is a fallacious argument. The argument is one in which the premises purport to give conclusive support to the conclusion. But, since it is invalid, the premises do not give such support to the conclusion. Consequently we can classify invalid arguments as fallacious. But typically it is more perspicuous — clearer — simply to note that they are invalid. In the case of inductive arguments, any argument in which the premises give no support to the conclusion, or such weak support as to be of no significance, is a fallacious argument.

Certain ways of arguing poorly — certain fallacious arguments — are so common that we shall identify them and give them labels. In this case we speak of them as committing a *fallacy*. (We could speak of any fallacious argument as committing a fallacy, but since we will not give labels to each and every mistake one could conceivably make, we will typically speak of an argument as committing a fallacy if we have a label, and simply as fallacious otherwise. The labels we will use are introduced at various later points in the text.)

It is important to bear in mind that the comment that an argument is fallacious is not typically a comment about the truth or falsity of either its premises or its conclusion. It is instead a comment about the fact that the premises would not support the conclusion even if they were true. Fallacious arguments may be of any of the following sorts:

Possibilities If an Argument is Fallacious

(1) The premises are all true and the conclusion is true.
(2) Not all the premises are true (that is, one or more of the premises is false) and the conclusion is true.
(3) Not all the premises are true (that is, one or more of the premises is false) and the conclusion is false.
(4) The premises are all true and the conclusion is false.

In other words, if an argument is fallacious all the possible combinations of truth and falsity remain open.

2.4 / The Form of Arguments

There are indefinitely many arguments that people could present, but we do not have to approach each and every argument on its own, as being absolutely unique. Typically, arguments will be of some particular kind, and we will evaluate them by using the criteria relevant to arguments of that kind. What primarily enables us to sort arguments into kinds is the fact that many particular arguments share the same structure or, as we shall say, have the same *form*.

Consider the following two arguments:

If the test is given on Friday, I will have to study on Thursday evening. The test will be given on Friday. So, I will have to study on Thursday evening.

If 13 is a prime number then it is divisible only by itself and 1. 13 is a prime number. So it is divisible only by itself and 1.

The subject matter of these two arguments is quite different, but if you look at them closely you should see that they do share the same structure, have the same form. We could represent this form as follows:

If p then q
p
Therefore, q

As we shall later show, any argument with this form is a valid argument.

Chapter Summary

Initially, in 1.1, we introduced the notion of an ***argument***: a sequence of statements that include statements put forward as supporting another statement and the statement to which this support is given. The statement to which the support is given is called the ***conclusion***, while each statement that purports to provide support is called a *premise*.

We then noted in 1.2 that there are a variety of uses of language. The ones we specified were:

1. *argument*
2. *description*
3. *explanation*
4. *advice*
5. *command*
6. *request*
7. *exhortation*
8. *other*

Our category of other was simply a "none of the above" category.

We learned in 1.3 that we can often identify arguments by taking note of the presence of ***indicators***. Certain terms, for example 'since', typically function as *premise indicators*. Other terms, for example 'therefore', typically function as *conclusion indicators*.

We then saw in 1.4 that passages may contain very complex argumentative structures, and we introduced a technique for diagramming these.

In 1.5 we noted that arguments may have missing premises or conclusions.

In Section 2 we introduced a broad classification of arguments. We discussed, in 2.1, what we called *would-be deductive arguments*. These are arguments in which the premises at least purport to provide conclusive support for the conclusion. Such an argument is said to be *valid* if and only if it does provide such conclusive support. That is, a would-be deductive argument is valid if and only if it is impossible that the premises should all be true while the conclusion is false. If such an argument is not valid it is said to be *invalid*. We identified any would-be deductive argument as *sound* if it is both valid and has true premises, and *unsound* if it either is invalid or has at least one false premise. We introduced, in 2.2, a class of arguments that we called *inductive arguments*. Inductive arguments are those in which the premises only purport to give some but not conclusive support to the conclusion. Even a strong inductive argument may then have true premises and a false conclusion.

In 2.3 we decided to characterize an argument as *fallacious* if the premises purport to give a certain kind of support to the conclusion but do not in fact do so. Certain fallacious ways of arguing are so common that they have received labels. In this case we speak of the argument in question as committing a *fallacy*.

Finally, in 2.4, we noted that certain arguments can exhibit the same basic structure. In this case we speak of them as having the same *form*.

CHAPTER 2

Analogy Arguments

We are all familiar with the use of analogies. They may be used to provide advice, to suggest alternate ways of understanding a situation, or simply to illustrate or make a point. But analogies may also be used to present arguments. Consider the following set of passages:

> **Think of Johnson as a bull: don't wave something in front of him or he will charge.**

> **"You see," he explained, "I consider that a man's brain originally is like a little empty attic, and you have to stock it with such furniture as you choose. A fool takes in all the lumber of every sort that he comes across, so that the knowledge which might be useful to him gets crowded out, or at best is jumbled up with a lot of other things so that he has a difficulty in laying his hands upon it. Now the skilful workman is very careful indeed as to what he takes into his brain-attic. He will have nothing but the tools which may help him in doing his work, but of these he has a large assortment, and all in the most perfect order. It is a mistake to think that that little room has elastic walls and can distend to any extent. Depend upon it there comes a time when for every addition of knowledge you forget something that you knew before. It is of the highest importance, therefore, not to have useless facts elbowing out the useful ones."**
> **— Arthur Conan Doyle, *A Study in Scarlet***

> **We are now in the position of Columbus. We are setting sail into space. We, like him, think we know what we will find, but we may be completely surprised.**

The first passage (that concerning Johnson) seems primarily designed to give us, in a colorful way, advice as to what to expect of him. The second (by Arthur Conan Doyle) does, however, seem to contain an argument to the effect that overcrowded brains, like overcrowded attics, are impediments to working effectively. However, it might be suggested that this is an "over-reading" of the passage, that the analogy is only used as illustrative. I personally think it is more than an illustration, but there is room for debate. The third passage is, I think, an argument. Our position is similar to that of Columbus. Just as he did not find what he expected, so we too may not find what we expect to find.

1 / Analogy Arguments

1.1 / Standard Version

Consider the following argument:

> **This CD has exactly the same kind of scratch on it as the last one I tried to play. The last one didn't play correctly. Well, I will try this one, but I don't expect that it will play correctly either.**

This familiar way of arguing seems, at least in this case, to be quite acceptable. The argument is an example of the kind of argument that we will call *analogy arguments*. The overt form of such arguments can be represented as follows:

Analogy Arguments: Overt Form

Object (or objects) **X** and object (or objects) **Y** are alike in having features **F, G, H** ...
Object (or objects) **X** has feature **Z**.
So, object (or objects) **Y** has feature **Z** as well.

We shall speak of the object (or objects) *X* as the *reference object*. In the case of our example the reference object was the CD that did not play well. Note that the reference object need not be, and is not in this case, the first object mentioned in the argument. The object (or objects) *Y* will be called the *target object*. In the case of our example the target object was the CD that the person was going to try out. The features *F, G, H* ... will be called the *reference features*. In the example the scratch was the reference feature. The feature *Z* will be called the *target feature*. The reference object is the one that is claimed in a premise of the argument to have the target feature. The target object is the one that is, in the conclusion of the argument, claimed to have the target feature. Let us look at another analogy argument just to make sure we can apply these terms.

> **The sauce in this bottle, the one we usually buy, and the sauce in this other bottle have the same ingredients. We like the one we usually buy, so we will probably like the other one. Since it's cheaper let's give it a try.**

This passage contains more than an analogy argument. But the analogy argument has as its conclusion that we will probably like the other one. The other one is then the target object. The one we usually buy is the reference object. The ingredients of the sauce are the reference features. Liking the stuff is the target feature. It should be apparent that when we present arguments of this sort, we are operating in the non-deductive realm. That is, while such premises might provide some support for the conclusion, they do not provide conclusive support for it.

Let us analyze this kind of argument in more detail. First note that we have a comparison between objects, a statement of respects in which the objects are similar. Our claim is that, in virtue of the similarity, the target object Y has the target feature Z that our reference object is said to have. What is it that makes for strength or weakness in such arguments?

We might at the outset think that the critical question is how similar the objects are, that is, how many features F, G, H and so on X and Y do have in common. This is not completely incorrect, but it is nonetheless misleading. The really critical question is whether the similarities are *positively relevant features*. Consider the following example:

> **This painting and the painting in the National Art Museum look much the same: both are on canvas, both are on oils, both are pictures of ships, and so on. The one in the museum is worth a million dollars. So the one here is probably worth a lot.**

Clearly, this is not a very good argument, but can we give an account of why it is not? There are two points to note. The paintings are, in this case, very similar indeed. It might even be that you could not even tell which was which if they were placed side by side. But what we must consider is whether these similarities are particularly relevant to the price. We will utilize the following account of *positive relevance*:

Positive Relevance

A feature or property **F** (any feature or property) is ***positively relevant*** to a feature or property **Z** if the presence of **F** in an object increases the likelihood that the object is **Z**.

Now we can state the obvious point that stating lots of similarities is important only to the to the extent that the features in question are positively relevant to the presence of the target feature. Note that features may be positively relevant to varying degrees, that is, their presence in an object may increase the likelihood of the presence of the target feature **Z** to a greater or lesser degree. So, when we speak of positive relevance we have in mind the degree of relevance as well. Generally the strength of an analogy argument is a function of the degree to which the reference features are positively relevant to the presence of the target feature.

We are now in a position to provide our account as to what we shall take to be our standard form for analogy arguments.

Analogy Arguments: Simple Standard Form

Object (or objects) **X** and object (or objects) **Y** are alike in having features **F, G, H** ...
Object (or objects) **X** has feature **Z**.
F, G, H ... are positively relevant to **Z**.
So, object (or objects) **Y** has feature **Z** as well.

Notice that this differs from the overt form in that the claim of positive relevance is made explicit. Let us return to one of our sample analogy arguments:

> **This CD has exactly the same kind of scratch on it as the last one I tried to play. The last one didn't play correctly. Well, I will try this one, but I don't expect that it will play correctly either.**

Put into diagram form this argument is:

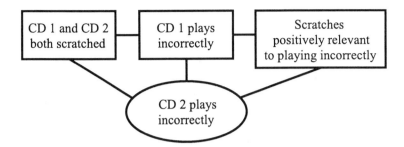

As we have indicated, we take the strength of this argument to be a function of the degree to which the scratches are positively relevant. Why then could we not simply put the argument as one in which we have two premises, one of which states that CD 2 is scratched, the other of which states that scratches are positively relevant to playing incorrectly? The answer is that we could, but we are at this point trying to stay as close as we legitimately can to standard presentations of analogy arguments. Let us continue for now with our discussion of factors relevant to assessing them.

Consider the following passages:

> **The first bird I bought was a young male cockatiel. He learned to talk very quickly. This second bird is a young male cockatiel, so he will very likely learn to talk quickly.**

> **The first bird I bought was a young male cockatiel found in Calgary. He learned to talk very quickly. This second bird is a young male cockatiel bought from the same store, so it is very likely that he will learn to talk quickly.**

The second passage includes mention of a similarity between the birds that is not mentioned in the first. But whether they present different arguments is dependent upon whether the passage's author wishes us to take, for example, being bought from the same store as a positively relevant feature. There is no mechanical way of answering this question. In the absence of further information we might suppose that she does. And if we do, then do we have two different arguments? Do they differ in strength? I would judge that the arguments are of equal value. My judgment is based upon the assumption that being young, male, and a cockatiel are features that are positively relevant to a bird's learning to talk, but being purchased from the same store is not. Given that, the similarity of the birds in that respect does not strengthen the argument at all. You might disagree. You might think that being purchased in the same store is relevant and might therefore judge the second argument to be a stronger one. Our disagreement is not a verbal one. It is one to be resolved by further study of cockatiels. But what we have just seen is that the assessment of the value of a particular analogy argument, indeed of any inductive argument, is not a simple mechanical task. We utilize here, as we will in all cases in which we are assessing inductive arguments, our background knowledge.

Regardless of how similar objects are, there will also be dissimilarities between them. Just as we might have been tempted to say that more similarities make for a stronger argument, we might be tempted to say that the more dissimilarities there are the weaker the argument. This would equally be a mistake. Here the fundamental question is one of relevance, but relevance of a negative rather than a positive sort:

Negative Relevance

A feature **F** (any feature) is **negatively relevant** to a feature **Z** if the presence of **F** in an object **decreases** the likelihood that the object is **Z**.

So even if an object is dissimilar to another in any number of ways, that does not matter unless, for example, a feature **F** negatively relevant to the presence of **Z** is absent in the reference object but present in the target object. Consider yet another version of our "bird" arguments:

> **The first bird I bought was a young male cockatiel. This bird is a young male cockatiel. Of course, this second bird has more white on his wings. But nonetheless he should, as the first bird did, learn to talk quickly.**

The argument here is:

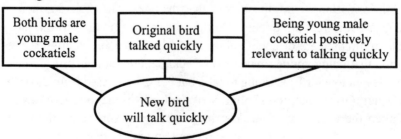

Notice that we have omitted the explicit mention of the dissimilarity. But as is indicated by the "nonetheless" present in the original passage, this dissimilarity is dismissed. It is only included to forestall an objection that the author of the passage anticipates as one that might be presented. If it is rightly dismissed, it is because having more white on the wings is not negatively relevant to a bird's ability to learn to talk quickly.

We have noted that a primary concern of ours is to become skilled at assessing arguments, determining how good they are. As we are operating in the inductive realm, our vocabulary of assessment will typically be a qualitative one using such expressions as "very strong", "strong", "weak", and the like. We have already seen, in our discussion of whether the store in which the bird was purchased matters, that carrying out these assessments involves an appeal to our background assumptions — what we take to be knowledge that we already have. In the sample argument we just considered, the one in which the second bird differed a bit in color, I dismissed the dissimilarity as irrelevant, while accepting being young, male, and a cockatiel as positively relevant. If I am right to dismiss the dissimilarity on the grounds that it is irrelevant, that is, on the grounds that it is not negatively relevant, then my judgment that the argument is a tolerably strong one is correct. It is not correct because I *think* it is; its strength is determined by whether or not the similarities are in fact positively relevant and the dissimilarity irrelevant. But neither you nor I are in a position to even begin assessing the argument unless we are in a position to make judgments about relevance and irrelevance.

Consider the following argument:

> **Chris is exceedingly agile, seven feet tall, quite strong, and very adept at playing Esterian Conquest. Patel is just as agile, just as tall, and just as strong. So, I would expect Patel to be a good Esterian Conquest player.**

Now — very quickly — assess this argument. It should be apparent to you that you cannot do so unless you know what Esterian Conquest is, and know enough to make some judgment about the relevance of the mentioned similarities. As it happens, this is not a very good argument; it is so poor an argument as to be fallacious. Again, that it is not a good argument is not dependent upon my viewing it as an argument that is not a good one. It is not a good argument simply because I say that it is not. It is not a good argument because Esterian Conquest is a game in which those physical abilities are utterly irrelevant; it is a computer game that one can win by thinking and planning rather than by using physical skills. Since I happened to be aware of this fact, I was in a position to judge that the argument was not a good one. And I chose this argument because I thought it unlikely that you would be able to assess it. But even though you are not able to make the assessment that the argument is a very poor one, it is nonetheless a very poor one.

1.2 / Analogy Arguments: Advanced Version

If this were the whole of the story, then life, while not entirely simple, would not be overwhelmingly complex. Unfortunately this is not the whole of the story so we will make the story more complex. It will hopefully not be overwhelmingly complex.

Consider the following argument:

> **My first cockatiel was a young male. My second cockatiel was a young male. Both the first and the second learned to speak quite quickly. This new one is a young male. So this new young male cockatiel will, as they did, learn to speak quickly.**

Notice that the primary difference between this argument and one presented above is that we now mention two previous cockatiels rather than one. Presented diagramatically in terms of what we called our simple standard form we have the argument:

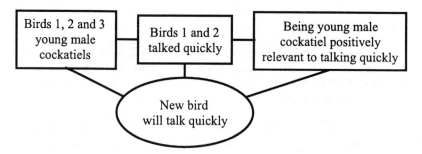

Note that the third premise is precisely the same in the case in which there is one initial cockatiel and the case in which there are two, or, in fact, any number of initial cockatiels. Insofar as the strength of an analogy argument is measured by the degree of positive relevance, these arguments are equally strong. But considerable care must be exercised here. Actual argumentation is a very complex affair, and there are various factors involved in the assessment of actual argumentation. You would probably judge this second argument to be somehow a more powerful argument. Here is one way of accounting for that. That we have encountered more than one young male cockatiel and that they typically learned to talk quickly will typically give us *better reason to believe* that being a young male cockatiel is positively relevant to quickly learning to talk. This is obviously important, but nonetheless having better evidence for a feature's being relevant is quite different from a feature's being relevant.

We can accommodate this point by noting that when we present an analogy argument, part of what we say is designed to indicate some or all of the evidence we have for the positive relevance. So we shall, from what we call our advanced standpoint, treat an analogy argument as a complex argument:

Analogy Arguments: Advanced Standard Form

(1) Object (or objects) **X** and object (or objects) **Y** are alike in having features **F, G, H** …

(2) Object (or objects) **X** has feature **Z**.

Since object (or objects) **X**, which have features **F, G, H** … are **Z**

(3) **F, G, H** … are positively relevant to **Z**.

So, object (or objects) **Y** has feature **Z** as well.

Let us look at our previous example from this standpoint in diagrammatic form:

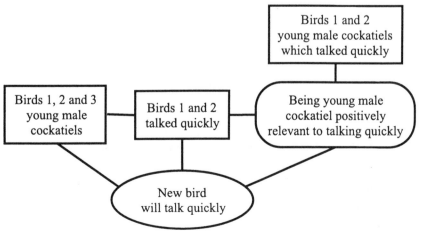

The lower portion of this diagram is precisely the same as it was before, save that we have utilized a rounded rectangle to indicate that the positive relevance statement is functioning as both a premise and a conclusion. The argument that moves from the premise that birds 1 and 2 are young male cockatiels which talked quickly to the conclusion that being a young male cockatiel is positively relevant to talking quickly is not itself an analogy argument. It is an argument of the sort we shall call an ***inductive generalization***, a sort that we shall study in a later chapter.

You might at this point be wondering which of the three forms that we have introduced — the overt form, the simple standard form, or the advanced standard form — is the "correct" representation of an analogy argument. This is the wrong question. We utilize whichever representation serves the purpose that we currently have. In the case above we were concerned not just with the analogy argument but with the question of how well-evidenced it was. So we utilized the advanced standard form. In other cases either the overt form or the simple standard form might suffice for us to make the point that we wish to make.

We noted earlier that insofar as we attend only to the analogy argument the strength of the argument is in large measure a function of the degree of positive relevance. How likely is it that the target feature will be present given that it has the reference features? So from this standpoint the argument in which one cockatiel is cited is of the same strength as the argument in which two are cited. But we also noticed that in the case in which we have two cockatiels we have better reason to believe that the reference features are positively relevant. The other argument, the one we spoke of as the inductive generalization, is stronger when we have two birds rather than one. We shall recognize this by speaking of the argument involving two birds as ***more completely evidenced*** than the argument in which only one bird was cited.

Let us work through two more arguments in order to fix our understanding of the vocabulary.

> **The last truck I had was built by company *T*. It was highly reliable. This truck is built by company *T*. So likely it will be highly reliable as well.**

> **The last two trucks I had were built by company *T*. They were highly reliable. This truck is built by company *T*. So likely it will be highly reliable as well.**

Here are the two arguments in standard form:

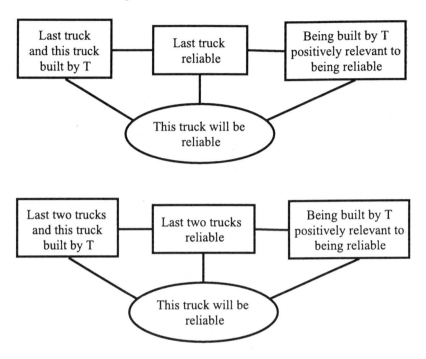

Again, we judge these to be of equal strength since the critical third premise is the same in both cases. But let us now look at them from our advanced vantage point:

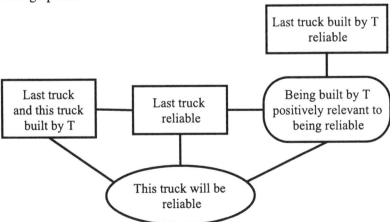

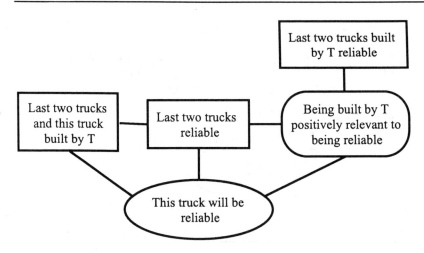

Now that we have revealed more of the underlying structure, we can see why we classify the second as more completely evidenced than the first. The second provides us with more reason to believe that being built by *T* is positively relevant. Whether the analogy argument itself is strong depends, as we have noted, upon the degree of positive relevance of the properties that the objects share. But there is the additional question of how well-evidenced the argument is. We noted above that we might not be in a position to judge whether an analogy argument is strong or weak. An argument that is more completely evidenced puts us in a better position to judge whether or not the properties are positively relevant. I should emphasize that the vocabulary we are using is mildly idiosyncratic. Many authors treat what I have labeled as more completely evidenced arguments as, simply, stronger arguments. Labeling is not in and of itself important; the important point to remember is that we have here two quite distinct questions:

Two Questions to Ask of Analogy Arguments

(1) Are the features positively relevant?
(2) How much evidence is offered that they are positively relevant?

If the answer to the first is that they *are* positively relevant, the argument has some strength. That is related to the degree of positive relevance. The argument may be a very strong one even if little or no evidence is offered that it is a strong one. But if little or no evidence is offered that it is strong, then the argument is *not* well-evidenced. This is the answer to our second question.

There is another kind of situation in which we can suggest that one analogy argument is more completely evidenced than another is. Consider the following argument:

> **The last BlueStorm computer I owned was very reliable. So this next BlueStorm computer will be as well.**

This may or may not be a strong analogy argument, but it is not a well-evidenced one. Note that the argument rests upon the supposed positive relevance of being a BlueStorm computer. Now consider the following argument:

> **I have owned five BlueStorm computers. Each one was very reliable. They were different models; each had a different motherboard, different CPU, and so on. So this next BlueStorm will be reliable as well.**

Put in diagram form we have:

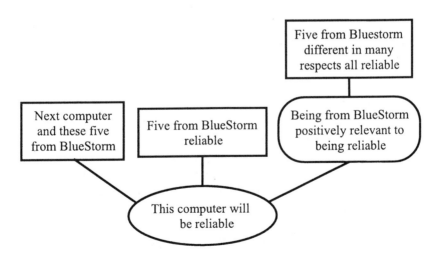

The analogy argument here appeals, as did the previous one, to the supposed positive relevance of being a BlueStorm. Given our vocabulary, this argument is of the same strength as the preceding one. However, the second argument is clearly more completely evidenced than the first. We are provided with evidence that just being a BlueStorm, rather than being one with a particular motherboard or a particular CPU, is positively relevant to being reliable. Notice that this argument is not simply an inductive generalization. It is rather more complex and of a sort that we shall look at in a later chapter. There is no single kind of argument that is always used to support a claim of positive relevance.

It is, of course, desirable if we appeal to an analogy argument that it be a strong one. But how important is it that it be well-evidenced? This depends on a variety of considerations. One very important consideration is how much background knowledge the people in the conversation can be presumed to have. If we all have reason to believe that a given feature, say being a young male cockatiel, is positively relevant, then there is no particular reason to include that information in our presentation of our argument. But if our intent in presenting an argument happens to be to persuade someone, then we may well need to present a more completely evidenced argument. This is particularly true when the person to whom we are talking cannot be presumed to share the background knowledge regarding positive relevance. And in some cases we simply will not have much background knowledge regarding positive relevance. If this is the case, we may well need more evidence if we are to be in any position to judge how strong the analogy argument is.

Let us now introduce what we shall call the *fallacy of false analogy.* One way in which any argument can go astray is by having a false premise. If my bird, which learned to talk, was not a young one, then any argument that appealed to a premise that stated that it was young would have a false premise. We have, however, already agreed that we will not typically identify an argument as fallacious merely in virtue of its having a false premise. One commits the fallacy of false analogy not by way of appealing to just any false premise, but by appealing in an analogy argument to similarities which are either not positively relevant or are relevant to such a minimal degree as to be insignificant. Consider the following argument:

A and B are similar in being enrolled at Harvard. A is planning on being a doctor. So B is planning on being a doctor.

Put in overt form the argument is:

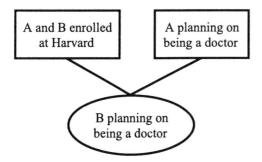

This is not a strong argument; indeed, I suggest that we should view it as one case of the fallacy of false analogy. It is not that going to Harvard is *utterly* irrelevant to planning on being a doctor. It is rather that its positive relevance is so minimal as to be insignificant. Put in simple standard form the argument is:

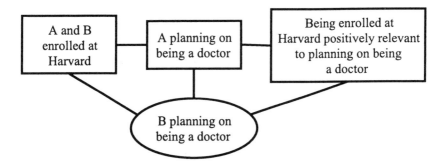

Here we have taken the claim of relevance as a third premise. It is not false but, as we said, too minimal. There is no precise point at which we are forced to say that an argument is fallacious as opposed to being very weak indeed. This is of no fundamental importance. What is important is that we understand what we are to take into account in assessing the argument. Of course, in some cases an argument will appeal to similarities that are not positively relevant. Consider the following argument:

A and B both have brown eyes. A is tall. So B is tall.

We immediately recognize this as a fallacious argument, as again one example of an argument that commits the fallacy of false analogy, since we know that eye-color is not positively relevant to height.

We earlier introduced the notion of a negatively relevant feature. Recall that a feature **F** is negatively relevant to a feature **Z** when it decreases the likelihood that an object which is **F** is also **Z**. Recall our overt form for analogy arguments:

Analogy Arguments: Overt Form

Object (or objects) **X** and object (or objects) **Y** are alike in having features **F, G, H** ...
Object (or objects) **X** has feature **Z**.
So, object (or objects) **Y** has feature **Z** as well.

We shall speak of a feature **K** (negatively relevant to **Z**) that is found in **Y** but not in **X** as a *relevant dissimilarity*.

Relevant Dissimilarity

If object (or objects) **X** has feature **K** and object (or objects) **Y** lacks feature **K** and **K** is negatively relevant to the target feature **Z** then **K** is a relevant dissimilarity.

If we are considering a particular analogy argument and find or know of a relevant dissimilarity, we have evidence that is not mentioned in the argument. We have then to take this relevant dissimilarity into account in assessing the strength of the analogy argument in question.

Consider the following argument:

> **Scott enjoyed the last movie he saw. It was a science fiction movie. This is a science fiction movie. So, probably he will enjoy this movie.**

This is not a strong argument, but it does have some force. (We are not currently operating in an area where we can specify a precise degree of relevance. To attempt to do so would be to impose more precision than the situation warrants.) But now let us suppose that the last movie Scott saw was a color extravaganza replete with spectacular special effects, whereas the second movie is a black-and-white one made in the fifties when special effects were, to say the least, typically less than spectacular. These would seem to be relevant dissimilarities. We are now operating from a different evidential base. In this kind of situation we will typically say that the new evidence weakens the argument. We can see this by considering a new argument, an argument that explicitly includes this new evidence. Here is this new argument:

> **Scott enjoyed the last movie he saw. It was a science fiction movie that was in color and had spectacular special effects.**
> **This is a science fiction movie that is in black-and-white and has very unspectacular special effects. So, probably he will enjoy this movie.**

This argument seems on the face of it to be a very poor one. Indeed, we might take it as another example in which the fallacy of false analogy is committed. In this kind of case what happens is that relevant dissimilarities (I am presuming they are relevant dissimilarities) are simply ignored. But let us look back at the original argument:

> **Scott enjoyed the last movie he saw. It was a science fiction movie. This is a science fiction movie. So, probably he will enjoy this movie.**

Should we classify this as fallacious given that we come to know of the relevant dissimilarities? The answer is that we should not automatically do so. After all, in this case the relevant dissimilarities are not mentioned in the argument. However, we shall classify an argument as fallacious if there are relevant dissimilarities of which we are aware, or relevant dissimilarities which are in some sense apparent but are ignored.

We do not have any mechanical means of distinguishing between relevant similarities or dissimilarities that are apparent and those that are not. The core of this idea may be illustrated in the following way. Suppose I present you with the following argument:

> **There is a post-secondary institution along the Crowchild Trail in the southwestern quarter of the city of Calgary.**
> **There is another post-secondary institution along the Crowchild Trail in the northwestern quarter of the city.**
> **The one in the northwest has a graduate program. So, the one in the southwest likely does too.**

It is true that being a post-secondary institution is relevant to having a graduate program. But if it is part of the background knowledge of the people in the conversation that the one in the southwest is a junior college we should, I think, classify the argument as one that commits the fallacy of false analogy. The information regarding the relevant dissimilarities is available to the parties to the conversation, and they should take it into account. As we noted, this in effect requires us to take the statement that the one in the southwest is a junior college as being a missing premise in the argument being assessed. And the argument, when it includes this missing premise, is not one in which the premises give any support to the conclusion.

Contrast this situation with one in which someone living, let us suppose, in the United States knows that the University of Calgary (which is the one in the northwest) is a post-secondary institution that has a graduate program. She finds out that there is another post secondary institution in Calgary called Mount Royal. Since she wishes to go to graduate school in a city near the mountains, she concludes that Mount Royal might be worth considering as a graduate school choice. Here it would be inappropriate to take her argument that since the one has a graduate school the other does too, as a fallacious argument. Being a post-secondary institution is a relevant similarity and, in this context at this time, the relevant dissimilarities are not apparent.

Suppose, though, that our U.S. student, on the basis of what she currently knows, sends off a $50 check to Mount Royal in order to apply to its graduate school. This would, to say the least, be rather rash. It is not that her original argument was fallacious; it is rather that, since something is at stake, it makes sense to investigate further, to see whether there are relevant dissimilarities that are not currently apparent.

Keep in mind, as you attempt to apply the above distinctions, that it is far more important to attempt to understand how to assess arguments and what kinds of considerations are relevant than it is simply to apply labels. Labels in these sorts of cases are at best guides as to how to proceed further.

Consider the following arguments:

> **Lorne and Larry look a lot alike. They are both named "Hanson". So there is some plausibility in the supposition that they are related.**

> **Lorne and Larry look a lot alike. They are both named "Hanson". So it is virtually certain that they are related.**

The premises of these arguments are the same. But the first argument is clearly superior to the second. The conclusion in the first is, as we shall say, **proportionate** to the evidence at hand. In the second the conclusion goes beyond the evidence provided. That evidence hardly warrants the claim that it is *virtually certain* that Lorne and Larry are related. We shall judge inductive arguments in general, not just analogy arguments, to be weakened to the extent that the conclusion goes beyond the evidence. I would in fact be tempted to classify the second argument as fallacious. We will not attempt to give any precise characterization of what it is to go beyond the evidence; it is simply a question that we have to consider when we are assessing the strength or weakness of inductive arguments. We have here to rely upon our own critical judgment.

Let us keep the point of the preceding paragraph in mind and consider the argument regarding movies that we looked at before.

> **Scott enjoyed the last movie he saw. It was a science fiction movie that was in color and had spectacular special effects.**
> **This is a science fiction movie that is in black-and-white and has very unspectacular special effects. So, probably he will enjoy this movie.**

I suggested that this argument might be fallacious. Claiming that it is probable that he will enjoy this movie disregards the relevant dissimilarities. But suppose instead that we conclude that he *might* enjoy the second movie. It is, after all, a science fiction movie. That he might enjoy the movie does seem to be justified by the evidence at hand. It is a conclusion proportionate to the evidence at hand. The moral to this is that in trying to decide how strong an inductive argument is, we have to take account of what is claimed by the conclusion.

Let us consider one more example to make this point clearer. Suppose you have misplaced the key to your postal box. You see one that, though not the same key, nonetheless looks like a key to a postal box. Suppose you say to yourself that since this key looks much the same, it will almost certainly open the box. This is not a strong argument: the conclusion is not proportionate to the evidence you have in hand. However, were you to say to yourself that since this key looks much the same, it *might* open the box, you would have a strong argument. Here the conclusion you draw, that the key might open the box, is proportionate to the evidence at hand.

Argument Strength

A non-deductive argument is strong only if the conclusion is proportionate to the evidence.

1.3 / The Use of Analogy Arguments to Refute

One common use of analogy arguments is to attempt to show defects in other arguments. This involves no new principles, but we shall look at a few examples just to ensure a secure grasp of the matter.

Suppose someone were to argue as follows:

> **A** **If Jean Chrétien is the prime minister of Canada, then a Liberal is prime minister of Canada.**
> **A Liberal is prime minister of Canada.**
> **So, Jean Chrétien is prime minister of Canada.**

This argument is, of course, a deductive one, but we are here concerned to see how we might use an analogy argument to suggest that it is not a good argument. You might respond by saying that's just like arguing:

> **B** **If John Kennedy is president of the United States, then a Democrat is president of the United States.**
> **A Democrat is president of the United States.**
> **So, John Kennedy is president of the United States.**

Your argument might be presented in the following way:

> **Argument A is similar to argument B (in particular, it has the same form or structure).**
> **Argument B is a bad argument.**
> **So, argument A is a bad argument.**

You are, obviously, taking for granted that the person to whom you are speaking will recognize that argument B is indeed a bad argument. Your argument here is an analogy argument, and is to be assessed in the way we have suggested any analogy argument is to be assessed. One critical question will be whether or not the form of arguments (or at least of deductive ones) is positively relevant to their goodness or badness.

This kind of tactic may be used even when one is not quite sure how the argument one is questioning is meant to work. One famous example of this arose in connection with a supposed proof for the existence of God that has come to be known as the ontological argument. Anselm, an eleventh-century monk, speaks of God as "that than which no greater can be conceived"; we shall substitute for this the phrase "the most perfect being conceivable". Significantly revised, Anselm's argument is:

> **A The most perfect being conceivable exists in the understanding, since we can understand the phrase "the most perfect being conceivable". But the most perfect being conceivable cannot exist only in the understanding. If it exists only in the understanding, then it can be conceived to exist in reality as well — and that is a more perfect being. Therefore, if the most perfect being conceivable exists in the understanding alone, then a being more perfect than it is conceivable. Since this is not possible, the most perfect being conceivable must exist in reality as well as in the understanding.**

Even in paraphrase, you will find this argument difficult at best. It is unlikely that you will find it persuasive. One of Anselm's fellow monks, a chap named Gaunilon, presumably felt just the same. He asked why this argument was not like the following argument (again significantly revised):

> **B The most perfect unicorn conceivable exists in the understanding, since we can understand the phrase "the most perfect unicorn conceivable" ...**

Argument B can be completed by simply replacing the occurrences of the phrase "the most perfect being conceivable" by the phrase "the most perfect unicorn conceivable". As was the case in the preceding example, Gaunilon may be construed as presenting the following argument:

> **Argument A is similar to argument B (in particular, it has the same form or structure).**
> **Argument B is a bad argument.**
> **So, argument A is a bad argument.**

Whether Gaunilon's argument is a good one depends upon whether it is a good analogy argument. Recall that Gaunilon is not arguing that God does not exist; he is using an analogy argument to attempt to show that Anselm's argument for the existence of God is a bad one. Whether Gaunilon is successful is not something we will attempt to decide here. (You should ask your instructor if you would like additional information regarding Anselm's argument and Gaunilon's response.) Suffice it to say that it is quite often useful to attempt to assess arguments—any arguments—by attempting to construct a formally similar argument.

1.4 / Negative Analogy Arguments

In 1.3, we considered how we might use analogy arguments to refute a claim. Here we introduce what we shall call *negative analogy arguments*. Consider the following argument:

> **Fish are unlike us in that they have very small brains and are not mammals. We feel pain, but it is likely that they don't.**

This argument seems to rest upon the supposition that having a brain that is not small and being a mammal are positively relevant to the capacity to feel pain, and the supposition that having a small brain and being something other than a mammal are negatively relevant to the capacity to feel pain. Note that merely lacking a positively relevant feature does not in and of itself guarantee the presence of a negatively relevant feature. Let us explain this by way of an example. Having a remote control device is positively relevant to being able to control a television set from a distance. Suppose a television set has no remote control device to carry around. So it lacks a feature positively relevant to being controlled from a distance. But we should not necessarily conclude from this that it is not controllable from a distance. It might, for example, be voice controlled. In the above example what was appealed to was not simply the absence of a positively relevant feature, but the supposed negative relevance of having a small brain and being other than a mammal.

Negative Analogy Arguments

Object (or objects) *X* and object (or objects) *Y* are not alike in that *Y* has features *F, G, H, ...* whereas *X* has features *F′, G′, H′*.
Object (or objects) *Y* has feature *Z*.
So, object (or objects) *X* does not have feature *Z*.

Here the features F', G', H', ... must be negatively relevant to the presence of feature Z if the argument is to be a strong one. At this point you should see how other aspects of our discussion of analogy arguments can be revised so as to apply to negative analogy arguments. For example, a negative analogy argument is fallacious if apparent relevant similarities are ignored. Can you see why?

Chapter Summary

In this chapter we introduced *analogy arguments*. In 1.1 we took their overt form to be:

Analogy Arguments: Overt Form

Object (or objects) *X* and object (or objects) *Y* are alike in having features *F, G, H...*
Object (or objects) *X* has feature *Z*.
So, object (or objects) *Y* has feature *Z* as well.

The object(s) X is the *reference object(s)*, while the object(s) Y is the *target object(s)*. The features F, G, H ... are the *reference features*, while Z is the *target feature*.

We introduced both *positive* and *negative relevance*:

Positive Relevance

A feature or property *F* (any feature or property) is **positively relevant** to a feature or property *Z* if the presence of *F* in an object **increases** the likelihood that the object is *Z*.

Negative Relevance

A feature *F* (any feature) is **negatively relevant** to a feature *Z* if the presence of *F* in an object **decreases** the likelihood that the object is *Z*.

In order better to understand the structure of analogy arguments we introduced:

Analogy Arguments: Simple Standard Form

Object (or objects) *X* and object (or objects) *Y* are alike in having features *F, G, H* ...
Object (or objects) *X* has feature *Z*.
F, G, H ... are positively relevant to *Z*.
So, object (or objects) *Y* has feature *Z* as well.

---

and, in 1.2:

Analogy Arguments: Advanced Standard Form

(1) Object (or objects) *X* and object (or objects) *Y* are alike in having features *F, G, H* ...
(2) Object (or objects) *X* has feature *Z*.
Since object (or objects) *X*, which have features *F, G, H* ... are *Z*
(3) *F, G, H* ... are positively relevant to *Z*.
So, object (or objects) *Y* has feature *Z* as well.

Using the advanced standard form we were able to assess whether one analogy argument was *more completely evidenced* than another. A more completely evidenced argument cites more evidence that the reference features are indeed positively relevant. Remember that there are two questions here:

Two Questions to Ask of Analogy Arguments

(1) Are the features positively relevant?
(2) How much evidence is offered that they are positively relevant?

We introduced the notion of a *relevant dissimilarity:*

Relevant Dissimilarity

If object (or objects) *X* has feature *K* and object (or objects) *Y* lacks feature *K* and *K* is negatively relevant to the target feature *Z* then *K* is a relevant dissimilarity.

Analogy arguments may commit what we called the *fallacy of false analogy*. One way of committing the fallacy of false analogy is by appealing in an analogy argument to similarities that are either not positively relevant or are relevant to such a minimal degree as to be insignificant. However, we shall classify an argument as committing this fallacy if there are relevant dissimilarities of which we are aware, or relevant dissimilarities which are in some sense apparent but are ignored.

In assessing not just analogy arguments but any non-deductive argument, we must try to ensure that the conclusion is *proportionate* to the premises, to the evidence we have. We are, for example, only infrequently in a position to claim that our evidence justifies the claim that our conclusion is virtually certain.

Argument Strength

A non-deductive argument is strong only if the conclusion is proportionate to the evidence.

We noted in 1.3 that analogy arguments are frequently used in attempts to refute other arguments. We do this by claiming that the disputed argument is like, in respects, an argument that we know to be fallacious.

Finally, in 1.4, we considered *negative analogy arguments:*

Negative Analogy Arguments

Object (or objects) **X** and object (or objects) **Y** are not alike in that **Y** has features **F, G, H,** ... whereas **X** has features **F′, G′, H′**.
Object (or objects) **Y** has feature **Z**.
So, object (or objects) **X** does not have feature **Z**.

The presumption here is that F', G', H', are negatively relevant to the presence of Z.

CHAPTER 3

Using Statistical Statements

In this chapter we will learn how what we shall call *statistical generalizations* can be utilized in arguments. In later chapters we will study some of the ways in which we attempt to establish such claims.

1 / Some Kinds of Statements

1.1 / Generalizations

If we are to classify arguments so as to be able to assess them, we will quite often find it necessary to classify various kinds of sentences. We will initially focus on two kinds of statements or sentences.

Consider the following two statements:

All residents of Mount Royal are wealthy.
Most residents of Mount Royal are wealthy.

The subject matter of the two statements is the same; that is, both make a claim about the wealth of residents of Mount Royal. But the claims they make are different in an important way. The first statement is the kind that we shall call a *universal generalization*; the second is the kind we shall call a *statistical generalization*. Keep firmly in mind that these terms are applied to statements, not to arguments.

Now consider the following two generalizations:

No people approve of his behavior.
Few people approve of his behavior.

The first statement is also one that we shall classify as a universal generalization, while the latter is a statistical generalization. If you consider all of these examples, you should see that the account we are using is:

Kinds of Generalizations

A statement is a ***universal generalization*** if and only if it states that all (100%) or none (0%) of the members of one group or class are members of another group or class.
A statement is a ***statistical generalization*** if and only if it states that some proportion (neither all nor none) of the members of one group or class are members of another group or class.

In either case the generalization may be expressed numerically or non-numerically. For example:

80% of the people here are vegetarians.
Most people here are vegetarians.
10% of the people here are vegetarians.
Few people here are vegetarians.

are all statistical generalizations. And:

0% of the animals have the disease.
100% of the animals have the disease.
None of the animals have the disease.
All of the animals have the disease.

are all universal generalizations. If you look carefully, you will note the first and the third of the statements say, in a quite straightforward sense, the same thing: 0% is none. The second and the fourth of these statements also say the same thing: 100% is all. As we shall frequently have occasion to see, we typically have various ways of saying the same thing. But we do have to be careful here. If you look back at the preceding examples of statistical generalizations you should see that although numerical and non-numerical statements are related in some way, there is no general way of translating a statement of one sort into one of the other sort. It is, I suppose, clear that if it is true that most people here are vegetarians then it must be true that more than 50% of the people here are vegetarians. A claim regarding "most" does seem to require, at the very least, a simple majority. But there is no simple numerical statement that says the same thing as our claim that most people here are vegetarians. To be sure, there is some definite percentage of vegetarians at the place in question, but in speaking of "most" we are not specifying that particular percentage.

Do not fall prey to the false view that numerical generalizations are somehow inherently superior to non-numerical generalizations. They are not. In the first place, with respect to universal generalizations we simply have, as noted above, different ways of saying the same thing. In the second place, with respect to statistical generalizations we must remember that the non-numerical statements do not typically say the same thing as the numerical ones. And often, as we shall have ample occasion to see, the non-numerical versions accord with the evidence we have much better than would any particular numeric statement. Consider the following example. Calgary, like many other cities, has an outdoor football stadium. As we know, not everyone who has purchased a ticket to a sporting event attends the event. If the weather is good I can with reasonable confidence predict that virtually all who have purchased a ticket will attend. If the weather is quite dreadful — for example, if there is one of Calgary's early fall blizzards — I know that many who have purchased a ticket will not attend. But in neither case do I have sufficient evidence to make some particular numeric prediction. It would typically be unreasonable to say, for example, that 75% of those who have purchased a ticket will attend. We should never make a more precise claim than is warranted by the evidence that we have. Any claim we make must be proportionate to the evidence that we have.

The word "many" is one of a number of words that we have to handle with some care. If I say that many people are very unhappy with the government, it does not seem that I am claiming that, for example, a majority of the people are very unhappy. It seems instead that I am claiming that some number of people above some floor, considered significant in the context, are unhappy. Consider the claim that many people get some disease while they are in the hospital. The actual figure might be between 5% and 10%, but we might here count this as "many". In this context we might well take the floor as near 0%. But consider a case in which around 10% of the population oppose a particular government policy. It seems dubious in this case to claim that many people oppose that policy. In this sort of case the significant floor seems to be considerably higher. In any given case we have to examine the context in order to determine just what claim is being made. Related points apply to claims involving "lots". If you call a bookstore and they say they have lots of copies of a particular book in stock you do not know how many that is. And, most likely, they are making that claim using as a base the expected sales of the book in question.

2 / Statistical Syllogisms

2.1 / The Basic Form

In the preceding section we identified certain statements as statistical generalizations. In this section we shall introduce a kind of argument which we shall call a *statistical syllogism*. Consider first this argument:

> **All whales are mammals.**
> **That is a whale.**
> **Therefore, that is a mammal.**

As you consider this argument, you should see that it is a valid deductive argument: there is no possibility that all the premises are true while the conclusion is false. Note that the first premise of this argument is a universal generalization. But now consider the following argument:

> **In almost all cases people with this sort of disease who take this medication are cured.**
> **You are a person who has this sort of disease and is taking this medication.**
> **So, you will be cured.**

It should be clear that these premises do give *some* support to the conclusion. But it should be equally clear that the argument is *not* a would-be deductive one. It is, instead, an inductive one of the sort that we shall call a *statistical syllogism*. One premise of any argument of this sort will be a statement that is a statistical generalization. Recall that statistical generalizations include both numeric and non-numeric statements. The arguments that we call statistical syllogisms all have a premise that states that:

> **A proportion of objects that are *F* are *G*.**

We shall say that the term *"F"* identifies what we shall call the *reference class*, and that the term *"G"* identifies what we shall call the *target class*. In the above example, the reference class was the class of people with this sort of disease who are taking this medication, and the target class is the group of people who are cured. Each statistical syllogism will also have a second premise. This premise will state that some particular individual or object *a* is a member of the reference class in question. The conclusion of such an argument is then that *a* is a member of the target class. In the above case, the conclusion is that you would be cured.

Statistical syllogisms will have both positive and negative forms. The positive form is:

Positive Statistical Syllogism

Most *F* are *G*.
a is an *F*.
So, *a* is, or very likely is, *G*.

Both the first premise and the conclusion may, on some occasions, be expressed numerically.

> **90% of *F* are *G*.**
> ***a* is an *F*.**
> **So, *a* is *G* (or it is likely that *a* is *G*).**

The negative form of the argument is:

Negative Statistical Syllogism

Few *F* are *G*.
a is an *F*.
So, *a* is not, or is very likely not, *G*.

There are numerical variants of negative statistical syllogisms:

> **10% of *F* are *G*.**
> ***a* is an *F*.**
> **So, *a* is not *G* (or it is likely that *a* is not *G*).**

Various points must be kept in mind in assessing the strengths of these arguments. Consider the following arguments:

> **80% of *F* are *G*.**
> ***a* is an *F*.**
> **So, *a* is *G*.**

> **99% of *F* are *G*.**
> ***a* is an *F*.**
> **So, *a* is *G*.**

Clearly one has better evidence for the conclusion that *a* is *G* in the second case than in the first. So the second argument is stronger than the first. The situation is the same in the case of negative statistical syllogisms. Consider:

> **25% of *F* are *G*.**
> ***a* is an *F*.**
> **So, *a* is likely not *G*.**

> **10% of *F* are *G*.**
> ***a* is an *F*.**
> **So, *a* is likely not *G*.**

Here, too, the second argument is stronger than the first. So how large, in the case of positive statistical syllogisms, or how small, in the case of negative statistical syllogisms, a proportion we have is one of the factors that determines our assessment of the strength of an argument. But it is not the sole factor.

We must also determine whether or not, as we put it, the conclusion is *proportionate* to the evidence at hand. We discussed this in Chapter 2. Consider the following arguments:

> **90% of *F* are *G*.**
> ***a* is an *F*.**
> **So, *a* is for sure *G*.**

> **90% of *F* are *G*.**
> ***a* is an *F*.**
> **So, there is a quite decent chance that *a* is *G*.**

In the first argument our unguarded conclusion seems to go beyond the evidence we have cited. Our more guarded conclusion in the second argument does, however, seem proportionate to the evidence at hand. So we would judge the first argument to be weaker than the second. In many cases, deciding whether a conclusion is proportionate to the evidence at hand involves making a judgment call. But it is a judgment call we have to make if we are reasonably to assess arguments. As we shall see later, when we study polls, for example, we will sometimes be in a position to determine with some precision whether a conclusion is proportionate to the evidence at hand.

So, assessing the strength of these arguments involves taking account of two factors — how large or small the proportion (or percentage) we have and whether or not the conclusion is proportionate to that evidence.

But, as is often true in the inductive realm, there is more to the story than this. Consider the following argument:

Most mammals do not have tusks.
That elephant is a mammal.
So, very likely, that elephant does not have tusks.

This argument should strike you as quite a suspicious one, because you and I know that elephants frequently have tusks. This is a sample of an argument that we shall identify as fallacious. Indeed, we shall say that it commits the *fallacy of incomplete evidence*. The point here is this: as the second premise makes clear, we have available additional relevant information about the creature in question. To be sure, it is a mammal; but it is also an elephant. This is relevant simply because the likelihood that an animal has tusks is very high if the animal in question is an elephant. In presenting our argument we have not taken this available additional relevant information into account. The conclusion drawn could not legitimately be drawn were that information taken into account. We shall say that an argument that does *not* take into account available relevant information that would significantly lower the likelihood that the conclusion is true commits the fallacy of incomplete evidence. Generally speaking, we can avoid this fallacy by using as narrow, or specific, a relevant reference class as is available to us. In the above case we should have considered not mammals, but those mammals that are elephants.

Fallacy of Incomplete Evidence

A statistical syllogism commits the fallacy of incomplete evidence if and only if available relevant information that would significantly lower the probability that the conclusion is true is ignored.

If an argument does *not* take into account available relevant information that would *raise* the likelihood that the conclusion is true, we shall not characterize the argument as fallacious, but simply note that the argument is weaker than one we could have provided. The general moral remains that we should narrow the reference class to one about which we have relevant information. In this way we hope to avoid fallacious arguments and simultaneously present the best argument we can.

But what information are we to count as available? I could, I suppose, run to the zoo and inspect the elephant in question above. But we do not wish to count information as available simply because it could in principle be obtained, that is, because we could obtain it if we were not subject to constraints of time, cost, and energy. In the case of the mammal we, as shown by the way we presented our argument, had the information that the creature was an elephant — this was explicitly mentioned in a premise of the argument. As we have noted, in drawing our conclusion we ought not to have considered the reference class of mammals, but the reference class of mammals that are elephants. Note that our premise did not give us information about that reference class: it mentioned only the reference class of mammals. So we had a quite clear case of our fallacy. We do not, however, want to restrict ourselves simply to what is explicitly stated. That is, we wish to impose more stringent conditions upon the choice of a reference class, to include more than what is explicitly mentioned in an argument.

What we must remember is that real arguments are presented in real contexts. It does not seem unreasonable to demand that the argument take account of the relevant information possessed by the persons in the context, information of which they are aware, or that is in some sense apparent to them. This is precisely the same point we made in connection with false analogies: there we demanded that the person presenting the argument take account of relevant dissimilarities that are, as we put it, apparent in the context.

The following is, let us suppose, true. Most students know little about history. I see a student sitting in a classroom. If there is nothing that distinguishes the student in any way it is perfectly legitimate to draw the conclusion that the student more likely than not knows little about history. Of course, the student could be an exception, an exceedingly knowledgeable history major. But the mere fact that this could be true does not in any way show that the argument is fallacious. In this situation the argument:

Most students know little of history.
That person is a student.
So, it is likely that that person knows little of history.

is an acceptable argument. Again, the person could be an exception, but nothing indicating this is apparent. If, by contrast, the student is carrying a sign that says "Join the History Club", this should be taken into account; in this situation it is apparent that we have additional relevant information. Presumably, students who carry signs promoting the History Club are more likely than other students to know something about history. In this situation we would count the above argument as committing the fallacy of incomplete evidence, since it does not take the student's advertising of the History Club into account.

Words like "apparent" and "available" are, of course, a bit vague. We may run across cases where there is a dispute over whether something is apparent. This is not, however, a dreadfully important point. What is important is that we take into account what we do know or come to find out. If we discover additional relevant information, we must include that in our specification of the reference class. That is, we must utilize the new reference class determined by the new information we have. Whether we had bothered explicitly to mention that reference class at the outset is, at least typically, not important; given that we have that specification, we must utilize it.

One question remains. What sort of obligation, if any, do we have to obtain further information? It is often possible to gather more information. I could, as noted above, have gone to the zoo and inspected the elephant in question. But, as we are using the phrase "fallacy of incomplete evidence", we shall not classify an argument as fallacious simply because we did not go to the zoo. Keep in mind that the notion of a fallacy is not the only notion of concern in critical thinking. Of course we should investigate further, go beyond the information at hand, if something important is at stake. If we fail to, we may not be arguing fallaciously, but might be acting irresponsibly. Consider the following cases. Imagine that you know most Albertans do not speak French and that most Quebecois do. You are hiring for a position requiring the person to speak French. A candidate from Alberta applies for the job. Even though it is unlikely that an Albertan speaks French, you would presumably not rest content with the information you have, but endeavor to find out more about the particular candidate. Or suppose that you know that few politicians favor affirmative action programs. If you were considering some particular candidates and did yourself favor affirmative action programs it would be important for you to find out what position they held on that issue. The simple, rough rule is that the more important the issue or question is, the more important it is to obtain information that may not be immediately apparent. Filling in this rough rule is, however, beyond the scope of this chapter.

Let us consider a few more examples illustrating the point that you should not too quickly classify an argument as fallacious. Suppose that you are walking around the campus of a university searching for, let us say, Building A. Consider the following argument:

> **Most persons walking around a campus know the location of the buildings on the campus.**
> **That is a person walking around the campus.**
> **So, likely that person will know the location of Building A.**

Given that the premises contain all the information available at this point, there is absolutely nothing wrong with this argument. The person approaching you could, of course, be a visitor who is herself lost. But this is merely to say that the conclusion of this argument might be false even though the premises are true. To say this is not to criticize the argument, but only to point out that the argument is not a valid deductive one. And that is something that we already know. The same point obtains with respect to the following argument:

> **Most dogs do not bite.**
> **So, likely that dog over there will not bite.**
> **(You then walk over to pet the dog.)**

Stating that the dog over there could be one of the rare ones who does bite is not a legitimate criticism of the argument. The argument is a good one. Any reluctance on your part to agree most likely arises from the fact that something is at stake: it is rather unpleasant, to say the least, to get bitten. To avoid being bitten you might well want to attempt to obtain more information, for instance by asking the owner whether the dog is friendly.

We have all heard that smoking is dangerous — in particular, that it significantly increases our chance of getting lung cancer. Suppose one were to respond to this argument by presenting the following statistical syllogism:

> **Most smokers do not die from lung cancer.**
> **I am a smoker.**
> **Therefore, I will probably not die from lung cancer.**

I decide, on the basis of this argument, that I need not worry about my smoking. Can we attack this decision by claiming that the argument on which it is based is somehow faulty? The answer to this is no — there is nothing at all wrong with the argument. The premises are true and do provide strong support for the conclusion. The problem here is that we are, in making our decision, not considering the relevant claim, which is, of course, that as a smoker I am more likely to die than I would be were I a non-smoker.

2.2 / Comparative Statistical Syllogisms

To account for cases such as that introduced at the end of the previous section, let us introduce a new form of argument that we shall call a *comparative statistical syllogism*.

Comparative Statistical Syllogism

F are more (less) likely to be *H* than are *G*.
a is an *F*.
b is a *G*.
So, *a* is more (less) likely to be *H* than is *b*.

Here we have, as before, one target class, namely that indicated by *H*. But we have two reference classes — the one introduced by *F*, the other by *G*. We may now consider the following argument. Your child says to you:

> **Smokers are more likely to die from lung cancer than are non-smokers.**
> **You are a smoker.**
> **I am not.**
> **Therefore, you are more likely to die from lung cancer than I.**

This is an example of what we have called the comparative statistical syllogism. I consider my current self, a smoker, and I compare this to the non-smoking self who could come to be. I reason as follows:

> **Smokers are more likely to die from lung cancer than are non-smokers.**
> **My current self is a smoker.**

> **A possible later self — a self who has quit — does not smoke.**
> **So, I am now more likely to die from lung cancer than I would be if I quit.**

It is presumably the fact that I am more likely to die if I do not quit that I should take into account when I decide whether to continue smoking, not simply or even primarily the point that I am not likely to die from lung cancer. That I am more likely to die from lung cancer if I continue my current ways than I would be if I altered my habits does not, of course, "force" a decision, but it is something that I should take into account when deciding.

What we are calling comparative statistical syllogisms are quite frequently used in practical situations. You might, for example, look at the marks from last term in two classes that you are considering taking. You note that the marks are virtually all high in class 1 and low in class 2. Since it appears that students in class 1 typically receive higher marks than those in class 2, you conclude that as a student in class 1 you would be more likely to receive a high mark that you would as a student in class 2. This is a quite reasonable conclusion to draw, although of course what you decide to do depends on other factors as well. (Perhaps, for example, you care about your marks but care equally that the subject matter of a class interests you.) At a later point we will turn to a more explicit discussion of decision-making; for now let us rest content with noting that various statistical syllogisms often provide us with the base that we utilize in making decisions.

Most of the points we made regarding the assessment of statistical syllogisms apply to the comparative variety as well. For example, in the case of the preceding argument involving two classes, suppose that class 1 was a math class and class 2 a history class, and that you have typically received dreadful marks in math but very good marks in history. If you do not take these facts into account, your argument is indeed a fallacious one.

We noted before that people quite often reject statistical syllogisms that are quite acceptable. In my experience this is particularly true when we are considering our own case. We often wish to think of ourselves as the "exception to the rule", that what happens to most people will not happen to us. Those who consider driving when they are drunk, or doing anything else for that matter, quite often reason in this kind of way. But unless we have some particular reason to exempt ourselves, some further information, we reason wrongly if we think of ourselves as the exception.

3 / Some Specific Kinds of Arguments

3.1 / Appeals to Individual Authority

Much of what we believe is obtained from others, from books, from newspapers, and the like. In such cases we often base our beliefs upon what we shall call an **argument from authority**. In this section we focus on appeals to individual authorities. In courts, for example, expert witnesses are called upon to testify regarding matters upon which they are in a special position to impart information or, as it is sometimes put, upon which they can provide an expert or professional opinion. We shall give an account of this kind of argument broader than the one standardly utilized in the courts, for what we are concerned with is any appeal to an individual or a source as being somehow in a special position, as being an authority, or being authoritative. When are such appeals legitimate, that is, what is required if such an argument is to be a good one?

Consider the following argument:

> **My history professor told me that England was invaded in the eleventh century.**
> **So, it was.**

That your history professor claimed England was invaded then clearly gives you some reason to believe it was. Pretty clearly, the core idea here is that when she talks about that subject matter she typically has it right. Let us inspect this situation more closely in order to see what conditions must be met if this kind of argument is to have any strength.

First, in these kinds of cases we are concerned with certain subject matters, areas, fields, or topics. In the preceding example we were concerned with English history. If our appeal to authority is not to be fallacious, the subject matter or field must be what we shall call a *genuine* one. What counts as a genuine subject matter or field? Is astrology, for instance, a genuine field? It is certainly true that many people study astrology. It is also true that a sizeable percentage of the population is half-inclined to believe in astrology in some sense or another. But there is good reason to believe that astrology is nonsense, that is, that it is not an area in which there is anything to know. If there is indeed nothing to know, then one of the conditions that must be met if an appeal to authority is to be a good one fails, namely the condition that the field be a genuine one. We shall count any appeal to authority that fails to meet the condition that it involve a genuine field as a *fallacious appeal to authority*.

It might be thought that we are being quite dogmatic, and just dismissing, for example, astrology without giving reasons. This is not our intent. A more cautious statement of the position being taken here is this. If an appeal to authority is to have any force, there must be a consensus that the matter at issue falls within an area of knowledge, an area in which there is something to know. We count a field as genuine if there is such a consensus. In speaking of a consensus here, we are not requiring that absolutely everyone agree there is an area of knowledge. We are requiring only that most reasonable members of society who are in a position to judge agree that we are operating in an area in which there is, or at the very least could be, knowledge.

It is quite clear that this condition is not met in the case of astrology. It is important to note that we are not claiming that what any given astrologer says is false. We are saying that since astrology is not a genuine field or area, we cannot accept claims on the basis of the kind of argument that we are calling an appeal to authority. Our notion of a field's being a genuine one should be viewed as restricted to cases where we are considering arguments from authority. If we wish to accept astrology or the claims made by astrologers we must have evidence other than the say-so of some person.

As well, be careful here to distinguish claims made by astrologers from claims made about astrology. We have suggested that we cannot appeal to astrologers as authorities regarding, for example, the future course of our lives. But there may nonetheless be individuals who are authorities on what astrology is. Suppose you wanted to find out how horoscopes are constructed. You might ask an astrologer how he constructs them. Presumably he is an authority about this. The situation here is in certain respects similar to the following: people throughout history, and even now, have attempted to construct perpetual motion devices. Such devices are physically impossible, so no one can in fact know how to build one. Nonetheless, you could study and become very knowledgeable about the various attempts people have made to construct the devices.

The question of authority is equally complex when we consider areas like morality. There is clearly no consensus here as to whether we have an area at all. Consider the following argument:

**Religious leader *X* says that abortion is wrong.
So, abortion is wrong.**

The conclusion of this argument is clearly contentious; however, that is not the point here. The point is that precisely because it is contentious whether morality is an area of knowledge, we cannot legitimately utilize an appeal to authority. Morality is in this sense not a genuine area of knowledge. Again, our claim is not that the conclusion of the preceding argument is false, but rather that we are considering questions with regard to which arguments from authority have no force. To say they have no force is, in our jargon, to say that they are fallacious, but, again, fallacious as arguments from authority. We are not saying that there is no circumstance in which the fact that a certain individual believes something to be immoral can count as evidence for a moral claim.

The second condition that must be met if such an argument is not to be fallacious follows in a straightforward way from the first: the source to which we appeal must actually be an authority in the relevant area, the area on which she or he is speaking. Individuals may count as authorities because they have engaged in a detailed study of the area, but practice and experience may count equally. For example, many excellent mechanics who specialize in repairing particular makes of car may never have gone to an automotive school. But if they say that your problem is such and so, you would be well advised to pay them heed. And consider the following:

Steven told me that he has been to Vancouver.
So (likely) he has been there.

It is a bit of stretch, but not too much, to consider this an argument from authority. That is, I, Steven, am presumed to know a fair bit about my own life, which is the area in question here. That I say I visited Vancouver does give you reason to believe that I did.

As an aside, we may note the following. We mentioned above the auto mechanic who has never been to school. If you have visited an auto dealer, however, you may have noticed signs up stating that the dealership's mechanic has gone to a school sponsored by the auto-maker whose cars the dealer sells. Does this matter? As a university student, you may have encountered persons who say that schools give one merely "theoretical" knowledge, and that it is better to have experience. It is important to realize that there is here no question that can be settled in the abstract. How best to become an authority, what is the best means to expertise, is a question to be settled in particular cases. To venture an opinion regarding our previous example, the schooling of mechanics has become more important as cars have become more computerized. The moral to be drawn from all of this is that what a source has to have done, what has to lie behind a source, if we are to accept that source as authoritative, is not a question that can be answered by laying down rules. Rather, we must exercise judgment. However, the fact remains that if the source is not an authoritative one then an appeal to authority is simply fallacious.

We noted earlier that an area, say astrology, may not count as a field of knowledge. Another kind of problem can arise: some areas, even though they are genuine areas of knowledge, contain particular subject matters with respect to which there is dispute. An argument from authority has force only if the particular conclusions being drawn are ones with respect to which there is consensus, ones regarding which experts would not typically disagree. (Keep in mind that, in speaking of consensus, we do not demand that absolutely all experts in the area agree, but rather that most reasonable persons who are authorities would agree.) Where there is such a consensus, and to the degree to which the consensus does approach unanimity, an appeal to an individual authority may be a strong one. But if there is no consensus among those who are authorities, then an appeal to an individual authority is fallacious.

One of the most common kinds of fallacious appeals to authority occurs when a person who is an authority in some area speaks outside of that area. Athletes sometimes are brought forward to speak about clothing or breakfast cereals. Unless they happen to have, for example, studied nutrition, we should not, so far as argumentation from authority is concerned, pay much attention to them. If you ask me a question about ancient Greek philosophy, my answers do have some claim to credibility, as that topic falls within my area of expertise. If you ask me about ancient Greek politics, my answers have no greater claim to accuracy than those of any tolerably well-educated person; I am not an authority on ancient Greek politics.

The bare skeleton of what underlies argument from authority is in effect:

Core of Arguments from Individual Authority

Most of what authority *a* says regarding area *S* is true.
a claims *p* (where *p* falls under area *S*).
So, *p*.

This is a statistical syllogism; therefore, we must take into account all relevant information. How might this requirement pose a problem regarding appeals to authority? One problem that can arise is that the person, though an authority, may have some vested interest that affects his or her credibility. For example, before you rush to embrace the claims of Jones, an authority on environmental problems, you should take into account that Jones may be employed by those who wish to build a massive pulp mill. It might be true that (most of what Jones says regarding area S is true), but false that (most of what Jones says regarding area S while she is acting on behalf of a pulp mill is true). We shall count an argument from authority as a fallacious argument if available relevant information regarding the authority is ignored. Here, the fallacy would be that of incomplete evidence. But you should recall the special conditions that an argument from authority must also meet if it is not to be fallacious.

Special Conditions for Arguments from Individual Authority

(1) The area must be a genuine area of knowledge.
(2) The person must be an authority or the source must be authoritative in the area in question.
(3) The statements must fall within that area.
(4) There must be a consensus among the authorities in the area regarding the statements made by the individual authority.

If an appeal to an individual authority violates any of the special conditions, it is a *fallacious appeal to authority*.

3.2 / Arguments from Consensus

We sometimes present arguments that have the following general form:

Arguments from Consensus

Most claims that are accepted by most people of kind K that fall in area S are true.
p is a claim falling in area S on which most people of kind K agree.
So, p is true.

The problem with this kind of argument is that the first premise is quite frequently false. Recall that, even though an exception was just made above, we do *not* typically call an argument fallacious simply because it has a false premise. What we should do instead is simply note that the argument has a false premise. But there is another problem that can render the argument from consensus fallacious. This argument is a statistical syllogism, with the reference class being *claims that are accepted by most people of kind K that fall in area S*. We are required to make use of all available relevant information. Well, *p* will be some particular statement. In most cases we will have other available relevant information. For instance, most claims that are accepted by most people who are Canadian citizens regarding which parties are in power are true. Now consider the particular claim that the Liberals hold power federally. That is, we may suppose, a claim on which most Canadian citizens agree. But it is also one that is supported by the evidence provided by news broadcasts, for example. This is available relevant information that I am ignoring. Given that this information supports the conclusion rather more directly, we should classify this particular argument from consensus as a weak one. (You may find it helpful to review the general discussion of statistical syllogisms.)

We will say that we have a *fallacious appeal to consensus* if relevant available information that would weaken our justification for accepting the conclusion is ignored. Note that what we are calling a fallacious appeal to consensus is simply our fallacy of incomplete evidence applied to a statistical syllogism which is an argument from consensus.

Let us illustrate this point again. Consider the following argument:

> **Most claims made by most people regarding the question of whether something is a genuine science are true.**
> **That astrology is a genuine science is a claim made by most people.**
> **So, astrology is a genuine science.**

I do not know whether the premises are true; let us suppose they are. Even so, the argument is a fallacious one. We do have available relevant information regarding the question of whether astrology is a science. And the reference class we should be considering is the class of claims made by most people regarding the question of whether astrology is a science.

3.3 / Some Seeming Consensus Arguments

There are certain arguments that look like inductive arguments from consensus, but are not. We most commonly find these in institutional contexts such as courts and legislatures, or in contexts where the fact that most people think something "makes" it true. Consider the following argument:

> **The majority of the Trade Commisson held that the Canadian tariff policy was in violation of the trade treaties.**
> **So, the policy was in violation of the treaty.**

Here we are supposing that we have an institutional set-up in which what a certain group of people find or hold determines the 'truth'. Note, though, that it is somewhat misleading to speak simply of what the people in question think or believe. Typically, the people must act in some way specified by the rules of the institution in question. Once they act in the specified way, what they say goes: the policy is held to be in violation and appropriate actions are undertaken.

In many countries the highest court of the land is placed in a very special position. Consider the following:

> **The majority of the Supreme Court of Canada found the abortion law in violation of the Canadian Charter of Rights and Freedoms.**
> **Therefore, the law is in violation of the Charter.**

(The Charter confers rights and freedoms similar to those given to Americans by the U.S. Constitution.) Once the Supreme Court of Canada reached this decision, the law was in violation of the Charter and was no longer in force. No further persons could be convicted under this law, and a person who had been so convicted was no longer a criminal. And of course, as many of you know, the Supreme Court of the United States is quite frequently called upon to determine whether a given law is constitutional. In such cases the decisions cannot be understood simply in terms of the thoughts or beliefs of the justices of the Court. The justices must present or concur in a decision. (A decision is typically a written document released in the proper time and proper circumstances.) Since neither of these examples is a case where the sole basis for the conclusion is what the individuals involved think or believe, neither is actually an argument from consensus at all. Given the institutional rules in place, it follows deductively from, for example, the fact that a decision was made by the majority of the justices in the Canadian case that the law in question violates the Charter and that the law is no longer in force. And, as you may know, the United States Supreme Court has decided that capital punishment is not in and of itself a violation of the constitutional prohibition of cruel and unusual punishments. Consequently, states can, within certain limits, introduce capital punishment as a punishment.

This kind of point can be made clear by considering votes in a majoritarian legislature. Precisely what the members of a legislature think or believe does not matter; what does matter is how they vote. If a majority votes for something to be a law, then that something becomes a law. Or rather, it becomes a law after such other steps prescribed in the structure have been taken.

3.4 / Arguments from Collective Authority

In section 3.1 we discussed arguments from individual authority. There is a related kind of argument, one which is also a special case of an argument from consensus, that we shall call an *argument from collective authority*.

Argument from Collective Authority

Most claims that are accepted by most authorities in area **S** that fall in **S** are true.
The authorities claim **p** (where **p** falls under **S**).
So, **p** is true.

What differentiates this from an argument from consensus is the appeal to the notion of an authority. Notice that arguments from individual authority differ from those from collective authority in that the former involve an appeal to one authority and the latter to more than one. An argument from collective authority must meet the same conditions as an argument from an individual authority:

Special Conditions for
Arguments from Collective Authority

(1) The area must be a genuine area of knowledge.
(2) The persons must be authorities or the sources must be authoritative in the area in question.
(3) The statements must fall within that area.
(4) There must be a consensus regarding the statements.

As was the case with arguments from individual authority, violation of any of the special conditions yields a *fallacious argument from authority*. Clearly questions may arise regarding the consensus condition and the truth condition. We shall turn to a discussion of these.

3.5 / Some Issues Regarding Arguments from Authority

If we think about it we should realize that much of what we think or believe, we think or believe on the basis of some argument from authority. But, as we noted, there are two problems that merit some further discussion.

The first, that regarding the consensus condition, can be made apparent if we consider court cases. In connection with some issues this is, typically at any rate, quite uncontentious. For example, if a ballistics expert testifies that a given bullet came from a particular gun, the testimony is typically accepted without question. But with respect to other issues there is often a conflict between authorities. In trials these might typically be conflicts between experts called by the prosecution and experts called by the defense. How are we to decide between experts, inside or outside the courtroom, when there are such conflicts? There is, unfortunately, absolutely no way to provide a general answer to such a question. But here are some of the kinds of considerations that we can bring to bear in such situations. First, we must remember that the consensus condition does not mean that each and every authority in a given area will agree. Typically there will be dissenters. We cannot claim that dissenters are invariably wrong and those on the dominant side invariably right. It is rather that, in the absence of any special knowledge of our own, we should at least incline toward the dominant view.

We might consider whether or not the experts in question have special interests. This would seem to apply in the seemingly endless disputes regarding the effects of smoking. Those who have spoken on behalf of the tobacco industry seem to have a special interest in the well-being of that industry. This might, depending on the circumstances, make us question their honesty (do they in fact believe what they say?) or question their ability accurately to assess the evidence available with respect to the issue at hand.

There may be other situations in which the disagreement seems to be such as to make us decide that the consensus condition is simply not met. We cannot simply decide this on the basis of counting. That is, it might well be that 7 out of 10 experts agree on a particular answer. From a simply numeric point of view the seven are dominant, that is, in the majority. But we should not view this as simply a question of numbers. We should not count a view as dominant if we judge the dissent to be significant. The dissenters' case might be strong enough for us to count their dissent as significant. In this case we should deny that the consensus condition is met. If we do judge this condition not to be met, then we should not ourselves choose between the answers unless we have some other kind of evidence supporting one or the other of the answers.

The absence of consensus may be significant in particular circumstances. In a recent case an *au pair* was accused of the murder of an infant. The claim was that the infant had died as a direct consequence of a severe shaking that occurred shortly before the death. This claim was supported by the majority, at least the majority of the physicians who treated the infant prior to its death. In this case the defense presented expert testimony that suggested that the infant had suffered an injury to its skull at some time prior to the day in question. It might have died without a *severe* shaking. I suggest that there is an absence of consensus in this case. If so, since it was a criminal case involving reasonable doubt, I would suggest that the absence of consensus brings about reasonable doubt. For her guilt to be established beyond a reasonable doubt would seem to require that it had been established beyond a reasonable doubt that the death of the infant required a *severe* shaking. As you may know, the jury did in this case convict the accused. But, unless there was some sort of additional evidence that they had of which I am unaware, their decision was simply wrong.

Here is an example of a position that, at the time of writing, I would take with respect to some issues concerning the depletion of the ozone layer. I would suggest that the view that there is such should be accepted. That claim is one with respect to which there is consensus, even though there are those who dissent. Beyond that there seems an absence of consensus, particularly in connection with how much of a danger this depletion poses. Is it the explanation of the seeming increase in the birth of abnormal frogs? Some authorities have said yes, but at this point there does not seem to be a consensus.

Another sort of problem arises with respect to the truth condition. Many people reject arguments from authority on the grounds that authorities have so often turned out to be wrong. And we all know that over time scientific opinion changes. Newtonian physics was for several centuries taken to be accurate. But, as you probably know, Newtonian physics has been replaced. There are two points to be kept in mind. First, we tend to exaggerate the number of cases of failure. Second, we have spoken in terms of truth. That is, we have taken as one premise that most of the authorities' claims in the area are true. If you doubt this, think of it in terms of reasonable belief. Authorities are typically in a position to base their views on the best evidence available at any given time. Given this we could replace our claim that most of what they say is true by the claim that most of what they say expresses the view that it is at the time in question most reasonable to accept. This would not really alter any of the fundamentals of our account of arguments from authority.

4 / *Ad Hominem* Arguments

You may recall the tale of the boy who cried wolf. The boy was a prankster: even when he knew there was no wolf threatening the village, he would scream out that there was one in the vicinity. The villagers initially heeded his cry and took the appropriate measures, but soon became angry and ceased to pay any attention to the boy. One day the inevitable happened: the wolf did show up, the boy gave the alarm, and it was ignored. The boy was, if I recall correctly, eaten. There is no doubt a moral to be drawn from this story, but it is the position of the villagers that interests us. On that fateful day they no doubt reasoned as follows:

> **Typically, when the boy cries wolf there is no danger.**
> **The boy is crying wolf.**
> **So most likely there is no danger.**

This is a good argument, one that is a statistical syllogism. But one often finds arguments that are like this one yet quite dubious. The family name for these is ***ad hominem arguments*** (*ad hominem* is Latin for "toward the person").

4.1 / Abusive *Ad Hominem*

Consider the following form of argumentation:

Abusive *Ad Hominem*

a is *F* (where *F* is an aspect of character) and most of what an *F* says that falls into area *S* is false.
a says *p*, which falls into area *S*.
So, *p* is false.

Given that *F* here picks out some aspect of the character of the individual, we shall speak of the argument as an *abusive ad hominem*. We include in character an individual's physical traits, mannerisms, personality, and the like. Here is one example.

Millikan is a real jerk, just extraordinarily nasty.
He said that he would go to the store. But I bet he won't.

The question to be asked here is whether Millikan's being a real jerk renders it likely that what he says (in area *S*) is false. Is being a real jerk at all relevant? If it is, if his being so *does* render it likely that what he says in that area is false, then the argument is not fallacious. (For example, perhaps his being a real jerk often manifests itself in deceiving people regarding his plans.) If his being a jerk is not relevant, if it *does not* render it likely that what he says in the area is false, then we do have a fallacious argument. And we saw in the case of the boy who cried wolf that the boy's being a prankster was relevant: the villagers' argument was a good one. But more often than not, abusive *ad hominem* arguments are fallacious. We should note that some authors reserve the term "abusive *ad hominem*" for an argument of this sort that is fallacious. We do not follow this practice, but utilize "abusive *ad hominem*" simply for this kind of argument. If a particular argument of this kind is fallacious, we shall use the term "fallacious abusive *ad hominem*" to characterize it.

A person's race is, as we use the term "character", an aspect of a person's character. We do here, unfortunately, often find *ad hominem* arguments used. I, for example, grew up in an extremely racist society in which many "whites" were quite prepared to dismiss claims made by persons who were not "whites". Arguments such as:

He says he wasn't there, but he's a black and you know how they lie.

were frequently presented.

In a slightly different vein, notice that some people tend to disbelieve others who have "shifty eyes", sweat profusely when they speak, or, as it is sometimes put, "appear nervous". The arguments here are cases of what we have called abusive *ad hominem*. Any such argument should be approached with extreme caution.

4.2 / Circumstantial *Ad Hominem*

A closely related argument has basically the same form:

Circumstantial *Ad Hominem*

a is *F* (where *F* is a circumstance of *a*) and most of what an *F* says that falls into area *S* is false.
a says *p*, which falls into area *S*.
So, *p* is false.

Note that here being an *F* identifies, to use the standard jargon, some circumstance that *a* is in. What is a circumstance? We would, for example, count being a Christian, a Communist, a Russian, a Jew, and so on as circumstances rather than aspects of the individual's character; whence the name *circumstantial ad hominem*. Now we ask our standard question regarding relevance. If being an *F* *does* render it likely that what individuals who are *F* say within area *S* is false, then the argument is not fallacious. If, however, being an *F* *does not* render it likely that what individuals who are *F* say within area *S* is false, then the argument is fallacious. More often than not, circumstantial *ad hominem* arguments are fallacious.

Consider now the following argument, where the Tall Tales is an organization for people who enjoy exaggerating:

Jones is a member of the Tall Tales Club. He told me he caught a northern pike that weighed forty pounds, but that it flopped out of his boat. I bet he didn't catch one.

This is not a fallacious argument. By contrast, consider the following argument:

> **Clinton is just another politician. He claims that he will
> run an honest government. But he probably won't.**

This argument is, I would suggest, a fallacious one. (Remember that this is *not* the claim that the conclusion is false.) A certain kind of stereotyping occurs here, namely that politicians are typically dishonest. Unless this is true (and it seems dubious), the argument is a fallacious one. Here again, some authors use the term "circumstantial *ad hominem*" as the name for a fallacy, but we shall use it to refer to a kind of argument. If a particular argument of that kind is fallacious, we shall state this fact explicitly.

4.3 / *Ad Hominem* Arguments and the Notion of a Fallacy

When we introduced, in the opening chapter, the notions of a fallacy and a fallacious argument, we noted that we would not typically apply these terms simply in virtue of an argument's having a false premise. However, if you survey the preceding two sections, you will see that in effect we have done just this. We took *ad hominem* arguments as having a premise:

> **Most people with that character or in that circumstance
> who say such-and-so are wrong.**

We labelled the argument a fallacious one when such a premise was false, as it frequently is. Why did we here make an exception to our general policy? There are two reasons. The first is simply that the classification of such arguments as fallacious is a common one. The second is that people who present such arguments frequently have formed their belief in the premise not on the basis of evidence, but on the basis of prejudice or some other non-reasonable basis. Given that the context in which such arguments are presented is frequently one in which the operative factors are not reasonable ones, it seems legitimate to extend our notion of a fallacious argument to cover such contexts.

4.4 / *Tu Quoque* Arguments

There is a kind of argument, typically treated as a special case of *ad hominem* argumentation, that is worth singling out with its own label: *tu quoque* (Latin for "you too"). We shall not treat it as a special kind of statistical syllogism, but will include it here, since it is traditionally considered along with the arguments we were just examining. This new kind of argument runs like this:

Tu Quoque

a has presented an argument against some claim *p*. *b* responds by saying: "But *a*, you believe that *p*" (or something close to *p*).

Or like this:

---

a has made an accusation against *b* or claimed that some-thing *b* did is wrong. *b* defends himself against the accusation or suggests that nothing is wrong by saying either (1) "But *a*, you did the same thing (or something close to the same thing) yourself" or (2) "But *a*, you ignored others who did the same thing".

Let us consider some examples of this kind of argument. Suppose I suggest to you that walking across the gym floor in your street shoes is wrong since it might damage the floor, to which you respond: "But Steven, you did it just the other day." Or, as a policeman is writing out your speeding ticket, you say, "I don't see why you're giving me a ticket. I was just passed by someone driving even faster than me." Typically, such argumentation is fallacious. To be sure, I was not practicing what I preach when I walked across the floor the other day. My behavior might give you some reason to believe that I am a hypocrite; but my having walked across the floor is not good evidence that it is right to do so. As a challenge, you might try to find or construct some *tu quoque* arguments that are not fallacious.

Chapter Summary

In Section 1 we considered some kinds of statements. In 1.1 we distinguished two kinds of generalizations.

Kinds of Generalizations

A statement is a *universal generalization* if and only if it states that all (100%) or none (0%) of the members of one group or class are members of another group or class.

A statement is a *statistical generalization* if and only if it states that some proportion (neither all nor none) of the members of one group or class are members of another group or class.

We also looked briefly at statements that speak of "lots" or "many", noting how they differed from, for example, statements speaking of "most".

In Section 2 we turned to *statistical syllogisms*: In 2.1 we introduced the basic form:

Positive Statistical Syllogism

Most *F* are *G*.
a is an *F*.
So, *a* is, or very likely is, *G*.

Negative Statistical Syllogism

Few *F* are *G*.
a is an F.
So, *a* is not, or is very likely not, *G*.

F introduced what we called the *reference class*, while *G* introduced what we called the *target class*.

We then introduced:

Fallacy of Incomplete Evidence

A statistical syllogism commits the fallacy of incomplete evidence if and only if available relevant information that would significantly lower the probability that the conclusion is true is ignored.

Generally speaking, to avoid this fallacy we should specify a reference class utilizing all our available information. And of course, as we noted in the preceding chapter, we should make our conclusion *proportionate* to the evidence we have.

We then turned, in 2.2, to *comparative statistical syllogisms*:

Comparative Statistical Syllogism

F are more (less) likely to be *H* than are *G*.
a is an *F*.
b is a *G*.
So, *a* is more (less) likely to be *H* than is *b*.

Suppose, for example, that people who take megadoses of vitamin C are less likely to get colds than people who do not. I take such doses whereas you do not. I would then conclude that I am less likely to get a cold than you are.

In Section 3 we turned to some specific kinds of arguments, some special cases of statistical syllogisms. The first, which we considered in 3.1, we called *arguments from individual authority*, the individual case of *arguments from authority*.

Core of Arguments from Individual Authority

Most of what authority *a* says regarding area *S* is true.
a claims *p* (where *p* falls under area *S*).
So, *p*.

Special Conditions for Arguments from Individual Authority

(1) The area must be a genuine area of knowledge.
(2) The person must be an authority or the source must be authoritative in the area in question.
(3) The statements must fall within that area.
(4) There must be a consensus among the authorities in the area regarding the statements made by the individual authority.

If any of the special conditions are not met then we have a *fallacious appeal to authority*. We also noted that since these arguments are special cases of statistical syllogisms we must consider whether or not they involve the *fallacy of incomplete evidence*.

We next turned to *arguments from consensus*:

Arguments from Consensus

Most claims that are accepted by most people of kind **K** that fall in area **S** are true.
p is a claim falling in area **S** on which most people of kind **K** agree.
So, **p** is true.

We will say that we have a *fallacious appeal to consensus* if relevant available information that would weaken our justification for accepting the conclusion is ignored. We noted in 3.3 that we should guard against taking certain implicitly deductive arguments as arguments from concensus.

In 3.4 we turned to *arguments from collective authority*:

Argument from Collective Authority

Most claims that are accepted by most authorities in area **S** that fall in **S** are true.
The authorities claim **p** (where **p** falls under **S**).
So, **p** is true.

Special Conditions for Arguments from Collective Authority

(1) The area must be a genuine area of knowledge.
(2) The persons must be authorities or the sources must be authoritative in the area in question.
(3) The statements must fall within that area.
(4) There must be a consensus regarding the statements.

Here again the violation of any special condition yields a *fallacious appeal to authority*.

In 3.5 we turned to a discussion of some general questions regarding arguments from authority. We focused here on the truth condition and the consensus condition.

In Section 4 we turned to *ad hominem arguments*. In 4.1 we identified *abusive ad hominem arguments*:

Abusive *Ad Hominem*

a is **F** (where **F** is an aspect of character) and most of what an **F** says that falls into area **S** is false.
a says **p**, which falls into area **S**.
So, **p** is false.

---

and, in 4.2, *circumstantial ad hominem arguments*:

Circumstantial *Ad Hominem*

a is *F* (where *F* is a circumstance of *a*) and most of what an *F* says that falls into area *S* is false.
a says *p*, which falls into area *S*.
So, *p* is false.

---

as special cases of statistical syllogisms. We noted that while *ad hominem* arguments are typically fallacious, we would leave open the possibility that some are not. In 4.3 we considered why we call arguments from authority "fallacious" when the typical problem is that the first premise is false.

In 4.4 we turned to *tu quoque* arguments. Some are like this.

Tu Quoque

a has presented an argument against some claim *p*. *b* responds by saying: "But *a*, you believe that *p*" (or something close to *p*).

---

or like this:

---

a has made an accusation against *b* or claimed that something *b* did is wrong. *b* defends himself against the accusation or suggests that nothing is wrong by saying either (1) "But *a*, you did the same thing (or something close to the same thing) yourself" or (2) "But *a*, you ignored others who did the same thing".

CHAPTER 4

A Miscellany of Arguments

In this chapter we shall examine various kinds of arguments that do not fall under any of our current categories. We will also examine various kinds of problems that can arise in argumentation and in the assessment of arguments.

1 / Some Common Kinds of Arguments

1.1 / Straw Man Arguments

Consider the following argument:

> **Proponents of abortion are child-killers. As long as they are active your children are endangered.**

You should not be too impressed with this argument; why? To be sure, the argument involves abusive language, but there is another kind of problem: it seems to rely upon the claim that individuals who are pro-choice also condone infanticide. Clearly, that premise is false—those who are pro-choice do not typically condone infanticide in the sense of killing extant children. The argument attacks such people by attacking a position they do not actually hold. The problem with this argument is not that the premises, if true, would not support the conclusion; the argument is not fallacious in that sense. One problem is, as noted, that a critical premise is false. But what centrally characterizes an argument of this sort is that those attacked do not hold the position in question. The use of this tactic is, unfortunately, common enough to warrant a label. We shall call these *straw man arguments*.

Straw Man Arguments

A straw man argument proceeds by attributing to those attacked a position they do not hold.

Do not forget that an argument that is a straw man may also contain other errors in reasoning.

One often finds that political and social campaigns frequently rely heavily upon not only *ad hominem* argumentation (which we examined in the preceding chapter), but also straw man arguments. There is, for example, much controversy concerning the logging industry and forestry policies. On the environmentalist side one sometimes finds a tendency to portray those who in a given case favor logging as endorsing the uncontrolled chopping down of every tree in existence; whereas the industrial side is sometimes prone to portray environmentalists as persons who place no value on the economic well-being of individuals involved in the forest industry. We cannot, of course, just assume that everyone holds some moderate position, but in this kind of heated exchange we should at the very least be on our guard. We should make some effort to try to identify the positions that the various protagonists actually hold, since such controversies are too often replete with straw man arguments.

It would seem that straw man arguments are often used with an eye to political effectiveness. For example, many people are opposed, in connection with social policy, to any group being granted "special rights". Special rights or privileges are in many contexts, particularly those in which a person holds some office or position, quite common. Queen Elizabeth II has many special rights and privileges as do chief executives, political leaders, and police officers. But in other contexts special rights are understood as giving some group some sort of competitive advantage which others lack. And, as I say, most people seem opposed to this. As you may know, various jurisdictions have considered legislation that precludes discrimination based upon sexual orientation. This legislation is often portrayed, by those who oppose it, as involving the granting of special rights to, for example, gays and lesbians. This characterization is clearly designed to invoke general opposition to giving anyone a competitive advantage. Whether or not you favor such legislation, it seems clear that this is a straw man argument. The legislation does not give anyone some special competitive advantage.

1.2 / Arguments from Ignorance

I suspect that you have heard people present arguments that in the end reduce to some one of the following:

Arguments from Ignorance

(1) There is no evidence against my position.
So, it is correct.
(2) There is no evidence available for **p**.
Therefore, **p** is false.
(3) My claim has not been conclusively refuted.
So, my claim is likely true, or my claim is just as respectable as any opposed claim.
(4) **p** has not been conclusively supported.
Therefore, **p** is false, or is no more respectable than any opposed claim.

Each one of these will be classified as an ***argument from ignorance***. Of course, the arguments are rarely put so bluntly. Let us discuss each in turn.

There is no evidence against my position.
So, it is correct.

The premise of this argument is that there is no evidence against the position in question, while the conclusion is that the position is correct. The problem with arguments of this sort is clearly that the absence of evidence against a position is not generally evidence for that position. Such arguments as these are, then, typically fallacious. The premise, even if true, does not in fact support the conclusion. For instance, as this is written I have no evidence against the claim that a car is driving by my house; but it is apparent that I ought not to conclude that therefore a car is driving by my house. Since the mistake here is so blatant, it is puzzling that anyone would ever make it. But, if you think back to arguments you have heard or even presented, you may remember some of this sort.

Part of the problem may be that there are certain special conditions in which an argument from ignorance has some merit. If we have made a thorough investigation and have not been able to find evidence against a claim, this fact may give us reason to accept the claim. This point is easier to see if we consider our second variant, in which we argue that there is no evidence for a claim and conclude that the claim is false:

There is no evidence available for *p*.
Therefore, *p* is false.

In my experience this kind of argument is rarely presented quite so baldly. Be careful in dealing with more subtle variations: this way of arguing is, for reasons similar to those presented in the first case, typically fallacious. I have no evidence right now that a car is driving by my house, but I should not thereby conclude that there is no car driving by my house. You should proceed with caution because this kind of argument is related to arguments that do have some merit. Since being reasonable involves forming beliefs in accord with such evidence as we have, it is not reasonable, given only the premise that there is no evidence available for *p*, to believe that *p* is false. It would be legitimate, however, to conclude that it is unreasonable to believe *p*. As this is a difficult point, let us consider some examples. Suppose it is true that there is no evidence for life after death, but you nonetheless believe that there is life after death. If I simply said to you that your belief is false because there is no evidence that there is life after death, I would be reasoning fallaciously. However, I would be right to claim that you have no reason to believe what you do. And if being reasonable involves forming beliefs in accord with the evidence, I would be right to suggest that you were being unreasonable in believing in life after death.

But, as we noted, we do have to be careful here. I do not, for instance, believe in unicorns. I do not believe in them because, after numerous active searches, we have not found what one would expect to find if there were unicorns. Much the same kind of point can be made in connection with flying saucers and alien visitation. We know perfectly well the kinds of things that would count as evidence for them. With respect to many kinds of claims *p* we know that:

If *p* is true, then *q*, *r* ... are to be expected.

If there are abominable snowmen then, by this time, we would expect there to be photographs, a plethora of reliable sightings, remains, and the like. We should expect this, for example, because of the numbers required to sustain a population. Various individuals have claimed that such evidence is available. Perhaps you have seen some of the photographs and films that have come to public attention. But these have, almost invariably to my knowledge, turned out to be bogus. What we would have expected does not seem to have happened. Consequently we should believe that the claim that there are abominable snowmen is very likely false. And, in the case of UFOs the sightings often involve misinterpretations of more mundane phenomena. It is very important to note that we are not denying the claim that it is possible that there are abominable snowmen or flying saucers. But that a claim is in this sense possible is, of course, not evidence for it. (See below for a more extended discussion of "possibility".)

Our third variant is:

> **The claim _p_ has not been conclusively refuted.**
> **So, _p_ is likely true, or _p_ is just as respectable as any opposed claim.**

This moves from the absence of a conclusive refutation of a claim to the truth of the claim or to a conclusion that the claim is just as good as any opposed claim. Part of the problem here is that "conclusive" refutation, like "conclusive" proof, is very hard to come by. We will consider this kind of point later. But it leads us now to our fourth variant:

> **The claim _p_ has not been conclusively proven.**
> **So, _p_ is likely false, or, _p_ is no more respectable than any opposed claim.**

This fourth variant differs from the third in that it moves from the absence of conclusive proof or support of the claim to the falsehood of the claim or to the conclusion that the claim is no better than any opposed claim. Perhaps the most common variants of the third and fourth variants are those that move to the conclusions concerning respectablility. Most of the points made regarding the first two variants transfer directly to this style of argument. Clearly, for example, the absence of a conclusive refutation of a claim is not generally evidence that the claim is true.

But some additional points may be made, as we shall illustrate with an example. This style of argument is very popular among so-called scientific creationists, whose argument may be viewed as starting with the following claim:

> **It is impossible to prove scientifically any particular concept of origins.**

or with:

Evolutionary theory has not been "proven" to be true.

Let us grant this. But suppose the creationist concludes from this that both creation and evolution are matters of faith and, as such, opposed positions that have an equal claim to acceptability. The problem here is simply this: from the fact that neither of two positions has been proved (even, as here, where such proof might be unattainable), it does *not* follow that we do not have better evidence for one position than for the other. Consequently, the argument presented by the creationist is a fallacious one. This, of course, is not to say that either his premises or his conclusion is false. It is to say that we need to consider a different question, namely, the question of what kinds of evidence we have for each of the opposed views. I would argue that we have very good evidence for evolution and, as well, evidence against creation; but again, my claim that the creationist's argument is fallacious does *not* depend upon my holding that evolutionary theory is the best theory of origins available to us. It is always important to remember that classifying an argument as committing this fallacy does not commit one to holding that the conclusion of that argument is false.

One might point to the legal systems common to United States, Canada, and many other countries. In these systems jurors are committed to voting "not guilty" if the guilt of the accused is not established beyond a reasonable doubt. The problem here is in part that the terms "guilty" and "not guilty" have both a specific legal sense and an ordinary sense. In one ordinary sense, the claim that someone is guilty is simply the claim that they committed a certain act, whereas the claim that they are not guilty is the claim that they did not commit that act. But in the courts we are concerned with guilt in the sense of convictability. A person is to be convicted — found guilty by the jurors — if and only if the evidence that the person did something is in a sense overwhelming, that is, it puts the claim that the person did it beyond a reasonable doubt. It is not our task here to give an account of reasonable doubt. What it is important to note is that a vote of not guilty — a vote against convicting the person on trial — may indicate either that one doubts that the person did it or that one thinks the evidence falls short of that required for a vote for conviction. In many cases, one should vote "not guilty" even though one thinks the evidence supports the claim that the person did it: those cases where the evidence, though it might be quite strong, is not strong enough to put the claim that the person did it beyond a reasonable doubt.

1.3 / Begging the Question

The problem we shall be discussing here is just as troublesome in the deductive as in the inductive case. However, it is so common a problem we do well to discuss it at this point. Consider the following argument, where, we shall suppose, the issue at hand is whether or not God exists:

> **The Bible is the word of God. It states very clearly in the Bible that God exists. Therefore, God exists.**

Clearly something is wrong with this argument, but what? To begin, note that the argument needs the premise that the Bible is the word of God; but this premise is one we would not have reason to believe unless we already had reason to believe that God exists, which is the very conclusion the argument is meant to support. We shall characterize this argument as one that *begs the question* (or as question begging). Arguments of this sort are also often spoken of as circular arguments. The problem here need not be that any claim made in the argument, either premise or conclusion, is false. If the argument is inductive, it may be a strong argument; if it is deductive, it may be valid. The problem lies elsewhere. The point of real argumentation is to provide evidence for claims, evidence that gives us independent grounds for belief in the conclusion. Arguments that beg the question cannot in this sense have a point for, as noted, they are arguments in which we do not have reason to believe a needed premise or premises unless we have antecedent reason to believe the conclusion.

Begging the Question

An argument begs the question if and only if one would not have reason to believe the premises are true unless one already had reason to believe the conclusion was true.

In some cases one begs the question by using the conclusion as one of the premises. If you argue for some claim *p* by stating, "It's just true, that's all", most of us would detect the circularity. But, more often, individuals beg the question by using some term or phrase that is in effect a synonym. That abortion is wrong because it is murder seems to suffer from this problem, as murder simply is wrongful killing. And occasionally students and others — myself included — when asked to write a paper defending a position, defend it by putting forward as premises various statements that are simply alternate phrasings of the conclusion in question.

1.4 / There's a Conspiracy

There are of course plots, conspiracies, and cover-ups. Documents that are now publicly available seem to indicate that tobacco companies, over an extended period of time, conspired to conceal information regarding the dangers of smoking. The Central Intelligence Agency in the United States has plotted, sometimes successfully, to overthrow governments that were disliked by the United States. Even though there are plots, conspiracies, and cover-ups, we should approach claims and explanations appealing to them with some caution.

One of the historically most significant "conspiracy" beliefs is that in an international Jewish or Zionist conspiracy to "control" the world. As you no doubt know, action upon this and related beliefs led, in World War II, to the Holocaust. There are today individuals who maintain these beliefs, or the belief that there was "really" no Holocaust. If you examine these beliefs, several features should serve to alert you to be very cautious. First, we should note that the "authorities" appealed to are, from the standpoint of the mainstream, cranks. As we noted in our discussion of appeals to authority this precludes our acceptance of the view on the basis of an appeal to authority. Again it is important to emphasize that we are not claiming that the dominant view is necessarily correct. It is rather a question of forming beliefs that are as reasonable as possible. Second, the evidence against the view seems to be overwhelming. In this case, that is to say that the evidence for the claim that there was a Holocaust seems overwhelming. This leads us to the third point. This evidence is dismissed as itself the product of the conspiracy. It is this latter feature which is one of the primary problematic features of many such conspiracy theories.

Governments do have the capacity to indulge in secret projects. The Manhattan Project, the project that led to the development of the atomic bomb, was kept highly secret during the Second World War. But note two features. It was in one sense a "large" project, but comparatively few people, in terms of the size of the government, were involved or, at the time, knew about it. And it did not remain secret. (Of course, this is a slightly special case — the project was successful and the weapons were used, but it still points out that secrets are difficult to keep over time.)

There are a number of conspiracy theories that have attracted and still do attract a considerable amount of public interest and belief. Various conspiratorial accounts of the assassination of John F. Kennedy have, virtually since the time of the assassination, attracted varying degrees of attentions. Some suppose involvement by either the FBI or the CIA. Others involve the claim that anti-Castro Cuban exiles arranged the murder due to Kennedy's "softness" on Castro. But all involve the rejection of the standard view that a lone gunman, Lee Harvey Oswald, did it on his own. More recently, many people believed that TWA Flight 800, which exploded near New York, was shot down by a missile, possibly one fired during U.S. military exercises. This is not in and of itself a conspiracy theory. At the outset it was one hypothesis that the initial evidence did not preclude. But it became a conspiracy theory when it became tied with the claim that there was a secret government plot to hide the evidence that the plane was indeed shot down by a missile. A CIA animation that provided the official account of what seemed most likely to have happened (which did not involve a missile) was dismissed by some as part of the cover-up.

And many people remain convinced of some or all of the following claims: At least one alien spacecraft crashed near Roswell, New Mexico. An alien survivor was kept alive for some years in a secret government site. Alien spacecraft have been tracked many times by NORAD (the North American Air Defense Command). Alien propulsion technology that would solve the problems regarding the emission of greenhouse gases is being kept secret by governments. Some current technology is based upon back-engineering of crashed alien spacecraft. The government is aware of many contacts that have been made with aliens. There are governments within governments that keep the evidence of all of this secret even from the elected officials. And so on.

It is not that any of these claims are certainly false. It is rather that they have some or all of a set of features that should alert us to be quite careful in assessing them. These are:

Watch For:

(1) Denial of positions that at least appear to meet the condition for a legitimate argument from authority.
(2) A slender, at best, evidential base.
(3) Lack of accounts of how the conspiracy or cover-up might be carried out.
(4) Explanation of the absence of evidence by an appeal to the cover-up or conspiracy.
(5) Involvement of large numbers of people in the cover-up or conspiracy.

It is not as if the presence of any or all of these factors shows a particular claim to be false. It is simply that they indicate that we should be especially cautious in assessing the claim.

2 / Some Questions of Meaning

2.1 / Semantic Pitfalls

It should be clear that both identifying and assessing arguments involves paying careful attention to meanings. It is not our intent to indulge in any full-scale study of meaning, but a few points are worth mentioning, to enable us to be on our guard.

Words, phrases, and sentences can be ambiguous. We noted one case of this in section 1.2: the word "guilty" may simply mean "did the act in question" or it may refer to a finding in a trial. Clearly, we would be making a mistake if we argued as follows:

She was (found) not guilty.
Therefore, she is not guilty (didn't do it).

We shall say that an argument like this commits the *fallacy of equivocation*.

Fallacy of Equivocation

An argument commits the fallacy of equivocation if and only if some word, phrase, or sentence is used ambiguously, and the argument depends upon the ambiguity.

We can often determine whether an argument depends upon an ambiguity for its evidential support by explicitly distinguishing the two (or more) meanings. In the above case, we could paraphrase the argument as:

She was not convicted (not found guilty).
Therefore, she did not do it.

Put in this way, the argument is obviously problematic.

It is not only single words that can be ambiguous. Phrases and sentences can be as well. Consider the statement that flying planes can be dangerous. This could mean that the activity of flying planes, the activity in which pilots engage, can be dangerous. On the other hand it could mean that planes that are flying are dangerous by way of, for example, posing a threat to migrating birds. Such ambiguities infrequently play a role in argumentation, but they can easily lead to misunderstandings.

Let us next look at some cases to see how problems involving equivocation may enter into arguments. First, we will consider two cases where arguments quite frequently rely upon equivocations. One involves the term "theory" and the other the term "possible".

People often say, "That's only a theory". There is certainly one ordinary sense of "theory" in which to be a theory is to be a guess or a bit of speculation. But "theory" is frequently used quite differently in science and mathematics. In mathematics one might take a course in set theory, in physics one might study the theory of special relativity, in biology one might study evolutionary theory. In these cases "theory" means, roughly, some sort of overall explanation or set of basic laws that specify how things work. (The term "law" is another problematic one, but we shall not concern ourselves with it at this point.) A theory in this sense may or may not be well supported. The critical point, though, is that if "theory" is used in this sense we have to look further to determine whether or not the theory is well supported, whether or not it is one that it is reasonable to accept. Hence arguments like the following:

**Evolution is a theory.
So, we need not accept it.**

rest upon an equivocation. Evolutionary theory is a theory in that it provides an overall explanation. It is not a theory in the sense of being speculation ungrounded in evidence. But it would have to be a theory in this latter sense for the premise to provide support for the conclusion.

The term "possible" and related terms like "might" and "could" occasion no end of difficulty. There are various ways of distinguishing kinds of possibility, some of which we shall present, but you should keep in mind that our purpose here is primarily to alert ourselves to problems that can arise in argumentation. The labels introduced are meant to be reminders of distinctions that may be drawn and points that should not be neglected.

Suppose you asked whether it could be true both that all whales have lungs and that some whales do not have lungs. I would respond that it is impossible that both could be true. The kind of impossibility that I am claiming to be present in this case is one we shall call *logical impossibility*. Statements that are logically impossible are contradictory. (Logical impossibility is discussed in more detail in other chapters of this text, in particular in Chapter 6.)

Let us consider whether it is possible to move objects by merely willing them to move. It does not seem to be logically impossible to do so. I might well concede that in that sense it could happen, that it is *logically possible*, but nonetheless assert that it is impossible. The claim I would be making is that it is inconsistent with the way in which the universe works. We shall call this kind of impossibility *empirical impossibility*.

A claim is then *logically possible* if it is not contradictory, and *empirically possible* if it is not inconsistent with the way in which the universe works. People sometimes say, "Anything is possible": this claim is simply not true if "possible" is taken to mean either logically or empirically possible. We might, of course, be mistaken in our judgments of whether some particular statement is or is not possible. But it does not follow from this that anything is possible.

People have often attempted to design perpetual motion machines, believing that such machines are possible. There is here most likely an equivocation on "possible". Such machines are perhaps logically possible, but they are not thereby guaranteed to be empirically possible. In fact there seems good reason to believe they are ***empirically impossible***, that is, incompatible with the way the world works. Attempting to construct such a device is, then, simply a waste of time.

There is also a use of "possible" that amounts to the claim that something is to some degree likely. Consider the following argument:

> **The chairperson is sometimes in her office in the morning.**
> **It is the morning.**
> **So, it is possible that she is now in her office.**

This is a statistical syllogism. Here ***possible*** is being used to indicate some degree of likelihood.

Finally, we may note that there seem to be uses of "possible" and related terms that arise in situations like the following. Suppose I am asked whether Ramraj is in the building, and I do not have any idea who Ramraj is. I might respond:

> **He could be. (For all I know he is.)**

Here I would be stating that there is nothing I know or believe that is inconsistent with Ramraj's being in the building. Or suppose I have just left a tenth-floor office in which the chairperson was sitting. You say you have just seen the chairperson walking down the street. I might well exclaim:

> **That's impossible! (I know it was not she.)**

The impossibility here might be characterized by noting that I know or believe something that is inconsistent with her walking down the street. Let us label this ***epistemic impossibility***.

One can utilize these distinctions by asking how to reformulate the possibility claims encountered in an argument. Consider the following:

> **It's impossible that their child should have learned**
> **advanced algebra in the last week.**

We have allowed that this claim may have the following interpretations:

1. **That their child has learned advanced algebra in the last week is logically impossible (contradictory).**
2. **That their child has learned advanced algebra in the last week is empirically impossible (inconsistent with the way the world works).**
3. **That their child has learned advanced algebra in the last week is not consistent with what I know about their child.**

The first and second claims seem to be false, but the third could be true: I might know that their child is not now capable of doing any advanced algebra problems.

We have looked at several examples of equivocation. But the main point remains that we should watch out for ambiguities in arguments, and endeavor to present arguments that do not trade on them. We shall close this part with a discussion of how equivocation enters into some discussions of abortion. (This example does not introduce any new concepts, so it may be omitted unless your instructor wishes to consider it.)

2.2 / The Abortion Argument

Perhaps one of the more common arguments against abortion runs, in one of its forms, as follows:

> **It is always wrong to kill an innocent human.**
> **A fetus is an innocent human.**
> **Therefore, abortion (the killing of a fetus) is always wrong.**

We should be on our guard in such cases. The argument here appears to be a valid deductive one, but there may be an equivocation. For example, the term "human" seems an ambiguous one. There is some sense of it, which we might call a biological or genetic sense, such that from the moment of conception we have a human. Let us call this sense "human$_1$". But we also usually distinguish between developed and undeveloped members of most biological species. We distinguish, for instance, between plant seeds and plants. Again, a chick may be a young chicken, but if your scrambled eggs were made from fertilized eggs you would not be eating chicken in at least one sense of the term. There is no doubt, then, that there is some sense of the term "human" such that to be a human is to be developed to the extent of having characteristic traits and characteristic features. (For example, one characteristic feature of a developed human is a functioning brain.) Let us call "human$_2$" the sense of "human" in which being human requires the presence of the characteristic traits and features, whatever these are. Finally, there is a sense in which something is human if it is a human$_1$ that has the potential to develop into a human$_2$. That is, other things being equal, a zygote will come to be a human in the sense of something that has the relevant characteristic traits and features. Let us call this sense of human, the sense in which there is the potential for development, "human$_3$".

If our argument is to be a good one, it must at least be true that "human" is used in the same sense throughout the argument. It must also be true that the premises are true. We are now in a position to see that our argument is in trouble. (Keep in mind that in saying this we are not taking a position on abortion.) If we substitute "human$_1$" in our initial premise, we have the following argument:

It is always wrong to kill an innocent human$_1$.
A fetus is an innocent human$_1$.
So, abortion is wrong.

The second premise is true, but the first premise seems to beg the question. That is, unless I already think that abortion is wrong, I will not accept this first premise. The first premise seemed innocuous enough when our argument was originally presented, but that might be because the interpretation that sprang to mind used the "human$_2$" sense. That is, I no doubt thought of myself, you, or a baby lying helplessly in a hospital bed. Again, let us emphasize that I am not suggesting the first premise is false, but only that its use here begs the question. Let us now read the argument as involving what we called human$_2$.

It is always wrong to kill an innocent human$_2$.
A fetus is an innocent human$_2$.
So, abortion is wrong.

Here, the problem is that the second premise is now false. That is, we do not have a fully developed creature from the moment of conception. Again, keep in mind that this is not meant to be a controversial claim; it only notes that, for example, a 32-celled creature does not have a brain or heart. We are left with our third sense of "human":

> **It is always wrong to kill an innocent human$_3$.**
> **A fetus is an innocent human$_3$.**
> **So, abortion is wrong.**

Here we have an argument that is not, or at least not so obviously, question begging. There is a minor problem regarding the second premise. It is not true that from the moment of conception on we always have a creature that could develop, could become a human$_2$. For example, an anencephalic fetus lacks certain portions of a brain and will never develop what we might call human consciousness. Such cases are, however, quite rare. To take account of them we can replace this deductive argument by the following argument:

> **It is always wrong to kill an innocent human$_3$.**
> **A fetus is almost invariably an innocent human$_3$.**
> **So, abortion is almost invariably wrong.**

After doing some work on the potential problems with equivocation, we now have an argument that we could proceed to discuss. This latter is not, however, our current task. Rather, we want to indicate that semantic problems can sometimes be eliminated so as to open the way for significant further discussion. We should not think that the elimination of semantic problems will automatically solve all problems: the argument with which we have ended is not one that will command either universal acceptance or universal rejection. But at least we have enabled discussion to focus upon an argument in which the premises are not ambiguous. And we can now clearly see that the first premise is the controversial premise. Since our argument no longer rests upon an equivocation, we are in a position to focus upon a claim that is actually in dispute.

2.3 / A Brief Note on Assessing Arguments

It should already be apparent to you that identifying and assessing arguments is a rather tricky business. One can certainly (and you probably will) disagree with the way in which I, for example, classify a given argument in a given passage. Quite often, though, this will not matter terribly much in that we may find ourselves agreeing in our assessment of the strength of the argument. But you must be prepared to defend and explain the way you classify an argument; simply unthinkingly attaching labels, even if they happen to be the correct labels, is of no particular benefit.

Divergence with respect to assessment is in a sense more troubling, for in those real cases where we both hold that the premises are true, this divergence will lead us to different beliefs. If you judge the argument a strong one, you will be committed to having some confidence in the truth of the conclusion. If I judge the same argument a weak one, I may well reject the conclusion; at the very least I will, if I do believe the conclusion, appeal to evidence other than that presented in the premises of the argument.

More often than not, as we shall see, a divergence in assessment will be explicable in terms of our background knowledge and background assumptions. I may know that an analogy argument is strong because I know that the similarities mentioned are positively relevant. If you do not know that they are relevant, you will not be in a position to judge the strength of the argument. It will sometimes be perfectly appropriate to note that one needs some further information in order to assess the strength of a given argument. At other times we may disagree in our assessments because we disagree, for example, as to whether certain similarities are positively relevant. In this case, the best we can do is to search for additional evidence in order to determine who is right.

Chapter Summary

In this chapter we considered a variety of distinct arguments. The first which we considered we identified as *straw man arguments*.

Straw Man Arguments

A straw man argument proceeds by attributing to those attacked a position they do not hold.

We noted that this sort of argument is often utilized in the political and social arena.

In 1.2 we turned to *arguments from ignorance*:

Arguments from Ignorance

(1) There is no evidence against my position.
So, it is correct.
(2) There is no evidence available for **p**.
Therefore, **p** is false.
(3) My claim has not been conclusively refuted.
So, my claim is likely true, or my claim is just as respectable as any opposed claim.
(4) **p** has not been conclusively supported.
Therefore, **p** is false, or is no more respectable than any opposed claim.

We considered a number of examples of these arguments, noting that they abound in discussions of "strange phenomena".

In 1.3 we turned to *begging the question*:

Begging the Question

An argument begs the question if and only if one would not have reason to believe the premises are true unless one already had reason to believe the conclusion was true.

We should particularly be on our guard against presenting arguments in which the premises are merely disguised statements of the conclusion.

In 1.4 we briefly considered some conspiracy theories. I suggested that we particularly:

Watch For:

(1) Denial of positions that at least appear to meet the condition for a legitimate argument from authority.
(2) A slender, at best, evidential base.
(3) Lack of accounts of how the conspiracy or cover-up might be carried out.
(4) Explanation of the absence of evidence by an appeal to the cover-up or conspiracy.
(5) Involvement of large numbers of people in the cover-up or conspiracy.

In Section 2 we discussed some questions of meaning, turning in 2.1 to a consideration of some semantic pitfalls.

Fallacy of Equivocation

An argument commits the fallacy of equivocation if and only if some word, phrase, or sentence is used ambiguously, and the argument depends upon the ambiguity.

We considered various examples involving, for example, the terms "theory" and "possibility".

Possibility and Impossibility

(1) A claim is *logically possible* if it is not contradictory or inconsistent, *logically impossible* if it is.
(2) A claim is *empirically possible* if it is consistent with the way the world works, *empirically impossible* if it is inconsistent with the way the world works.
(3) A claim is *epistemically possible* if is not inconsistent with what we know, *epistemically impossible* if it is inconsistent with what we know.

We then turned, in 2.2, to some arguments that involve positions regarding abortion to provide an extended illustration of some of our points. In 2.3 we considered some general points regarding the assessment of arguments.

CHAPTER 5

Forms of Reasoning

Deductive logic is a rich and complex field, and, as we shall later see, there are various approaches to it that are useful in various circumstances. One approach is to study certain arguments whose validity derives from what we shall speak of as the structure of the statements involved. In this chapter we will be identifying certain forms of argument; in a later chapter we will undertake some more general, less restricted approaches. We will also consider whether validity and soundness guarantee that we have a non-fallacious argument.

1 / The Forms

1.1 / Modus Ponens and Some Core Concepts

Consider the following argument:

> **If that animal is a cat, then that animal is vicious.**
> **That animal is a cat.**
> **Therefore, that animal is vicious.**

This is a valid argument. (Keep in mind that to say an argument is valid is only to say it is impossible for its premises to be true and its conclusion false.) We may represent the form or structure of this argument as follows:

Modus Ponens (mp)

If p, then q.
p.
So, q.

We shall say that particular arguments of this form are instances of the application of **_modus ponens_** (abbreviated as "mp"). Note that any statements may be put in place of *p* and *q*. We could, for example, obtain the argument above from this form by replacing the *p* and *q* by the particular statements in question. *Particular arguments have a given form if they may be obtained in this way from the form.* Note that the order in which the premises are spoken or written does not matter. Consider this argument:

> **If both of them will stay at home if I want them to, then I can safely go out.**
> **Both of them will stay at home if I want them to.**
> **Therefore, I can safely go out.**

This argument has the same basic structure as the argument regarding the cat. In this case, the more complex statement "Both of them will stay at home if I want them to" replaces the *p*, but the basic structure remains the same. This form is a valid argument form in the sense that any particular argument that is an instance of it (has this structure) is valid. We shall say.

Validity of an Argument Form

An ***argument form*** is *valid* if and only if it is impossible that any particular argument of that form has true premises and a false conclusion.

Argument forms may also be invalid:

Invalidity of an Argument Form

An ***argument form*** is *invalid* if and only if some particular arguments of that form can have true premises and a false conclusion.

One of the major tasks of deductive logic is to distinguish argument forms that are valid from ones that are not. We will do that in a more general way in later chapters; for now, we will simply look at some common argument forms.

Notice that we can characterize the above argument form as one involving the application of what we shall call a ***rule of inference***. We present rules of inference as follows:

Modus Ponens (As a Rule of Inference)

From: *p* and *if p, then q*
To: *q*

This says that if we are given some statement *p* and some statement *if p then q*, then we may legitimately infer — move to — the statement *q*. This is a good rule of inference in that it will never lead us from premises that are true to a conclusion that is false. If you think about this, you should see that it guarantees that any argument constructed by the use of the rule will be a valid argument. And the argument form that involves that rule will be a valid argument form. We shall use the name "modus ponens" for both the form and the rule of inference. We are in effect viewing an argument of the form modus ponens as having arisen via an application of the rule of inference modus ponens.

We shall utilize the following vocabulary in connection with rules of inference:

Truth Preservation

A rule of inference is *truth-preserving* if and only if it is impossible that an application of it leads from truths to falsehoods.

We shall also say:

Rule Validity

A rule of inference is valid if and only if it is truth-preserving.

Valid argument forms or valid (particular) arguments may be viewed as having been constructed by the use of valid rules of inference. We shall not talk further about rules of inference in this chapter; they will be reintroduced in later chapters.

So much, for now, for that portion of our vocabulary. Certain argument forms and rules of inference are so common that they have been given names. (We will often use the same name to refer to both argument form and rules of inference.) Above we mentioned the argument form modus ponens:

Modus Ponens (mp)

If *p*, then *q*.

p.

So, *q*.

The first premise is a kind of statement that we will call a ***conditional***. As we noted, modus ponens is a valid argument form.

We must keep in mind, though, that English and other natural languages are quite complex. There are various ways of saying much the same thing, various ways of stating something that has, for example, the force of a conditional. In order to apply our system, we have to learn some of the different ways in which we can say something that can be represented as *if p then q*. Later on we shall do this in considerably more detail, but for now we shall consider a few common and comparatively easy cases. Consider the claim:

Sampras will win if he plays up to his ability.

It should be apparent that this is simply a variant of:

If he plays up to his ability, then Sampras will win.

Given that the sentence can be so restated, we take the following argument:

Sampras will win if he plays up to his ability.
He will play up to his ability.
Therefore, he will win.

as an argument of the form we called modus ponens. There are many other variants of the first premise. For instance:

His playing up to his ability is a sufficient condition of his winning.

is again a variant of:

If he plays up to his ability, he will win.

Consider now the claim that:

> **Passing the final is a necessary condition for passing the course.**

Note that this does *not* say:

> **If you pass the final, then you pass the course.**

Instead it says:

> **If you (are to) pass the course, then you (have to) pass the final.**

Two last variants are:

> **Provided that he plays up to his ability, he will win.**
> **He will win provided that he plays up to his ability.**

We shall, as noted, study these and other variants in much more detail later. But you should on your own be able to recognize other statements that may be paraphrased as conditionals. Doing this simply involves paying careful attention to what English statements mean.

One more point must be emphasized: we placed no restrictions upon the complexity of the statements that could replace the *p* and *q* in our argument form. Consider the following argument:

> **If Brown or Valdez comes, then the party will be wild and fun.**
> **Brown will come or Valdez will come.**
> **So the party will be wild and fun.**

This argument is one we will count as of the form modus ponens. We have replaced the *p* by a statement that amounts to:

> **Either Brown will come or Valdez will come.**

and we have replaced *q* by a statement that amounts to:

> **The party will be wild and the party will be fun.**

In using the phrase "amounts to" we are signifying that the statements in question differ only stylistically. Sometimes, for example, we include the word "either" and sometimes we do not; this is a mere stylistic variation. What is important is that we replace each occurrence of *p* and *q* by the same thing, however complex that thing happens to be. (Recall that is the way in which particular arguments that have a certain form are obtained.) The argument:

> **If John or Roberto comes, then the party will be wild and fun.**
> **John will come.**
> **So, the party will be wild and fun.**

is not a case of modus ponens. We cannot obtain it by replacing each occurrence of *p* by some one statement. We are not saying that it is not valid (as it happens, it is). We are only saying that, whether valid or not, it is not an argument of the form modus ponens. For a particular argument to be a case of modus ponens it must fit the form or pattern. This one, as we can see, does not fit that form.

1.2 / More Arguments Involving Conditionals

There are several other forms involving conditionals that we will be concerned with in this chapter. We now turn to a survey of these. Consider the following valid argument:

> **If Gupta has taken the trash out, then the garbage bin is empty.**
> **The garbage bin is not empty.**
> **So, Gupta has not taken the trash out.**

Let us agree that we will use ~ as our means of saying "it is not the case that", our means of constructing the *negation* of a statement. (The negation ~*p* of a statement *p* comes out true if the statement *p* was false, false if the statement *p* was true.) We can now exhibit the form of the argument as:

Modus Tollens (mt)

If *p*, then *q*.
~*q*.
So, ~*p*.

The name of this argument form, as you can see, is *modus tollens* ("mt" will be our shorthand). It is a quite familiar argument form, and is indeed a valid one. As we noted when we were discussing modus ponens, we are allowing *p* and *q* to be replaced by any statement. But be very careful: the second premise *must* be the negation of the statement that replaces *q*, and the conclusion *must* be the negation of the statement that replaces *p*. In requiring these precise negations we are, of course, indicating that if they are lacking, the argument is not an argument of the form modus tollens.

Keeping this in mind, let us turn to some examples. The following are cases of modus tollens:

(1) **If his bike is gone, Curtis is on his way home.**
He is not on his way home.
So, his bike is not gone.

(2) **If Wilson failed, he would be both crying and**
complaining right now.
He is not both crying and complaining right now.
So, he did not fail.

(3) **If my pet is a bird or a dog it is warm-blooded.**
My pet is not warm-blooded.
So, my pet is not either a bird or a dog.

However, the following arguments are *not* cases of modus tollens; they do not have the requisite form:

(1′) **If his bike is gone, Curtis is on his way home.**
His bike is not gone.
So, he is not on his way home.

(2′) **If Wilson failed, he would be both crying and**
complaining right now.
He is crying, but is not complaining.
So, he did not fail.

(3′) **If my pet is a bird or dog, it is warm-blooded.**
My pet is not warm-blooded.
So my pet is not a dog.

You should examine these last three carefully to ensure that you see why they are *not* cases of modus tollens. (Keep in mind that in saying they are not cases of modus tollens, we make no claim regarding their validity or invalidity. As it happens, 1′ is invalid and both 2′ and 3′ are valid.) In argument 2′, for example, the second premise is not the negation of the statement that has replaced *q,* and in argument 3′ the conclusion is not the negation of the statement that replaced *p*.

We now turn to what are sometimes termed "formal fallacies". Consider the following argument form:

Affirming the Consequent (Invalid) (ac)

If *p*, then *q*.

q.

So, *p*.

This looks a bit like modus ponens, but if you look carefully you will see that it is not at all the same. This is not a valid argument form. We shall speak of it as the fallacious or invalid form ***affirming the consequent***. (Our short label will be "ac".)

Where does the name for this argument form come from? The first premise of the above argument form is what we have called a conditional statement. It has become part of the standard vocabulary to speak of the *p* in any conditional statement *if p then q* as the ***antecedent*** of that statement, and the *q* as the ***consequent***. This vocabulary explains the above choice of label: in the preceding argument we affirmed (asserted) a conditional statement, then affirmed a statement that was the consequent of that conditional, and proceeded to our conclusion. We could in a similar fashion have named modus ponens "affirming the antecedent", and some authors do just that. We did not, simply because the name "modus ponens" has become entrenched in the tradition.

An argument form is valid if and only if every particular argument that has that form is valid. To say that a form is not valid (is invalid) is to say that not every particular argument that has that form is valid. Note that this claim *is not equivalent to* the claim that every argument of that form is invalid. Recall that for an argument form to be invalid it need only be true that some particular arguments of that form can have true premises and a false conclusion. We must then exercise some care when we assess particular arguments of that form, since we cannot automatically conclude that they are invalid. Nonetheless, many particular arguments such as:

> **If John is at home, then the door is open.**
> **The door is open.**
> **So, John is at home.**

are clearly fallacious. So what we shall do is the following: we shall say

that a particular argument is a case of (the fallacy of) affirming the consequent if and only if (1) it is invalid and (2) is of the form:

If *p* then *q*.
q.
Therefore, *p*.

Most real arguments that are of this form are invalid. (Real arguments are
ones people actually present.) But here is one example that should indicate
to you why we need to exercise some care:

If John comes, then both John and Mary will come.
John and Mary will come.
Therefore, John will come.

This argument is of the form we are currently discussing (make sure you
see why). But it is valid. It is not, of course, valid because it has the form
we call "ac". It is valid because the second premise is one from which the
conclusion follows. Our account above was designed to take care of this
sort of case. But, again, most real arguments of this form are invalid; it is
not very likely that anyone would actually present such an argument.

Now let us consider the following argument form:

Denying the Antecedent (Invalid) (da)

If *p*, then *q*.
~*p*.
So, ~*q*.

This too is an invalid argument form, one that, as you see, we are calling *de-*
nying the antecedent. (Our short form will be "da".) The discussion we had
above regarding invalid argument forms applies equally here. So we say that
a particular argument is a case of (the fallacy of) denying the antecedent if
and only if that particular argument is (1) invalid and (2) is of the form:

If *p*, then *q*.
~*p*.
Therefore, ~*q*.

Given that the kind of conditionals with which we are concerned are those
that come out true save in the case where the antecedent is true and the

consequent is false, we can identify another valid form. Consider the following argument:

> **If the bird is loose, then the cage door is open.**
> **If the cage door is open, then the bird can re-enter the cage.**
> **So, if the bird is loose, then the bird can re-enter the cage.**

The form of this argument is:

Hypothetical Syllogism (hs)

If *p*, then *q*.
If *q*, then *r*.
So, if *p*, then *r*.

This is a valid argument form. We have called it a *hypothetical syllogism* ("hs" for short). Now consider the following argument:

> **She will win if she plays well.**
> **Her winning is a sufficient condition for remaining on the team.**
> **Therefore, if she plays well she will remain on the team.**

This is a case of hypothetical syllogism. However, you do have to exercise care. Consider the following argument:

> **If she plays well, then she will win.**
> **She will remain on the team if she plays well.**
> **So, if she wins, then she will remain on the team.**

This is *not* a case of hypothetical syllogism. The second premise is the statement that if she plays well, she will remain on the team. The antecedent of the conditional that is the conclusion is not the antecedent of either premise. You should see that the form of this argument is:

> **If *p* then *q*.**
> **If *p* then *r*.**
> **So, if *q* then *r*.**

Now, as it happens this is an invalid argument form (not, however, one we shall bother naming). But that is not the main point. The main point is that the argument simply is not a hypothetical syllogism.

1.3 / Some Other Common Argument Forms

There are three additional argument forms that we shall consider in this chapter. Here is an example of the first:

Either the dog is in the living room or he is outside.
He is not in the living room.
So, he is outside.

The argument form here involved is:

Disjunctive Syllogism (ds)

Either *p or q*.	Either *p* or *q*.
~*p*.	~*q*.
So, *q*.	So, *p*.

We label this argument form a *disjunctive syllogism* (or "ds"). Note that we have allowed two versions. It should be clear to you that this is a valid argument form.

Consider now the following argument:

If the party is held at my house, then my house will be a mess.
If the party is held at your house, then your house will be a mess.
The party is either at my house or at yours.
So, either your house or mine will be a mess.

The argument form here is:

Constructive Dilemma (cd)

If *p* then *r*.	If *p* then *r*, and if *q* then *s*.
If *q* then *s*.	Either *p* or *q*.
Either *p* or *q*.	So, either *r* or *s*.
So, either *r* or *s*.	

Here we have two versions of a valid form of argument that we are calling *constructive dilemma*. (Our shorthand will be "cd".) Why two versions? The version on the left has three premises (as you should recall from the opening chapter, we count any number of sentences connected by "and" as one statement), and the version on the right has only two.

Do not confuse constructive dilemmas with arguments like the following:

> **If his pet is a bird, then it is warm-blooded.**
> **If his pet is a reptile, then it is cold-blooded.**
> **His pet is either warm-blooded or cold-blooded.**
> **So his pet is either a bird or a reptile.**

This particular argument has the form:

> **If *p* then *r*.**
> **If *q* then *s*.**
> **Either *r* or *s*.**
> **So, either *p* or *q*.**

This argument form is, of course, invalid. We will not introduce any special name for arguments of this sort.

Here is another argument to consider:

> **If Jones aided in the crime, then he was the driver.**
> **If Lubnic aided in the crime, then he was the driver.**
> **Either Jones was not the driver or Lubnic was not the driver.**
> **So either Jones did not aid in the crime or Lubnic did not.**

The argument form here is:

Destructive Dilemma (dd)

If *p* then *r*.	If *p* then *r*, and if *q* then *s*.
If *q* then *s*.	Either ~*r* or ~*s*.
Either ~*r* or ~*s*.	So, either ~*p* or ~*q*.
So, either ~*p* or ~*q*.	

This argument form, again given in two versions (for precisely the same reason as above), is a valid one that we shall call *destructive dilemma* (or "dd"). It should not be confused with the follow invalid argument form:

If *p* then *r*.
If *q* then *s*.
Either ~*p* or ~*q*.
So, either ~*r* or ~*s*.

We shall not bother with a special name for this invalid argument form.

1.4 / Are Valid Arguments Ever Fallacious?

Clearly, would-be deductive arguments that are invalid are to be dismissed. But can we safely conclude that any valid — or indeed any sound — argument cannot be fallacious? The answer is a resounding *No*. The following is a valid form:

New Valid Form

p.
So, *p*.

But if you present an argument that consists only of this, your argument will of course be one that begs the question. A less obvious, but also common, problem arises from the use of disjunctive syllogisms and dilemma arguments. Consider the following argument:

> **Either the famous football player killed them or a drug dealer did.**
> **A drug dealer didn't.**
> **So, a famous football player did.**

This argument is valid and it may be sound. There is good reason to believe the second premise to be true as written. In fact, I personally believe the second premise. But, as written, this is a very bad argument. Let us inspect the first premise. There clearly are alternatives not mentioned, for example, what of a burglar? In this particular case there is no reason now for me to believe that the first premise is true unless I already have reason to believe the conclusion. (Don't forget I have reason to believe the second premise is true.) So we can accuse this argument of begging the question. More generally, we can introduce the concept of what is often called a *false dilemma* (the name relates to dilemma arguments that we introduced in 1.3).

False Dilemma

An argument involves a ***false dilemma*** if it relies upon the specification of a set of alternatives (typically by use of statements involving "or") that does not exhaust — that is, include — all the alternatives that, in the circumstances, there might reasonably be supposed to be).

We shall later have occasion to see in more detail how false dilemmas often enter into ordinary argumentation. But for now let us simply look at one example.

> **Either UFOs are real alien spacecraft or people reporting sightings are lying. If they are real alien spacecraft, then we are being visited by aliens. If the people reporting sightings are lying, then we have so many frauds in our society that we should just give up. So either we are being visited by aliens or there are so many frauds we should just give up.**

No one, to the best of my knowledge, has presented just this valid argument. That aside, while the argument as a whole suffers from many problems, it may strike you that the first premise is a blatant case of a false dilemma.

Chapter Summary

In this chapter we studied a number of valid and invalid forms of argument. You should review precisely what it means to say that an argument form is valid or is invalid. The valid forms introduced were:

Valid Forms

Modus Ponens (mp)
If *p*, then *q*.
p.
So, *q*.

Valid Forms *(continued)*

Modus Tollens (mt)
If *p,* then *q.*
~*q.*
So, ~*p.*

Hypothetical Syllogism (hs)
If *p,* then *q.*
If *q,* then *r.*
So, if *p,* then *r.*

Disjunctive Syllogism (ds)

Either *p or q.*	Either *p* or *q.*
~*p.*	~*q.*
So, *q.*	So, *p.*

Constructive Dilemma (cd)

If *p* then *r.*	If *p* then *r,* and if *q* then *s.*
If *q* then *s.*	Either *p* or *q.*
Either *p* or *q.*	So, either *r* or *s.*
So, either *r* or *s.*	

Destructive Dilemma (dd)

If *p* then *r.*	If *p* then *r,* and if *q* then *s.*
If *q* then *s.*	Either ~*r* or ~*s.*
Either ~*r* or ~*s.*	So, either ~*p* or ~*q.*
So, either ~*p* or ~*q.*	

We also specifically labelled two invalid forms.

Invalid Forms

Affirming the Consequent (ac)
If *p,* then *q.*
q.
So, *p.*

Denying the Antecedent (da)
If *p,* then *q.*
~*p.*
So, ~*q.*

All the forms involving *conditionals* were discussed in 1.1 and 1.2. The other forms were introduced in 1.3.

We also discussed, primarily in 1.1, validity and related concepts in connection with rules and forms. Here is a summary of our account:

Some Core Concepts

Validity of an Argument Form

An *argument form* is valid if and only if it is impossible that any particular argument of that form has true premises and a false conclusion.

Invalidity of an Argument Form

An *argument form* is invalid if and only if some particular arguments of that form can have true premises and a false conclusion.

Truth Preservation

A rule of inference is *truth-preserving* if and only if it is impossible that an application of it leads from truths to falsehoods.

Rule Validity

A rule of inference is valid if and only if it is truth-preserving.

We then turned, in 1.4, to an initial consideration of whether valid, or even sound, arguments are necessarily non-fallacious. There we introduced:

False Dilemma

An argument involves a *false dilemma* if it relies upon the specification of a set of alternatives (typically by use of statements involving "or") that does not exhaust — that is, include — all the alternatives that, in the circumstances, there might reasonably be supposed to be).

CHAPTER 6

Symbolizing, Truth Tables and Validity

In this chapter we will turn to a more detailed study of arguments like those we encountered in the previous chapter. Our study will be much more comprehensive. In particular, we shall develop a system that is complete in that it enables one to answer any question regarding the validity of arguments involving our conditionals (*if p then q* sentences) and such terms as "and", "or", "not", and "if and only if".

1 / Our Formal Language

1.1 / Basic Definitions

Our primary concern is to assess arguments. In order to facilitate this we will introduce a formal language. In this language we will be able to represent or, as we shall say from now on, *symbolize* certain real sentences and arguments. There are certain words in English (or any other language) that can be used to construct new sentences from already existing ones. For example, here we have two sentences:

The wind is blowing. The sun is shining.

From these we can construct the following single sentences:

> **The wind is blowing and the sun is shining.**
> **The sun is shining and the wind is blowing.**
> **It is not the case that the wind is blowing.**
> **If the wind is blowing, then the sun is shining.**
> **The wind is blowing or the sun is shining.**
> **The sun is shining if and only if the wind is blowing.**

(Note that the first and second sentences on the list say much the same thing. Nonetheless, we count them as *different sentences.*) These sentences have been constructed by the use of:

**and; it is not the case that;
if ... then; or; if and only if**

We shall speak of terms like these, terms that can be used to construct new sentences from previously given ones, as ***connectives***. The sentences constructed by means of their use will be spoken of as ***complex*** (or, on occasion, ***compound***) sentences.

Let us now turn to our language. It will have certain sentences that we shall call our ***atomic sentences***. For our atomic sentences we shall use capital letters either with or without superscripts. Thus

A, B, ... Z, ... A^1, B^1, ... A^n, B^n ...

will all count as distinct atomic sentences. Our language will also contain certain connectives:

Connectives

&	(our "and" or *conjunction* sign)
∨	(our "or" or *disjunction* sign)
→	(our "if ... then" or *conditional* sign)
↔	(our "if and only if" or *biconditional* sign)
~	(our "it is not the case that" or *negation* sign)

We will also need left and right parentheses: "(" and ")". We are now in a position to define what will count as a sentence of our language:

Definition of a "Sentence of Our Language"

1. Every atomic sentence is a sentence of our language.
2. If *p* and *q* are both sentences of our language, then each of:

   (p & q)
   (p ∨ q)
   (p → q)
   (p ↔ q)

   is a sentence of our language. (Note that *p* and *q* can be any sentence of our language.)
3. If *p* is a sentence of our language, then ~*p* is a sentence of our language.
4. The only strings of symbols that are sentences of our language are those strings constructed by the use of the above rules.

This may seem very formidable, but it simply tells us that all of the following are sentences of our language:

(R & (~S ∨ Q))
(~~P → (~W & (R ∨ S)))
~(B & (Q ∨ S))
(~B ↔ (Q → S))
(R ↔ R)

These can all be constructed in accord with our rules. You should not really have any problem in recognizing something as a sentence of our language. Here, for the sake of contrast, are some strings of symbols that are not sentences of our language:

((R & (S → Q))

(Note that sentences of our language must contain an even number of parentheses.)

(R & S)) → Q

(Note that the parentheses in this cannot be paired.)

Again, it is pretty easy to distinguish those strings that are sentences of our language from those that are not. (Another common vocabulary uses the term "well-formed formulas" to refer to what we have called sentences of our language. Strings that we have said are not sentences are in that vocabulary said not to be well-formed.)

You may wonder why we bother with parentheses. We bother here for the same reason we bother in arithmetic: they enable us to avoid ambiguity. Suppose one were to say or write:

Juan will come and Amil will come or Karen will come.

As it stands, this sentence is ambiguous; we have no way of knowing which of the following two it is saying:

Either both Juan will come and Amil will come or Karen will come.
Juan will come and either Amil will come or Karen will come.

These are two different statements, different in the sense that they do not come out true or false under precisely the same conditions. The statements are not, as we shall say, logically equivalent. English has various devices to avoid ambiguity. Note that the explicit introduction of the words "both" and "either" did serve to disambiguate. When writing, we can also use punctuation to the same purpose (notice that our initial sentence would, since it lacks punctuation, be viewed as ungrammatical). When speaking, our intonation and pauses may help us disambiguate. When either speaking or writing, we would often say (for the first interpretation):

Juan and Amil will come or Karen will.

For the second interpretation we might well say:

Juan will come and Amil or Karen will as well.

But in our language we use parentheses. Using obvious abbreviations, we would symbolize the first sentence above as:

((J & A) ∨ K)

and the second as

(J & (A ∨ K))

Each of our sentences can be said to be of a unique type. If a sentence is a single capital letter it is an atomic sentence. Here are the other types, of which each complex or compound sentence is one:

Types of Compound Sentences

1. If the sentence is formed by placing the negation sign before a previously constructed sentence, it is a negation. The negation sign is said to be the main connective of the sentence.

   ~*p* is a ***negation***

2. If the sentence is formed by putting the conjunction sign between two sentences and surrounding the result with parentheses, the sentence is a conjunction. The conjunction sign is said to be the main connective of the sentence.

   (*p* & *q*) is a ***conjunction***

3. Same as 2 save that if we use the disjunction sign we get a disjunction.

   (*p* ∨ *q*) is a ***disjunction***

4. Same as 2 save that if we use the conditional sign we get a conditional.

   (*p* → *q*) is a ***conditional***

5. Same as 2 save that if we use the biconditional sign we get a biconditional.

   (*p* ↔ *q*) is a ***biconditional***

We have already agreed that we will call the left sentence in a conditional the ***antecedent*** and the right sentence the ***consequent***. We shall call the left sentence in a conjunction the ***left conjunct*** and the right sentence the ***right conjunct***, and the left sentence in a disjunction the ***left disjunct*** and the right sentence the ***right disjunct***. We do not have a special name for the left and right sentences in a biconditional.

1.2 / Substitution Instances

As you have seen, we are utilizing capital letters to form the actual sentences of our language. We will utilize lowercase letters to represent sentences of our language, however complex those sentences might be. The lowercase letters form part of what is often called a *metalanguage* — a language that we utilize when we wish to speak about another language. If you have studied a language, say French, by reading a textbook written in English, then English is the metalanguage you used on that occasion. The language that you are speaking about is often called the *object language*. If we replace the uppercase letters in any sentence of our language by lowercase letters, without ever replacing two different uppercase letters by the same lowercase letter, we obtain what we shall call a *sentential form* for that sentence. Thus:

((p & q) → r)

is a sentential form for the sentence:

((A & B) → D)

Recall also that the sentences of our language, other than atomic sentences, are constructed from previously formed sentences of our language. We may then obtain a sentential form for a given sentence of our language by replacing sentences from which it was constructed — these are often called *subsentences* — by lowercase letters. Again, we may not replace different subsentences by the same lowercase letter. Thus:

(p → q)

is also a sentential form for the sentence:

((A & B) → D)

Here we replaced the subsentence **(A & B)** by *p*. Finally, any lowercase letter is a sentential form for any sentence of our language. Thus:

p
q
r

and so on are each a sentential form for the sentence in question.

These sentential forms are part of our metalanguage. If a sentence of our language has some particular sentential form, then we shall speak of that sentence as being a *substitution instance* of that sentential form. Thus, our sentence:

((A & B) → D)

was a substitution instance of each of:

p; q; r; (p → q); and ((p & q) → r)

Remember that in any given case a lowercase letter may stand only for some one sentence. Thus:

(A & B)

is not a substitution instance of:

(p & p)

and

((A & B) → (A ∨ B))

is not a substitution instance of, does not have the sentential form of:

(q → q)

Keep in mind that a sentence of our language will not have a unique sentential form. Any given sentence of our language is a substitution instance of any number of sentential forms. Let us consider the following sentence of our language:

~(~P & (Q ↔ R))

This as a whole is a sentence of our language, so as a whole it has the sentential form:

p

or the form identified by any other lowercase letter. It is also a negation, so it has the sentential form:

~p

It is not a conjunction, so it does *not* have the form:

(p & q)

It does, however, have the form:

(1) **~(p & q)**

and the form:

(2) **~(~p & q)**

This might seem very strange; let us see exactly why it is so. In (1) we allowed our lowercase p to stand for the **~P** in our sentence, and the lowercase q to stand for the **(Q ↔ R)** of our original sentence. In (2) we allowed p to stand for the **P** rather than the **~P**. Again, recall that our lowercase letters stand for any sentence whatsoever. Given this, you should note that:

(3) **~(q & p)**

and

(4) **~(~q & p)**

serve just as well as sentential forms for the original sentence:

~(~P & (Q ↔ R))

In (3) we have allowed the lowercase q to stand for **~P**, whereas in (4) we have allowed the lowercase q to stand for **P**. In both (3) and (4) we have allowed the lowercase p to stand for **(Q ↔ R)**.

If we look back to the original sentence we can also see that it has the sentential forms:

~(~p & (q ↔ r))

and

~(~q & (r ↔ p))

If you think about it a bit, you should see that these two sentential forms have precisely the same substitution instances.

The original sentence does not have the form (is not a substitution instance of):

~~p

The original sentence does not contain any double negation. It is the negation of a conjunction that in turn has a negation as its left conjunct.

The sentence:

   ~~A

is a substitution instance of each of:

   q
   ~q
   ~~q

In the second case the **q** replaces the sentence **~A**, whereas in the third case it replaces the sentence **A**. Finally, the sentence:

   (~~A ∨ C)

is a substitution instance of each of:

   p
   (p ∨ q)
   (~p ∨ q)
   (~~p ∨ q)

but is not a substitution instance of either of:

   ~p
   ~(p ∨ q)

The sentence is a disjunction, not a negation.

1.3 / Basic Truth Conditions

The connectives of our language will be interpreted as what are known as *truth-functional connectives*. A connective is truth-functional when the truth or falsity of a sentence formed by its use depends simply on the truth or falsity of the sentences from which it was formed. Consider any sentence:

   (p & q)

This sentence is clearly true if and only if both **p** and **q** are true; it is false otherwise. We can capture this by the following chart — a chart that is in effect our definition of how our conjunction sign is to be understood:

```
         Basic Chart for Conjunctions

      p           q              (p & q)
      T           T                 T
      T           F                 F
      F           T                 F
      F           F                 F
```

We are using "T" and "F" for "true" and "false", which we shall call our *truth-values*. This chart exhibits what we said above. Any conjunction (*p* & *q*) receives the truth-value T just when *p* receives a T and *q* receives a T.

Next we shall concern ourselves with our disjunction sign, the chart for which is:

```
         Basic Chart for Disjunctions

      p           q              (p ∨ q)
      T           T                 T
      T           F                 T
      F           T                 T
      F           F                 F
```

This says that any disjunction (*p* ∨ *q*) receives the truth-value T just in case at least one of *p*, *q* receives the truth value T.

Next we shall concern ourselves with conditionals and biconditionals. Here is the chart for the conditional:

```
         Basic Chart for Conditionals

      p           q              (p → q)
      T           T                 T
      T           F                 F
      F           T                 T
      F           F                 T
```

Our conditionals receive the truth-value T in every case except the case where the antecedent receives a T and the consequent receives an F.

Here is the chart for the biconditional:

Basic Chart for Biconditionals

p	*q*	*(p ↔ q)*
T	T	T
T	F	F
F	T	F
F	F	T

A biconditional comes out true just in case *p* and *q* are assigned the same truth-value.

Our final connective is our negation sign.

Basic Chart for Negations

p	*~p*
T	F
F	T

As you would expect, a negation *~p* comes out true where *p* is false, and false where *p* is true.

We will study the construction of truth-tables in more detail in Section 2. We will now turn to symbolizing.

1.4 / Symbolizing: Basic Cases

The core idea behind symbolizing is quite simple. Consider the sentence:

The (C)at is on the mat and the (D)og is on the rug.

Notice that this sentence is a conjunction. We shall utilize our atomic sentences to symbolize the sentences from which this conjunction is formed. We will always try to make fairly obvious choices of the letters for atomic sentences. Here we will take **C** as the atomic sentence symbolizing the statement that the cat is on the mat, and **D** for the statement that the dog is on the rug. (We will enclose an initial capital letter in parentheses in order to indicate the letter we will use in symbolizing the sentences.) Noting that the whole sentence is a conjunction, we would symbolize it as:

(C & D)

That is all there is to it. One note here: you will recall that we utilize parentheses to eliminate ambiguities. We will relax our use of parentheses in the text by way of allowing that we may drop the *outermost pair of parentheses*. Thus:

C & D

will be accepted as a symbolization of the sentence we were considering. (You should ask your instructor whether he or she wishes to allow you to drop the outermost pair of parentheses.) But there is one point with respect to which you must exercise considerable care. Consider the sentences:

~(A & B)
(~A & B)

The first sentence is a negation. It does *not* have an outermost pair of parentheses. So you cannot eliminate any parentheses from it. The second sentence is not a negation; it is a conjunction that has a negation as its left conjunct. But conjunctions do have an outermost pair of parentheses, so you could omit them to obtain the sentence:

~A & B

which you can still distinguish from the first sentence:

~(A & B)

We noted that symbolizing can be quite tricky. One of the reasons is that English contains a number of different terms that, for example, enable one to construct sentences that have the truth conditions of a conjunction. Here are some of them:

however
but
moreover
although
whereas

If I say any of:

The (C)omputer is on, but the (R)adio is off
The (C)omputer is on, however the (R)adio is off.
The (C)omputer is on, although the (R)adio is off.
The (C)omputer is on, moreover the (R)adio is off.

I have said something that is true if and only if the computer is on and the radio is off. The sentences may differ in other ways, but we are concerned with the conditions under which they come out true or false. So, all of them (using the specified atomic sentences) would be symbolized as:

C & R

Notice that I have omitted the outermost pair of parentheses.
There is another kind of problem. Consider the sentence:

Amil and Lupe will both be at the party.

This sentence can happily be viewed as a conjunction. But now consider:

Melanie and Kristos will come to the party together.

This sentence is not a genuine conjunction of our sort. You can see this if you ask yourself what conjunction it is:

(1) Melanie will come to the party together and Kristos will come to the party together.
(2) Melanie will come to the party and Kristos will come to the party.

Sentence 1 is nonsense. Sentence 2 does not say the same thing as the original sentence. So we would simply take our sentence "Melanie and Kristos will come to the party together" as a single chunk, as symbolized in our language by a single atomic sentence. To be sure, the sentence is a complex one, but the type of complexity is one that our language cannot capture.

Let us move on to disjunctions. There is one problem here that you may have already noted. Our disjunctions have the property of coming true unless both disjuncts are false. But consider the following situation: A menu in a restaurant says you can order mashed potatoes or fried potatoes. You would no doubt meet with an annoyed rejection if you said you would have both. The menu is using a sense of "or" that our language does not employ. To mark this distinction in senses of "or", some languages (Latin, for example) contain two words meaning "or". One is *"vel"*, which means what our symbol "∨" means. So, if I were to say:

A *vel* B

I would be saying something that has the truth conditions of our disjunctions. We shall speak of our disjunctions as ***inclusive disjunctions***. But there is another Latin word, *"aut"*, that has, or so some claim, the following truth conditions:

p	*q*	*p aut q*
T	T	**F**
T	F	**T**
F	T	**T**
F	F	**F**

This is what we shall call an ***exclusive disjunction***. We will not introduce a connective for exclusive disjunction. This is not really any loss, for, though we have no single symbol conveying its sense, if we were to encounter a sentence, say:

You can order (M)ashed potatoes or you can order (F)ried potatoes.

that we thought was an exclusive disjunction, we could capture its meaning (albeit more long-windedly) by symbolizing it as:

(M ∨ F) & ~(M & F)

This can be read as "You can have one or the other but not both".

However, unless the evidence to the contrary is overwhelming, we will take all of the terms "or" we encounter as inclusive.

There is one kind of mistake you should carefully avoid. Consider the sentence:

Either it will (R)ain or it will not rain.

Some people want to take the "or" here as an exclusive one. After all, they say, **R** and ~**R** cannot simultaneously both be true. It is true that **R** and ~**R** cannot both come out true; but that is a fact about those sentences, not about the meaning of "or". Here is a symbolization of the sentence with the truth conditions included:

R	**(R** ∨ **~R)**
T	**T** F
F	**T** T

Never construe an "or" as an exclusive one when it is the disjuncts that are mutually exclusive.

We shall now consider conditionals, our "if ... then ___" sentences. We have already noted that there are many variants of such sentences. Here is a (non-comprehensive) list of them:

> **Provided that R, S.**
> **S provided that R.**
> **R is a sufficient condition for S.**
> **S is a necessary condition for R.**
> **R only if S.**
> **S if R.**

all of which are correctly symbolized as:

> **R → S**

The one on this list that tends to cause the most problems is "only if". One approach you might take is simply to accept an argument from authority and simply remember that "... only if ___" is to be taken as precisely the same as "if ... then ___" and to be symbolized as such. However, we shall spend some time looking at examples in order to persuade ourselves that this approach is correct.

Consider the following case:

> **You will pass this (C)ourse only if you pass the (E)xam.**

We have said that this is to be symbolized as:

> **C → E**

That this is correct can be seen by contemplating the truth conditions. Suppose I state to you on the first day of class that you will pass the course only if you pass the exam. We can determine the truth conditions by asking in which possible situations I could legitimately be accused of breaking my rules, of having lied to you. Here are the four possible situations.

(1) You pass the course and you pass the exam.
(2) You pass the course and you do not pass the exam.
(3) You do not pass the course and do pass the exam.
(4) You do not pass the course and do not pass the exam.

Situations 1 and 4 are clearly unproblematic; that is, I have not lied to you. Hence our sentence is true in those cases. It seems equally clear that in situation 2 I have lied to you. I said that you would pass the course only if you passed the exam. I have violated that policy. You would not necessarily be unhappy that I violated the policy, but the fact remains that I did. What about situation 3? You did not pass the course, but you did pass the exam. The thing to note is that I did not give you any guarantee that passing the exam would yield a pass in the course. It is only a requirement, a necessary condition, for passing the course. So you could not accuse me of having lied. Consider as well a person having the following dialogue with herself:

This can be table salt only if it contains sodium.
I have run the first test and it does contain sodium.

Clearly the person could not yet conclude that what she has is table salt. This, again, indicates that our account of "only if" is correct. For our final example, suppose that I visit my doctor. He says:

Steven, you are going to (S)urvive for more than six months only if you (Q)uit smoking today.

I have said that this should be taken as:

(1) If I am going to survive for more than six months, then I quit smoking today.

The alternative that students often choose is to take the statement as:

(2) If I quit smoking today, then I am going to survive for more than six months.

But here is the rest of the story. I do quit smoking. Unfortunately I die in a car crash five months later. Claim 2 is false, whereas claim 1 is not false. What the doctor said is clearly not to be taken as false because I die in the car accident. The moral of all these examples is to take "… only if ___" is as the same as "if … then ___".

"Necessary" and "sufficient" can also cause some difficulty. Consider the following two sentences:

> **That you (W)ork hard is sufficient for your being (P)raised.**
> **It is sufficient for (R)eceiving a commendation that you (S)ave a life.**

On first inspection you might think that these two had the same structure. But they do not. The first, as we would expect, comes out as:

> **If you work hard, then you will be praised.**
> **W → P**

But the second comes out as:

> **If you save a life, then you will receive a commendation.**
> **S → R**

A similar point obtains with respect to:

> **That you pass the (E)xam is necessary for (P)assing the course.**
> **It is necessary for (R)eceiving the refund that you (S)end in the form.**

The first comes out as:

> **If you pass the course, then you pass the exam.**
> **P → E**

But the second comes out as:

> **If you are to receive the refund, then you must send in the form.**
> **R → S**

Such differences will, given the complexity of our language, arise frequently. All you can do is to utilize your knowledge of the language and come up with a symbolization that does capture what is being stated.

Another word of warning: certain English sentences that do include an "if ... then" statement are not our sort of conditional. One sort of example of this is provided by sentences that we shall call *counterfactuals*. Imagine I have in my hand a lump of butter that I did not put into my very hot oven, and consider the following two sentences:

If I had put the butter in the oven it would have melted.
If I had put the butter in the oven it would have frozen.

It seems clear that we would take the first as true but the second as false. If we take them as conditionals of our truth-functional sort (as material conditionals) we would have to count both as true. (Look back at the account we gave of conditionals: a conditional whose antecedent is false gets an overall value of true.) Counterfactuals are a special case of what we shall call *subjunctive conditionals*. For example, consider the statements:

If I were to turn on the TV, then I would do little work.
If I were to play Civilization II, then I would do little work.

These might be true or false, but their truth or falsity is not determined simply by the truth or falsity of the constituent statements. The moral to draw from this is not that there is something wrong with our conditionals, but that counterfactuals and subjunctive conditionals are a different kind of statement; they are not truth-functional conditionals. We would represent them simply by an atomic sentence. They are, of course, complex, but the complexity is a sort that our language cannot cope with. The same sort of thing happened with the statement that Melanie and Kristos would come to the party together: it had a kind of complexity with which we could not cope.

We will now turn to biconditionals. The main point to keep in mind here is that all of the following:

R if and only if S.
R just in case S.
R is both necessary and sufficient for S.
R exactly when S.

can typically be symbolized as:

R ↔ S

You should not have too much trouble here.

Negations, by contrast, can be a bit of a problem. If someone says:

It's not true that (J)ohn will come and (B)ill will come.

it is hard to tell whether to take this as:

(1) (~J & B)

or as

(2) ~(J & B)

Notice that these do not say the same thing. English has various devices that allow us to distinguish between statements to be taken as of the sort of (1) and those to be taken as of the sort of (2). For example:

It's not true that (J)ohn and (B)ill will both come.

clearly comes out as (2), whereas:

(J)ohn won't come, but (B)ill will.

clearly comes out as (1). There is little to say here save that one symbolizes by making a plausible decision as to what a "not" is negating. Our original statement:

It's not true that (J)ohn will come and (B)ill will come.

would seem simply to be ambiguous. More often than not, though, common sense and an appreciation of the context will help us to disambiguate. There are, as we have seen, English sentences that just are ambiguous. There is nothing we can do about that except encourage people to speak and write less ambiguously. For English does have, as we have seen, numerous devices that enable us at least to minimize ambiguity.

There is a point to keep in mind about the conventions we are here using. Note that when we write the following:

(F)elicia won't come, and (G)uzman is not in town.

we are taking the letters to stand for the "positive" sentences "Felicia will come" and "Guzman is in town". We would therefore symbolize this as:

~F & ~G

People often have other sorts of difficulty in identifying what a "not" is negating. Consider:

(C)arbon's presence is not a sufficient condition for the presence of (L)ife.

Here the "not" negates the whole sentence:

It is not the case that if there is carbon around, then there is life around.
~(C → L)

The sentence cannot be construed as either of:

~C → L
C → ~L

The first says that if there is not carbon around, then there is life around. The second says that if there is carbon around, then there is not life around. Neither of these say the same thing as the original. A similar point obtains with respect to any statement of this sort:

q is not a necessary condition of p.

Such statements are correctly symbolized as:

~(p → q)

You might have noticed that we have nowhere discussed "unless" or "neither ... nor". "Neither ... nor" is rather simple. We do not have a connective in our language for it, but we can symbolize:

Neither p nor q.

as either:

~(p ∨ q)

or

~p & ~q

Both of these give the same, correct, account of our sentence. Let us consider an example in order to see why they are correct. Suppose I say that neither (R)alph nor (B)ill is at the party. If either Ralph or Bill is at the party, my statement that neither is there is false:

R	B	Neither Ralph is at the party nor Bill is at the party.
T	T	F
T	F	F
F	T	F
F	F	T

Next note that both

~(R ∨ B) (It is false that either Ralph or Bill is here.)

and

~R & ~B (Ralph is not here and Bill is not here.)

come out true and false in precisely the same circumstances as our "neither … nor" statement.

"Unless" is rather more troublesome. What we want to do is to determine how to symbolize sentences involving it by figuring out the truth conditions of those sentences, or by paraphrasing it as some sentence that we already know how to symbolize. Consider the following sentence:

(J)ohn will stay at home unless the family (H)ires a baby-sitter.

It should strike you that we can exactly paraphrase this by:

If the family doesn't (H)ire a baby-sitter then (J)ohn will stay at home.

If this is right, we can symbolize it as:

~H → J

We will allow this symbolization but, even though it might sound strange at first, we have available a much simpler symbolization. If, as agreed, the first symbolization is correct, what does that tell us about the truth conditions of our "unless" sentence? The world can come out in any of the following four ways:

T	T	John stays at home, the family can hire a sitter.
T	F	John stays at home, the family can't hire a sitter.
F	T	John doesn't stay at home, the family can hire a sitter.
F	F	John doesn't stay at home, the family can't hire a sitter.

Our sentence comes out false only in the fourth case. But notice that the sentence:

J ∨ H

comes out true or false in precisely those conditions. So:

John will stay at home unless the family can hire a babysitter.

could have been taken as:

John will stay at home or the family can hire a babysitter.

at the outset and symbolized as:

J ∨ H

Our conclusion is that we can typically symbolize any sentence:

p unless q

as:

p ∨ q

As people usually find this a rather strange claim, let us consider the following example. Suppose I tell you:

You will (P)ass the course unless you fail the (E)xam.

Let us consider the possible situations, saving the tricky ones for last, and taking P to be the statement that you pass the course and E the statement that you fail the exam.

P	E	P ∨ E
T	T	T
T	F	T
F	T	T
F	F	F

Row 3 represents the case where you do not pass the course and do fail the exam. There is no problem here. Row 2 represents the case where you do not fail the exam and you do pass the course. There is no problem here.

Row 4 represents the case where you do not fail the exam but nonetheless you do not pass the course. Clearly what I said is false in this case. Now we turn to row 1. Here you failed the exam, but you did pass the course. Surely there is no problem here. I did not tell you that you would not pass the course if you failed the exam; I merely said that you would pass unless you failed the exam, that if you didn't fail the exam then you would pass.

Consider the sentence:

Unless (S)he goes, I will stay (H)ome.

We shall consider this a variant of:

I will stay home unless she goes.

Hence we will normally symbolize it as:

(H ∨ S)

However:

(S ∨ H)

will typically be accepted as well. These two sentences are logically equivalent, so the difference is not one that makes a logical difference.

You may still be quite dissatisfied with our approach to "unless" sentences so let us return to our initial sort of examples. Suppose I were to say:

I will watch the (F)ootball game unless I have (V)isitors.

As noted before most of us would agree that I could have made precisely the same claim by saying:

If I do not have visitors, then I will watch the football game.

The truth conditions for this are, as we have noted, exactly the same as those for:

Either I will watch the football game or I will have visitors.

Deciding upon a way of symbolizing, if we do not have an obvious answer available using the connectives we have, is always a question of finding a symbolization that captures the truth conditions of the statement that we are symbolizing.

1.5 / Symbolizing: More Complex Cases

Hitherto, we have attended to sentences that, although they were sometimes complex, were comparatively simple. Very few connectives were used and there was very little embedding. Let us now consider such a sentence as the following:

I will not (A)rrive on time if the (B)abysitter is late or the (C)ab is late.

The first question to ask in symbolizing a relatively complex English sentence is, "What kind of sentence is it that I am trying to symbolize?" Here the most plausible answer is that the sentence as a whole is a conditional. It is paraphrasable as:

If (the babysitter is late or the cab is late) then I will not arrive on time.

So, you know that your whole sentence will end up as a conditional:

$$(\ldots \rightarrow \underline{\quad})$$

The antecedent is the sentence:

(The baby sitter is late or the cab is late.)

which is, of course:

(B $\vee$ C)

So now we have:

$$((B \vee C) \rightarrow \underline{\quad})$$

The consequent is:

I will not arrive on time.

which is:

~A

So, finally, we obtain:

$$((B \vee C) \rightarrow \text{~}A)$$

as our symbolization. What we did here is to work from the outside in. We decided what the sentence as a whole was and went on from there. Generally speaking, this is the best way of proceeding.

Consider next:

> **(J)ames will not be on time if the (F)ight goes the full twelve rounds, while (W)ilson will not be on time if his (P)lane is delayed.**

Again we work from the outside in, deciding what the sentence as a whole is; here we have a conjunction so we know that it will as a whole have the structure:

> **... & ___**

The left conjunct is:

> **(J)ames will not be on time if the (F)ight goes the full twelve rounds.**

which comes out as:

> **(F → ~J)**

So at this point we have:

> **(F → ~J) & ___**

The right conjunct is:

> **(W)ilson will not be on time if his (P)lane is delayed.**

which is:

> **(P → ~W)**

So our final symbolization is:

> **(F → ~J) & (P → ~W)**

As we noted, negations may cause problems, in particular problems of ambiguity. Consider the following statement:

> **It's false that they will win the (C)hampionship if they win this (G)ame.**

Our initial problem is that the sentence as a whole can, it seems, be construed as being either a negation or a conditional. That is, it can be taken as:

> **It's false that (they will win the (C)hampionship if they win this (G)ame).**

or as:

> **(It's false that they will win the (C)hampionship) if they win this (G)ame.**

But notice that on the second construction we have:

> **If they win this game, then they won't win the championship.**

It is hard to imagine a situation in which this would be the correct construction. So it seems here that we should take the statement as a negation:

> **~...**

And it is a negation of:

> **They will win the (C)hampionship if they win this (G)ame.**

which is:

> **(G → C)**

So our final symbolization will be:

> **~(G → C)**

In this case we were able to make a reasonable guess as to how to construe an ambiguous sentence, but in other cases we may simply have to note the ambiguity.

2 / Truth Tables and Their Use

2.1 / Truth Tables: An Introduction

In 1.3 we specified the basic truth conditions for statements constructed using our connectives. You will recall that such statements are truth-functional, that is, once you know the truth-values of the atomic or basic statements you can compute the truth-value of any complex statement involving those basic statements. We shall now turn to a mechanical means of doing this; we will introduce ***truth tables***.

Suppose we are given that **A** receives a T and **B** receives an F. We can utilize our basic charts to determine what the following complex sentences will receive:

~A ∨ **B**
F **F** F

Note that ~A receives an F, since A received a T. The whole sentence received an F because it is a disjunction, and a disjunction with an F on the left and an F on the right receives an F. Next consider this sentence:

~(A & B)
　T　　F

This sentence is as a whole a negation. In order to determine what it receives we need to know what (**A & B**) receives.

~(A & B)
　T **F** F

The sentence (**A & B**) receives an F, since a conjunction with a T on the left and an F on the right receives an F.

~(A & B)
T　F

The whole sentence, then, receives a T, since it is the negation of a sentence that received an F. Let us now consider:

~A → **~(A** ∨ **B)**
　T　　　T　F

This whole sentence is a conditional. In order to determine what it receives we need to know what the sentence on the left receives (in this case it is the sentence ~A and it receives an F).

~A → **~(A** ∨ **B)**
F　　　　T

The sentence (**A** ∨ **B**) receives a T, since it is a disjunction with a T on the left and an F on the right. Next we consider:

~A → ~(A ∨ B)
F   F

The negation ~(A ∨ B) receives an F, since the sentence it negates received a T. Finally:

~A → ~(A ∨ B)
F **T** F

Our conditional receives a T, since it has an F on the left and an F on the right.

We shall now turn briefly to full truth tables. Consider the sentence of our language (~A → B). Note that it contains two atomic sentences. The number of rows that a full truth table for a sentence has to have is strictly determined by the number of atomic sentences the sentence contains. If a sentence contains n atomic sentences then a truth table for that sentence will contain 2^n rows. If there are two letters there will be four rows, if three letters then eight rows, and so on. The reason is quite simple. Consider two claims:

John will come. Kristin will come.

There are four ways the world might turn out. Both might come, John might come while Kristin doesn't, John might not come while Kristin does, and neither might come. Our truth tables are our means of encoding all possible combinations of truth and falsity: all the possible ways, with respect to the sentences we are considering, that the world might turn out. Here is the way the truth table for the sentence (~A → B) would look.

A	B	(~A → B)	
T	T	F	T
T	F	F	T
F	T	T	T
F	F	T	F

Note that on the left we have encoded the four possible combinations of truth and falsity. For the sake of convenience we usually take the atomic sentences in alphabetical order. Our sentence as a whole is a conditional. But to enter the truth-values for it (the ones found under the conditional sign) we had to know the truth-values assigned to the antecedent and the consequent. The ones for the consequent we already knew, since it is just **B**.

The antecedent is a negation, so we used the rule for negation to make the entries there. Then we used the rule for a conditional to make the entry for the whole sentence, which appears in bold. Let us do one more:

A	B	C		~(A & (B ∨ ~C))		
T	T	T	**F**	T	T F
T	T	F	**F**	T	T T
T	F	T	**T**	F	F F
T	F	F	**F**	T	T T
F	T	T	**T**	F	T F
F	T	F	**T**	F	T T
F	F	T	**T**	F	F F
F	F	F	**T**	F	T T

We shall explain the construction of this by looking at the construction of the first row. The sentence as a whole is a negation. In order to assign a truth-value to it, we needed to know the truth-value of the sentence it negates, the conjunction (**A** & (**B** ∨ ~**C**)). The left conjunct of this sentence is the sentence **A**, and we already knew the truth-value for that. But we needed to know the truth-value of the right conjunct, the (**B** ∨ ~**C**). This sentence is a disjunction. We first placed an F under ~**C**. Since **B** received a T and ~**C** received an F, we placed, in accord with the rule for disjunctions, a T under the disjunction sign. We now know that **A** receives a T and that (**B** ∨ ~**C**) receives a T. So we placed a T under the conjunction sign. Since the conjunction received a T, the final result was that, on that row, the whole sentence received an F. Put verbally, this may all sound quite confusing, but when you begin to construct truth tables you will find that it is simply a mechanical task. It involves nothing other than following strict rules. It may be helpful to repeat what we just said as a sequence of steps visually displayed:

Step 1:

A	B	C	~(A & (B ∨ ~C))
T	T	T	F
T	T	F	T
T	F	T	F
T	F	F	T
F	T	T	F
F	T	F	T
F	F	T	F
F	F	F	T

Since we know the entry for **B** already, we can proceed to figure out the value of the disjunction (**B** ∨ ~**C**).

Step 2:

A	B	C	~(A & (B ∨ ~C))	
T	T	T	T	F
T	T	F	T	T
T	F	T	F	F
T	F	F	T	T
F	T	T	T	F
F	T	F	T	T
F	F	T	F	F
F	F	F	T	T

We are now in a position to compute the value of the conjunction.

Step 3

A	B	C	~(A & (B ∨ ~C))		
T	T	T	T	T	F
T	T	F	T	T	T
T	F	T	F	F	F
T	F	F	T	T	T
F	T	T	F	T	F
F	T	F	F	T	T
F	F	T	F	F	F
F	F	F	F	T	T

And, finally, we are in a position to determine the final entries.

Step 4:

A	B	C	~(A & (B ∨ ~C))			
T	T	T	**F**	T	T	F
T	T	F	**F**	T	T	T
T	F	T	**T**	F	F	F
T	F	F	**F**	T	T	T
F	T	T	**T**	F	T	F
F	T	F	**T**	F	T	T
F	F	T	**T**	F	F	F
F	F	F	**T**	F	T	T

All truth table construction involves the same mechanical, deterministic, procedures.

Recall that each row of the truth table tells us what happens to our whole sentence given one of the 2^n possible assignments of truth-values to the atomic sentences. We shall speak of such an assignment as an ***interpretation***. As our truth tables indicate, a given sentence will come out true or false on each interpretation. We utilize this notion of an interpretation to classify each sentence of our language as *contingent*, a *contradiction*, or a *tautology*.

Classification of Sentences

A sentence is *contingent* if and only if it is true in at least one interpretation and false in at least one interpretation.

A sentence is a *contradiction* if and only if it is false in all interpretations.

A sentence is a *tautology* if and only if it is true in all interpretations.

Tautologies are sometimes spoken of as *logical truths.* A sentence that is a contradiction (in our sense of the word) is sometimes spoken of as being *logically false* or *logically impossible* or *logically inconsistent.* We can, of course, use our truth tables to determine whether a given sentence is, for example, a contradiction by looking to see whether or not it comes out false on all rows. Notice that if we determine that a sentence is a tautology we know, without further investigation, that it is true. Tautologies are one kind of logical truth. And if a sentence is a contradiction we know, without further investigation, that it is false. However, if a sentence is contingent further investigation will be required to determine whether it is true or false. Here are examples of each kind of sentence:

R	S	R & S	
T	T	**T**	
T	F	**F**	**(R & S) is contingent.**
F	T	**F**	
F	F	**F**	

A		~(A → A)	
T		**F** T	
F		**F** T	**~(A → A) is a contradiction.**

A	B	A → (B → A)		
T	T	**T** T		
T	F	**T** T		
F	T	**T** F	**(A → (B → A)) is a tautology.**
F	F	**T** T		

Truth tables are deterministic; what is not deterministic is the language we use to symbolize statements and arguments. That is not because English or any other natural language is flawed, but because they are rich and diverse. As we have already noted, we have many ways of saying much the same thing.

2.2 / More on Constructing Truth Tables

Symbolizing can be difficult, but constructing truth tables is quite easy, because it is simply a matter of routine. It is strongly recommended that you learn how to construct truth tables by going off and practising. You should read this part only if you find that you are making too many mistakes.

Recall that the number of rows a truth table will have is strictly determined by the number of atomic sentences in the sentence for which you want to construct a truth table: 2^n where n is the number of atomic sentences. Usually, it is convenient to arrange the atomic sentences in alphabetical order and to place them on the left. It is also convenient to have some habitual method for entering the possible combinations of truth and falsity. If you look back at the tables I have done, you will see that I have proceeded in the following fashion. Under the leftmost atomic sentence, I entered $1/2k$ Ts (where k is the number of rows), followed by $1/2k$ Fs. Under the second I entered, alternately, $1/4k$ Ts and $1/4k$ Fs until done. If there is a third I enter $1/8k$ Ts followed by $1/8k$ Fs until done; and so on.

Consider, first, the following biconditional sentence:

A	B	C	$\sim(A \vee B) \leftrightarrow (\sim A \;\&\; C)$
T	T	T	
T	T	F	
T	F	T	
T	F	F	
F	T	T	
F	T	F	
F	F	T	
F	F	F	

As can be seen, a full truth table for this will have eight rows. Let us construct the truth table row by row, completing only the first row. We found it convenient when symbolizing to work from the outside in; by contrast, in doing truth tables we work from the inside out, from the smaller contained sentences to the larger ones. (The smaller contained sentences, the *subsentences*, are of course the ones that we used in the construction of the larger ones.)

A	B	C	~(A ∨ B) ↔ (~A & C)
T	T	T	F

~A receives an F because A receives a T in this row.

A	B	C	~(A ∨ B) ↔ (~A & C)
T	T	T	T F F

(A ∨ B) receives a T because A and B both received a T. (~A & C) receives an F because ~A receives an F and C receives a T. Note that we are using our basic charts to determine what entry to make.

A	B	C	~(A ∨ B) ↔ (~A & C)
T	T	T	F T F F

~(A ∨ B) receives an F, since (A ∨ B) receives a T.

A	B	C	~(A ∨ B) ↔ (~A & C)
T	T	T	F T **T** F F

The whole sentence receives a T, since the sentence on the left of the biconditional received an F and the sentence on the right received an F.

Now consider this more complex sentence:

A	B	C	D	~((A ∨ ~B) → ~(C → (D ∨ A)))
T	T	T	T	
T	T	T	F	
T	T	F	T	
T	T	F	F	
T	F	T	T	
T	F	T	F	
T	F	F	T	
T	F	F	F	
F	T	T	T	
F	T	T	F	
F	T	F	T	
F	T	F	F	
F	F	T	T	
F	F	T	F	
F	F	F	T	
F	F	F	F	

Again, we can proceed row by row, using the same technique as in the preceding case.

Let us look at our next step for the first row:

A	B	C	D	~((A ∨ ~B) → ~(C → (D ∨ A)))
T	T	T	T	F

We know the value of the atomic sentences already, though you may re-enter them if you find that convenient.

A	B	C	D	~((A ∨ ~B) → ~(C → (D ∨ A)))
T	T	T	T	T F T

We enter a T under the first "∨" since the left disjunct **A** gets a T and the right disjunct an F, and our rule says that in this case a disjunction gets a T. Since **D** and **A** both get a T, we enter a T under the second "∨".

A	B	C	D	~((A ∨ ~B) → ~(C → (D ∨ A)))
T	T	T	T	T F T T

We now enter a T under the second conditional sign. The antecedent has received a T, as has the consequent, so the entire conditional receives a T.

A	B	C	D	~((A ∨ ~B) → ~(C → (D ∨ A)))
T	T	T	T	T F F T T

Next we place an F under the third negation sign. It negates the whole conditional that follows it. That conditional had received a T, so the negation receives an F.

A	B	C	D	~((A ∨ ~B) → ~(C → (D ∨ A)))
T	T	T	T	T F F F T T

Now we know that the whole conditional, which has (A ∨ ~B) as its antecedent and ~(C → (D ∨ A)) as its consequent, gets an F, since the antecedent gets a T and the consequent gets an F, and our rule for conditionals says that in this case a conditional gets an F.

A	B	C	D	~((A ∨ ~B) → ~(C → (D ∨ A)))
T	T	T	T	**T** T F F F T T

The whole sentence is a negation. It gets a T, since the sentence it negates got an F.

You do not have to write all this down if you construct a truth table; you might merely make the entries. Again, there is absolutely nothing here that requires any insight. The whole procedure is strictly mechanical. There is absolutely no reason (save exhaustion, boredom, or carelessness) to make a mistake in the construction of truth tables.

2.3 / The Use of Truth Tables

We have learned how to construct truth tables. Now, of what use are they? In one sense, they are not very useful. They get too large too quickly. But they can in principle be used to answer almost any question about sentences and groups of sentences from our language. And, as we shall see, they provide a mechanical means of determining whether an argument is or is not valid or, to be more precise, whether an argument formulated in our language is truth-functionally valid or truth-functionally invalid (see p. 167). We shall now turn to an explanation of all of this.

We have already seen that certain sentences are contradictions: they come out false in all circumstances. But now consider the following set of sentences (suppose they represent sentences that Jones has claimed are all true):

> **P** ∨ **Q**
> **~P** ∨ **~Q**
> **~P** ∨ **Q**

To ask whether this set or group of sentences is **consistent** is to ask whether or not there is a possible circumstance in which *all* the sentences could be true. Since our truth table tactics involve surveying all possibilities, you would be right to suspect that we can use those tactics to answer the question at hand. Consider the following:

P	**Q**	**P** ∨ **Q**	**~P** ∨ **~Q**	**~P** ∨ **Q**
T	T	**T**	F **F** F	F **T**
T	F	**T**	F **T** T	F **F**
F	T	**T**	T **T** F	T **T**
F	F	**F**	T **T** T	T **T**

You can see that row 3 represents a possible situation in which all three of these sentences are true. Note that in various ways we can form a conjunction of these sentences. Such a conjunction will come out true in an interpretation if and only if all three of the sentences of our set come out true in that interpretation. Here is one such conjunction constructed via the recipe or procedure we will commonly use. (There are other procedures; we simply arbitrarily choose to use this one.)

(((P ∨ Q) & (~P ∨~Q)) & (~Q ∨ P))

Next we should note that the above set of sentences is inconsistent if and only if such a conjunction is a contradiction (a proof of this claim is, strictly speaking, required but we do not wish to be technical here), and the set is consistent if and only if this conjunction is consistent. (To say that a sentence is *consistent* is merely to say it is not a contradiction, that it gets a T on at least one row of its truth table.)

We might also ask, of a pair of sentences, whether they are logically equivalent. Recall that to say two sentences are *logically equivalent* is to say they cannot differ in truth-value. Consider the following pair of sentences:

Neither A nor B.
Either not A or not B.

Are these sentences logically equivalent?

A	B	~A & ~B			~A ∨ ~B		
T	T	F	**F**	F	F	**F**	F
T	F	F	**F**	T	F	**T**	T
F	T	T	**F**	F	T	**T**	F
F	F	T	**T**	T	T	**T**	T

Clearly, they are not, as you can see from rows 2 and 3. But what of "If A then B" and "Either not A or B": are they logically equivalent?

A	B	A → B	~A ∨ B	
T	T	**T**	F	**T**
T	F	**F**	F	**F**
F	T	**T**	T	**T**
F	F	**T**	T	**T**

These are logically equivalent. There is no possible situation (no row) in which they differ in truth-value. There is another way in which we could proceed. We could have formed a biconditional with one of the pair on the left and the other on the right.

A	B	(A → B)	↔	(~A ∨ B)		
T	T	T	**T**	F	T	
T	F	F	**T**	F	F	
F	T	T	**T**	T	T	
F	F	T	**T**	T	T	

Notice that this sentence is a tautology. The sentences of the pair with which we begin are logically equivalent if and only if the biconditional formed from them is a tautology. Why is this so? It should simply be apparent that it is so. Recall that ~**A** & ~**B** and ~**A** ∨ ~**B** differed in truth-value on rows 2 and 3. A biconditional formed from them would receive an F on both those rows; hence it would not be a tautology. However, **A** → **B** and ~**A** ∨ **B** differed in truth-value on no row. Since a biconditional gets a T on any row on which the left and the right get the same truth-value, a biconditional formed from these two would be a tautology. So you can check whether a pair of sentences are logically equivalent by forming a biconditional and then constructing a truth table to determine whether that biconditional is a tautology. As noted, the sentences are logically equivalent if and only if the biconditional is a tautology.

We will now turn to arguments. How can we use truth table techniques to check arguments for validity? Before you read further you should sit back and think. If you are catching on to what we are doing, you should be able to figure out for yourself a way of checking arguments for validity.

Thought enough? Then let us continue. Here is an argument:

> **A** → **B**
> **A** ∨ **C**
> **C** → **B**
> **Therefore, B**

Is this a valid argument? It is valid just in case there is no possible situation in which all the premises are true and the conclusion is false. So let us simply list the possible situations and see whether there is one such.

A	B	C	A → B	A ∨ C	C → B	/ B
T	T	T	T	T	T	T
T	T	F	T	T	T	T
T	F	T	F	T	F	F
T	F	F	F	T	T	F
F	T	T	T	T	T	T
F	T	F	T	F	T	T
F	F	T	T	T	F	F
F	F	F	T	F	T	F

We have used the "/" simply to mark off the conclusion. As you can see by inspection, there is no row on which all the premises are true but the conclusion is false. So the argument is, as we shall now say, ***truth-functionally*** *valid*. Why this slight shift in vocabulary? In part, it is because the argument is valid for the kinds of reasons we are looking at here. All truth-functionally valid arguments are valid, but they are valid because of the kinds of reasons we are now considering. There is, however, another reason, which we shall now proceed to explain. Consider the following argument:

A → B
B
So, A

A	B	A → B	B	/ A
T	T	T	T	T
T	F	F	F	T
F	T	T	T	F
F	F	T	F	F

(We re-entered **B** because it is a premise, **A** because it is the conclusion; we want these facts to be visually evident.)

Obviously, this is not a truth-functionally valid argument: there is a row on which all the premises are true and the conclusion is false. It is a ***truth-functionally invalid*** argument. We will now give our primary reason for the slightly modified vocabulary. As we noted above, all truth-functionally valid arguments are valid; but not all truth-functionally invalid arguments are invalid. Consider the following argument:

All whales are mammals.
Some whales live in the Pacific.
So, some mammals live in the Pacific.

We could only symbolize this argument in some such way as the following:

A
B
So, C

Note that this argument is truth-functionally invalid. But the argument it symbolizes, concerning mammals in the Pacific, is valid. We have no means of capturing the type of complexity possessed by the sentences in this argument. We have given it the best symbolization available to us. We cannot say that the argument is invalid, for it is not, but we do want to say that it is truth-functionally invalid. And it is that; its validity is not explained by the kinds of factors we are now considering.

We saw previously that we could determine whether a pair of sentences were logically equivalent by checking to see if a related biconditional was a tautology. Can we find a way of determining whether an argument is valid by way of checking some related sentence?

Let us first consider a very simple case, which will provide the basis for laying down a quite general technique. Consider the argument:

> **R** ∨ **S**
> **~R**
> **So, S**

Now recall that if this argument is truth-functionally valid (and it is), there will be no case in which all the premises are true and the conclusion is false: no case in which ((**R** ∨ **S**) & **~R**) is true and **S** is false. Notice that what we have done is to form a conjunction of the premises. Now consider the following sentence:

> **((R** ∨ **S) & ~R)** → **S**

This is a conditional sentence of our language. It is *not* an argument. But this sentence is related to the argument we are considering in a certain way. We conjoined the premises and then constructed a conditional that had this conjunction as its antecedent and the conclusion of the argument as its consequent. Now note the following: if there is no case in which the antecedent of a conditional is true and the consequent false, then the conditional in question is a tautology. Arguments are not tautologies; they are valid or invalid. But the argument we are considering is valid if and only if the conditional we are considering is a tautology. Let us look at another case:

> **~P** ∨ **Q**
> **Q**
> **So, ~P**

This is not a valid argument. There is at least one case in which both premises are true and the conclusion is false. So there is at least one case in which:

> **((~P** ∨ **Q) & Q)**

is true and

> **~P**

is false. Now form the following conditional:

$$((\sim P \vee Q) \mathbin{\&} Q) \rightarrow \sim P$$

Since there is at least one case in which the antecedent is true and the consequent false, this sentence (it is not an argument) is not a tautology. Given that the sentence is not a tautology, we can conclude that the argument to which it is related is a truth-functionally invalid argument.

We now wish to generalize. Any argument will consist of a sequence of premises and some conclusion *c*:

$$p_1$$
.
.
.
$$p_n$$
$$c$$

We will now define what we will call the ***corresponding conditional*** of an argument. We want every argument to have a unique corresponding conditional. A precise definition could be given, but we shall proceed by way of example. Where an argument has one premise *p* and a conclusion *c*, the corresponding conditional is simply

$$p \rightarrow c$$

Where an argument has two premises *p* and *q*, the corresponding conditional is:

$$(p \mathbin{\&} q) \rightarrow c$$

It is the cases after this that require a bit of care, given that we wish to have, for each argument, a unique corresponding conditional. Consider an argument with three premises:

$$p$$
$$q$$
$$r$$
So, *c*

The antecedent of our corresponding conditional will be the conjunction:

$$((p \mathbin{\&} q) \mathbin{\&} r)$$

So the corresponding conditional will be:

((p & q) & r) → c

Here is an example for an argument with four premises:

p
q
r
s
So, c

The antecedent of our corresponding conditional will be the conjunction:

(((p & q) & r) & s)

So the corresponding conditional will be:

(((p & q) & r) & s) → c

and so on, as we encounter arguments with increasingly many premises. As you should see, we are forming a conjunction in the following way: We first conjoin the first *n* premises in this way, coming up with a conjunction *a*. We then add the *n* + 1th premise — call it *q* — by forming the conjunction (*a* & *q*). If you look closely at the above examples, you should see that this is just what we did. We then formed a conditional sentence in which that conjunction was the antecedent and the conclusion of the argument was the consequent.

We can now state, though we will not here prove, the following theorem:

Theorem regarding Corresponding Conditionals

An argument is truth-functionally valid if and only if its corresponding conditional is a tautology.

Again, *arguments* and *corresponding conditionals* are *not* the same thing; they are distinct things related in just this way. Given that they are so related, you can always find out whether an argument is valid by seeing whether its corresponding conditional is a tautology.

Chapter Summary

In Section 1 of this chapter we introduced our formal language. In section 1.1 we specified its structure. Our basic symbols were our *atomic sentences*:

A, B, ... Z, ... A^1, B^1, ... A^n, B^n, ...

and our *connectives,* which enable us to form *complex* or *compound* sentences:

Connectives

&	(our "and" or *conjunction* sign)
∨	(our "or" or *disjunction* sign)
→	(our "if ... then" or *conditional* sign)
↔	(our "if and only if" or *biconditional* sign)
~	(our "it is not the case that" or *negation* sign)

We utilized parentheses as our punctuation.

Definition of "Sentence of Our Language"

1. Every atomic sentence is a sentence of our language.
2. If *p* and *q* are both sentences of our language, then each of:

   (*p* & *q*)
   (*p* ∨ *q*)
   (*p* → *q*)
   (*p* ↔ *q*)

   is a sentence of our language. (Note that *p* and *q* can be any sentence of our language.)
3. If *p* is a sentence of our language, then ~*p* is a sentence of our language.
4. The only strings of symbols that are sentences of our language are those strings constructed by the use of the above rules.

Each of our complex sentences had a name:

> ## Types of Compound Sentences
>
> ~*p* is a *negation*
> (*p* & *q*) is a *conjunction*
> (*p* ∨ *q*) is a *disjunction*
> (*p* → *q*) is a *conditional*
> (*p* ↔ *q*) is a *biconditional*

We will utilize this formal language to 'represent' or *symbolize* ordinary statements and arguments.

In 1.2 we introduced substitution instances. The language in which we talk about our formal language, which we call the *object language*, is our *metalanguage*. The sentences in our metalanguage that involve the lower-case letters such as those above we called *sentential forms*. We noted that all the sentences of our language had a number of sentential forms. If a sentence of our language has some particular sentential form, then we shall speak of that sentence as being a *substitution instance* of that sentential form.

In 1.3 we identified the basic truth conditions for the sentences of our language. We identified our connectives as *truth-functional connectives*. Our basic charts specified the truth conditions for each kind of complex sentence.

Basic Charts

Conjunction

p	q	(p & q)
T	T	T
T	F	F
F	T	F
F	F	F

Disjunction

p	q	(p ∨ q)
T	T	T
T	F	T
F	T	T
F	F	F

Conditional

p	q	(p → q)
T	T	T
T	F	F
F	T	T
F	F	T

Biconditional

p	q	(p ↔ q)
T	T	T
T	F	F
F	T	F
F	F	T

Negation

p	~p
T	F
F	T

In 1.4 we discussed how to symbolize certain basic statements, while in 1.5 we turned to a discussion of more complex cases of symbolization.

In Section 2 we turned to *truth tables* and their use. In 2.1 we saw how we utilize our basic charts to calculate the truth-value of complex sentences. We noted that if a sentence contains *n* atomic sentences then a truth table for that sentence will contain 2^n rows. We also introduced a classification of sentences:

Classification of Sentences

A sentence is *contingent* if and only if it is true in at least one interpretation and false in at least one interpretation.

A sentence is a *contradiction* if and only if it is false in all interpretations.

A sentence is a *tautology* if and only if it is true in all interpretations.

In 2.2 we simply illustrated the way to construct more complex truth tables, while in 2.3 we turn to a discussion of some applications of truth tables. We saw that we could utilize truth tables to determine whether a set of sentences was *consistent*, that is, whether there is a possibility that all of the sentences in the set could be true at the same time. *Truth-functionally valid* arguments are a special case of valid arguments, in which the validity of the argument is due to the considerations discussed in this and the preceding chapter. We developed various techniques for checking arguments for truth-functional validity. One was simply, by using truth tables, looking and seeing whether there is no possible circumstance in which all the premises are true and the conclusion false. If there is such a possible circumstance, then the argument is *truth-functionally invalid*. However we noted that a truth-functionally invalid argument may be valid for other reasons. We also saw that we could test any argument for truth-functional validity by seeing whether its *corresponding conditional* was a tautology. We stated, but did not demonstrate, a theorem:

Theorem regarding Corresponding Conditionals

An argument is truth-functionally valid if and only if its corresponding conditional is a tautology.

CHAPTER 7

A Deductive System

There are various ways in which deductive logic can be approached. In the previous chapter we approached logic by means of truth tables, which have the advantage of being mechanical, but also have certain disadvantages. Truth tables quickly become unwieldy if there are more than a few atomic sentences. And they bear no obvious relation to reasoning. Finally, though the topic is one beyond the scope of this book, there are situations in which there is no device similar to truth tables that will enable us to determine whether an argument is valid or not. For all these reasons, we will now introduce a formal deductive system. In this system we will be able to show that truth-functionally valid arguments are indeed truth-functionally valid.

Our system will be developed in the following way. An argument begins with certain premises. We will first list those premises. Each one will be entered on a separate line. If an argument is valid, we should be able to move from the premises to the conclusion in a sequence of steps. Each step, each additional line, will be one that the rules of inference (explained below) will allow us to add. If we reach a conclusion in this way, we shall say that we have a *derivation* or *proof* of the conclusion from those premises, or, to be slightly more formal, a derivation of our conclusion from that set of premises. In order to keep track of where a line comes from, we shall enter on the left an account — we shall call it a *justification* — that tells us how the line was derived, where it came from.

1 / Basic Rules

1.1 / Modus Ponens and Modus Tollens

Let us first set up a short argument, one in which we wish to show that:

> **Q & R**

follows from the premises:

> (P & S) → (Q & R)
> (P & S)

We will set this up as follows:

> **premise**   1.   (P & S) → (Q & R)
> **premise**   2.   (P & S)

Now we wish, in accord with our rules, to add lines until we reach our conclusion. Of course, we need some rules. Here is our first one:

Modus Ponens (mp)

From:

$p \rightarrow q$ and p

To:

q

This is, of course, a rule that we encountered in Chapter 5. Our rule says that given two previous lines, one of which is a conditional sentence and the other the antecedent of that conditional sentence, it is permissable to add a new line containing the consequent of that conditional. Put another way, of the two previous lines one must be a substitution instance of $p \rightarrow q$ and the other must consist of the same sentence that the p in the $p \rightarrow q$ stood for. The order in which these two occur does not matter. We will now use this rule in connection with the argument we were considering.

> **premise**   1.   (P & S) → (Q & R)
> **premise**   2.   (P & S)
> **1,2 mp**   3.   (Q & R)

We added as line 3 the consequent of the conditional that we had on line 1. We could do this because on line 2 we had the antecedent of the conditional. On the left of line 3 we entered, so as to keep track, our justification for the line. This says that we obtained line 3 from lines 1 and 2 by way of applying the rule mp. We have now reached our conclusion by means of the use of a valid rule of inference.

Here is another familiar rule:

Modus Tollens (mt)

From:

$p \rightarrow q$ and $\sim q$

To:

$\sim p$

The following argument involves a legitimate application of modus tollens:

premise	1.	$(P \rightarrow (\sim R \ \& \ S))$
premise	2.	$\sim(\sim R \ \& \ S)$
1,2 mt	3.	$\sim P$

The first premise is a substitution instance of $p \rightarrow q$ and the second premise of $\sim q$. Put in another way, premise 2 is the negation of the consequent of the conditional sentence that is premise 1. What is needed for a case of modus tollens is that we have a line that is a conditional and some other line that is the negation of the consequent of that conditional.

Here is one example of a slightly more complex argument, one in which we are heading for **S** as a conclusion:

premise	1.	$(P \vee Q) \rightarrow R$
premise	2.	$\sim R$
premise	3.	$\sim(P \vee Q) \rightarrow S$
1,2 mt	4.	$\sim(P \vee Q)$
3,4 mp	5.	S

Notice that the rules can be applied over and over again. They are not applied only to premises, but also to lines that we add in accordance with the rules.

1.2 / Simplification and Conjunction

Now suppose we have the following premises from which we wish to derive **Q** as our conclusion:

premise	1.	**P → (Q & S)**
premise	2.	**P**

To start with, we can utilize modus ponens:

premise	1.	**P → (Q & S)**
premise	2.	**P**
1,2 mp	3.	**Q & S**

But we do not yet have any rule that would allow us to move to **Q**.

We now need to add a rule:

Simplification (simp)

From:	From
p & q	*p & q*
To:	To:
p	*q*

This is a straightforward rule. It says that where we are given a conjunction *p & q* as a line, we may legitimately infer *p* and may legitimately infer *q*. We all know that, of course. Our goal, however, is to construct a system in which we do not rely upon intuition to tell us whether or not a line can legitimately be added, whether or not a given claim follows from previous lines. We want our rules to be valid rules of inference, and we want each line to be justified by being added in accord with the rules. (Recall that a valid rule of inference is one that is truth-preserving, one that will never lead us from a truth or truths to something false.) Insofar as we want to use valid rules, and do not want to rest our claims upon our intuitions, we must pay careful attention to the argument forms.

With the rule simplification, we are now able to complete the argument we were considering:

premise	1.	**P → (Q & S)**
premise	2.	**P**
1,2 mp	3.	**(Q & S)**
3 simp	4.	**Q**

We have reached **Q** via the application of valid rules of inference.

We emphasized above that it is important to pay attention to the kind of sentence we are encountering. Each sentence is of a certain kind, and that kind is, if the sentence is not an atomic one, determined by the main connective. The rule simplification, like all of the rules that we are now considering, is one that can be applied only to a whole line, which line must be a substitution instance of p **&** q. Let us see why it is important to apply a rule only to a whole line. Consider this argument:

premise	1.	**(P & Q)** ∨ **R**
1 simp	2.	**P**

The first point to note is that this argument does not fit our pattern. Line 1 is a disjunction, not a conjunction. It says only that either both **P** and **Q** are true or **R** is true. It would obviously be a mistake to infer from this that **P** is true; premise 1 guarantees no such thing. At the very least, we shall make no such mistakes if we attend to the form of the sentences — if we apply the rules of inference only when sentences are of the correct form.

Our system of rules is not yet a complete one, that is, one in which we could show any truth-functionally valid argument to be truth-functionally valid by deriving the conclusion from the premises by the use of our rules. We are, however, heading toward such a system, step by step.

We have re-introduced two old friends, modus ponens and modus tollens. And we have introduced the rule simplification. Let us now consider the following rule:

Conjunction (conj)

From:

p and *q*

To:

p **&** *q*

Clearly this rule allows the following:

premise	1.	**A** ∨ **B**
premise	2.	**C**
1,2 conj	3.	**(A** ∨ **B) & C**

But it also allows the following:

premise	1.	(A ∨ B)
premise	2.	C
1,2 conj	3.	C & (A ∨ B)

This might seem strange, but let us think about it a bit as it relates to a point we have made before. An argument stands or falls on the basis of whether or not the premises support a given conclusion. If the sentence(s) that I claim provide conclusive evidence for another sentence do in fact do so, then they do so regardless of the order in which I happen to say them or write them down. So, all of the following are cases of the rule that we call conj:

premise	1.	A
premise	2.	B
1,2 conj	3	A & B

premise	1.	B
premise	2.	A
2,1 conj	3.	A & B

premise	1.	A
premise	2.	B
2,1 conj	3.	B & A

premise	1.	B
premise	2.	A
1,2 conj	3.	B & A

1.3 / Disjunctive Syllogism and Addition

We have not yet introduced any rules that pertain to disjunctions. Here is one that should seem familiar (notice, though, that we have added some variations):

Disjunctive Syllogism (ds)

From:
$p \lor q$ and $\sim p$
To:
q

From:
$p \lor q$ and $\sim q$
To:
p

Disjunctive Syllogism *(continued)*

From:	From:
~$p \lor q$ and p	$p \lor$ ~q and q
To:	To:
q	p

It should be clear that this is indeed a valid rule of inference. Here is an example of the use of this rule (our conclusion will be $R \rightarrow S$):

premise	1.	$(A \lor (R \rightarrow S)) \lor D$
premise	2.	~D & ~A
2 simp	3.	~D
2 simp	4.	~A
1,3 ds	5.	$A \lor (R \rightarrow S)$
4,5 ds	6.	$R \rightarrow S$

Notice, however, that you cannot do the following:

premise	1.	$(A \lor (R \rightarrow S)) \lor D$	
premise	2.	~D & ~A	
2 simp	3.	~D	
2 simp	4.	~A	
1,4 ds	5.	$(R \rightarrow S) \lor D$	**erroneous**
3,5 ds	6.	$R \rightarrow S$	

Look very carefully at the parentheses in line 1. Line 5 is neither the left disjunct nor the right disjunct of that line. Hence you cannot move directly to it by an application of ds. Again, you must always be careful that you are identifying the main connective on any given line.

We need to include the following rule as well:

Addition (add)

From:	From:
p	p
To:	To:
$p \lor q$	$q \lor p$

That this is a valid rule should be clear if one thinks about our disjunction. Our inclusive disjunctions come true just in case at least one of *p*, *q* is true. And where *p* is true, at least one of *p*, *q* is true. This might seem like a very odd rule, but consider the following argument:

Wilson will support Cheung.
If either Wilson or Sanchez supports Cheung, then Cheung will win.
Therefore, Cheung will win.

It should be apparent that this is a truth-functionally valid argument. With our new rule, we can show it to be such in the following way (using the obvious symbolization):

premise	1.	W
premise	2.	(W ∨ S) → C
1 add	3.	W ∨ S
2,3 mp	4.	C

Notice here that I entered line 3 precisely because it would enable me to work toward the conclusion **C**.

Remember that when you use addition you may add as a right or left disjunct any sentence whatsoever. Your decision about what to add is guided by your goal, which is to reach a particular conclusion. You use addition when it is useful in reaching that conclusion. Developing the ability to determine what is useful, alas, involves a bit of practice.

1.4 / Hypothetical Syllogism and Constructive Dilemmas

We will now introduce two more rather familiar rules. The first is:

Hypothetical Syllogism (hs)

From:
p → *q* and *q* → *r*
To:
p → *r*

Again, we must keep in mind that the order of the lines (or premises) from which we move to $p \to r$ does not matter. Both of the following are cases of the application of hs:

premise	1.	$(A \lor B) \to {\sim}C$
premise	2.	${\sim}C \to D$
1,2 hs	3.	$(A \lor B) \to D$

premise	1.	$R \to S$
premise	2.	$A \to R$
1,2 hs	3.	$A \to S$

However, the following is not a case of the application of hs:

premise	1.	$R \to S$	
premise	2.	$R \to W$	
1,2 hs	3.	$S \to W$	**erroneous**

In Chapter 5 we talked about constructive dilemmas. We will now introduce our versions thereof.

Constructive Dilemma (cd)

From:
$p \to r$, $q \to s$, and $p \lor q$
To:
$r \lor s$

From:
$(p \to r)$ & $(q \to s)$ and $p \lor q$
To:
$r \lor s$

Here is a case of the application of this rule:

premise	1.	$(A \to C)$ & $({\sim}B \to D)$
premise	2.	$A \lor {\sim}B$
1,2 cd	3.	$C \lor D$

And here is a slightly more complex case:

premise	1.	$((A \& B) \to C)$ & $((D \lor C) \to E)$
premise	2.	$(A \& B) \lor (D \lor C)$
1,2 cd	3.	$C \lor E$

But consider the following set of premises, from which we would like to derive **(A & B) ∨ (C & D)**.

premise	1.	**R → (A & B)**
premise	2.	**S → (C & D)**
premise	3.	**R ∨ S**

Employing the first, left-hand version of our rule, we can move directly to the conclusion we want. We must only be careful to state the justification correctly.

premise	1.	**R → (A & B)**
premise	2.	**S → (C & D)**
premise	3.	**R ∨ S**
1,2,3 cd	4.	**(A & B) ∨ (C & D)**

Often we shall have to use various rules in combination in order to reach our conclusion. The only way to learn how to do this is by practice. However, after we complete our description of our system we will provide some tips and tricks that may help you to construct proofs. Two cautions: these tips and tricks will often help but will not always solve your problems; and even if they do help, they may not lead to a very short derivation.

1.5 / Biconditional Introduction and Elimination

We have not as yet introduced any rule that applies to biconditionals. A biconditional $p \leftrightarrow q$ in effect asserts that both $p \to q$ and $q \to p$ are true. So our rule (which we will abbreviate by "bc") will be:

Biconditional (bc)

From:	From:
$p \leftrightarrow q$	$(p \to q) \, \& \, (q \to p)$
To:	To:
$(p \to q) \, \& \, (q \to p)$	$p \leftrightarrow q$

Here is an example of the use of this rule:

premise	1.	$A \to B$
premise	2.	$B \to (R \lor S)$
premise	3.	$(R \lor S) \to A$
1,2 hs	4.	$A \to (R \lor S)$
3,4 conj	5.	$(A \to (R \lor S)) \& ((R \lor S) \to A)$
5 bc	6.	$A \leftrightarrow (R \lor S)$

And here is another example:

premise	1.	$A \leftrightarrow B$
premise	2.	~A
1 bc	3.	$(A \to B) \& (B \to A)$
3 simp	4.	$B \to A$
2,4 mt	5.	~B

We do not have a rule like modus tollens that applies directly to biconditionals. But this example shows how we can obtain the effect of having such a rule.

1.6 / Commutation, Idempotence, and Double Negation

We shall add three more rules to our group of basic rules. From arithmetic you are probably familiar with an operation that we shall call commutation. You know, for example, that $(m + n) = (n + m)$. In certain cases we allow a related move:

Commutation (comm)

From:	From:
$p \lor q$	$p \& q$
To:	To:
$q \lor p$	$q \& p$

You know from arithmetic that commutation, while it obtains with respect to addition and multiplication, does not apply to subtraction and division. It is not in general true that $(m - n) = (n - m)$. A similar point holds here. A move from, for example, $p \to q$ to $q \to p$ is not in general a valid one. Conditionals are not commutative, but both disjunctions and conjunctions are. Here is an example of the use of commutation:

premise	1.	$P \vee Q$
premise	2.	$(Q \vee P) \rightarrow S$
1 comm	3.	$Q \vee P$
2,3 mp	6.	S

Next, we need a rule that we shall call idempotence:

Idempotence (idem)

From:

$p \vee p$

To:

p

Where might we have occasion to use this rule? Consider the following argument:

> **If (J)ulio goes the (P)arty will be a success. If (C)han goes the (P)arty will be a success. One or the other will go. So the (P)arty will be a success.**

This is a valid argument, and if our system is to be a complete one we should be able to show it to be such. Here is a way to do that:

premise	1.	$J \rightarrow P$
premise	2.	$C \rightarrow P$
premise	3.	$J \vee C$
1,2,3 cd	4.	$P \vee P$
4 idem	5.	P

Step 4 is a perfectly legitimate use of constructive dilemma: we replaced the r by P and the s by P. And our new rule idem allowed us to move to line 5. Let us see why idempotence is a valid rule of inference, that is, one that does not allow us to move from a truth to a falsehood. Where p is false, $p \vee p$ is false, so when we move from $p \vee p$ to p we will not be moving from a truth to a falsehood. Where p is true, $p \vee p$ will be true, so when we move from $p \vee p$ to p we will again not be moving from a truth to a falsehood.

The following rule enables us to work with double negations:

Double Negation (dn)

From:

$\sim\sim p$

To:

p

From:

p

To:

$\sim\sim p$

Again, you can see that these are valid inferences. Here is an example of the use of double negation. Suppose we wish to get to **P** ∨ **Q**. We have as premises:

premise	1.	~(P ∨ Q) → ~R
premise	2.	R

We cannot yet apply mt, but we can proceed as follows:

premise	1.	~(P ∨ Q) → ~R
premise	2.	R
2 dn	3.	~~R

Premise 1 is a substitution instance of $p \to q$ and line 3 a substitution instance of $\sim q$, where p stands for ~(P ∨ Q) and q stands for ~R. So, next we can derive:

premise	1.	~(P ∨ Q) → ~R
premise	2.	R
2 dn	3.	~~R
1,3 mt	4.	~~(P ∨ Q)

We could not obtain (P ∨ Q) at line 4: modus tollens does not allow us to delete a negation sign. But now that we have dn, we can finish our derivation:

premise	1.	~(P ∨ Q) → ~R
premise	2.	R
2 dn	3.	~~R
1,3 mt	4.	~~(P ∨ Q)
4 dn	5.	P ∨ Q

2 / Modes of Proof: Conditional and Indirect

2.1 / Conditional Proof

Our first mode of proof is one that we shall call ***conditional proof*** (cp). It is designed to capture the following, rather familiar pattern of reasoning: We suppose that *p* is true. We then show that given that *p* is true, some claim *q* must be true as well. We conclude that therefore "If *p* then *q*".

Let us consider a case where we know the following:

> **Either (J)ones will do it or (P)atel will do it.**
> **If Patel does it then there will be (N)o problems.**

We might wonder what would happen if Jones doesn't do it. If we did, we might reason as follows:

> **Suppose Jones doesn't do it.**
> **Then Patel will.**
> **Then there will be no problems.**
> **So, if Jones doesn't do it there will be no problems.**

It is this mode of proof that our cp is designed to mimic. Let us write this out in the way in which we would write it out in our system. The initial set-up remains the same, that is, we list at the outset whatever premises we have at hand:

premise	1.	J ∨ P
premise	2.	P → N

The conclusion that we wish to obtain from this is ~J → N. How shall we attempt to derive this conclusion? Well, suppose that ~J is true. We encode this as follows:

premise	1.	J ∨ P
premise	2.	P → N
acp	⌐ 3.	~J

We should stop for a second and account for the appearance of something new on line 3. First, the justification acp indicates that our line is an assumption, not a genuine premise. In the English version we indicated this by our use of the word suppose. The c in acp indicates that our intent is to utilize a conditional proof. The symbol "⌐" indicates that we have made an assumption, that we are beginning what we shall call a *subderivation*. The lines will continue until the assumed premise has been, as we will say, *terminated*. This all needs a bit of explaining.

premise	1.	J ∨ P
premise	2.	P → N
acp	⌐ 3.	~J
1,3 ds		4.	P

Notice line 4. It is set off by vertical lines; this indicates that line 4 is a line that depends upon the assumed premise. Each line added after an *undischarged* assumption depends upon all the undischarged assumed premises that are above it. One of these will be the nearest. But what is it to discharge an assumption?

premise	1.	J ∨ P
premise	2.	P → N
acp	⌐ 3.	~J
1,3 ds		4.	P
2,4 mp	⌊ 5.	N

The symbol "⌊" indicates that this subderivation is terminated. Once we have terminated an assumption, no one of lines 3 to 5 is accessible at any point later on. That is, none of them may be appealed to as justification for a subsequent line in the derivation. We could not, for example, do the following:

premise	1.	J ∨ P	
premise	2.	P → N	
acp	⌐ 3.	~J	
1,3 ds		4.	P	
2,4 mp	⌊ 5.	N	
3,4 conj	6.	P & ~J	**erroneous**

In writing line 6 without the double lines, we are claiming that it follows from our premises. But **P & ~J** does not follow from our premises: **~J** is our assumed premise, our assumption, and **P** was derived by the use of that assumption. Let us cover the same ground in natural language: recall that in English our premises were:

Either Jones will do it or Patel will do it.
If Patel does it then there will be no problems.

It does not follow from these premises that Patel will do it and there will be no problems.

What we did conclude was that if Jones does not do it, then there will be no problems. A derivation cannot end at the point at which the assumption is terminated. We must add a line to the derivation that indicates what we are concluding from the subderivation. In the case of conditional proof, it is easy to determine what the line to be added is: it must be a conditional sentence that has our assumed premise as its antecedent and the sentence that terminated the subderivation as its consequent. The only kind of sentence that can be established by conditional proof is a conditional sentence. At this point, the nearest assumption will be said to be discharged. We exhibit this in the particular case under consideration as follows:

premise	1.	$J \vee P$
premise	2.	$P \to N$
acp	3.	$\sim J$
1,3 ds	4.	P
2,4 mp	5.	N
3-5 cp	6.	$\sim J \to N$ **(Assumption now discharged)**

We utilize the dash in the justification for line 6 to indicate that we are appealing to the entire subderivation. In that subderivation we showed that where $\sim J$ was supposed true, it followed that N was true. So we concluded at line 6 that $\sim J \to N$, just as we did in the English version.

The pattern of a conditional proof is, then, as follows:

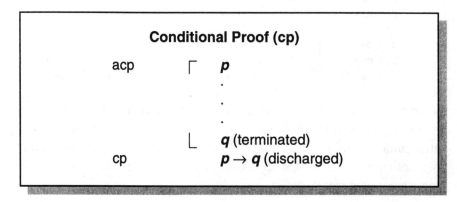

Conditional Proof (cp)

acp	⌐	*p*
		.
		.
		.
	L	*q* (terminated)
cp		$p \to q$ (discharged)

(In actual cases we will have line numbers as well. The acp must be the nearest undischarged assumption above the cp.)

You will be given some exercises in which you will be asked to provide the justification. It is relatively easy to fill in justifications; it is a bit more difficult to construct derivations for yourself. We shall consider two more examples. You might then go and try some problems on your own.

Suppose we wished to show that $P \rightarrow ((R \vee S) \vee Q)$ was derivable from $P \rightarrow Q$. Since the sentence that we wish to derive is a conditional sentence, we might contemplate a conditional proof. So, our initial set-up would look like this:

premise	1.	$P \rightarrow Q$
acp	2.	P

We know where we want to go, so let us get there:

premise	1.	$P \rightarrow Q$
acp	2.	P
1,2 mp	3.	Q
3 add	4.	$Q \vee (R \vee S)$
4 comm	5.	$(R \vee S) \vee Q$
2-5 cp	6.	$P \rightarrow ((R \vee S) \vee Q)$

Notice that for line 6 to be a legitimate application of cp, line 2 had to be the antecedent of the conditional found on line 6, and line 5 had to be the consequent of that conditional.

Suppose now that we wished to derive $(A \,\&\, B) \rightarrow C$ from $A \rightarrow C$. Again, our procedure is relatively straightforward: we wish to derive a conditional, so it is natural to use cp. We start as follows:

premise	1.	$A \rightarrow C$
acp	2.	$A \,\&\, B$

We move onward in a very natural way:

premise	1.	$A \rightarrow C$
acp	2.	$A \,\&\, B$
2 simp	3.	A
1,3 mp	4.	C
2-4 cp	5.	$(A \,\&\, B) \rightarrow C$

2.2 / Indirect Proof

The second mode of proof is one we shall call *indirect proof* (ip). (In some texts it is called a *reductio ad absurdum*, a reduction to absurdity. But we shall avoid introducing any more Latin.) The idea here is quite simple. If we can show that an assumed premise (aip) leads to a contradiction, we can legitimately infer that it is false. We insert the "i" in "aip" in order to indicate that our intent is to use an indirect proof.

The initial set-up remains the same: we list at the outset whatever premises we have at hand. Let us consider a particular argument in which our premises are:

premise	**1.**	$A \rightarrow B$
premise	**2.**	$A \rightarrow \sim B$

The conclusion that we wish to obtain from this is $\sim A$. How shall we attempt to derive this conclusion? Well, suppose that **A** is true. Then **B** is true and ~**B** is true. But that is a contradiction, so **A** must be false. That is, ~**A** is true. We shall reconstruct this argument in our system in the following fashion:

premise		**1.**	$A \rightarrow B$
premise		**2.**	$A \rightarrow \sim B$
aip	$\ulcorner$	**3.**	A

We should stop for a second and account for line 3. First, the justification aip indicates that our line is an assumption, and one we have made for the sake of using an indirect proof. As before, the symbol "$\ulcorner$" indicates that we have made an assumption, that we are beginning what we shall still call a *subderivation*. The lines will continue until the assumed premise has been, as we say, terminated.

premise		**1.**	$A \rightarrow B$
premise		**2.**	$A \rightarrow \sim B$
aip	$\ulcorner$	**3.**	A
1,3 mp	$\vert$	**4.**	B

Notice line 4. It is set off by vertical lines, which indicates that line 4 is a line that depends upon any assumed premises, just as in the case of conditional proof. Each line added after any undischarged assumed premises depends upon those premises. And one assumed premise (there is only one in this case) is the nearest one. Let us continue, as we have not yet explained the difference between an ip and a cp.

premise	1.	A → B
premise	2.	A → ~B
aip	3.	A
1,3 mp	4.	B
2,3 mp	5.	~B
4,5 conj	6.	B & ~B

The symbol "⌊" indicates that this subderivation is terminated. The nearest undischarged assumption above it is then said to be terminated. As before, once we have terminated an assumption no one of lines 3 to 6 is accessible at any point later on: none of them may be appealed to as justification for a subsequent line in the derivation. We could not, for example, do the following:

premise	1.	A → B	
premise	2.	A → ~B	
aip	3.	A	
1,3 mp	4.	B	
2,3 mp	5.	~B	
4,5 conj	6.	B & ~B	
3-6 ip	7.	~A	
4,7 conj	8.	~A & B	**erroneous**

In writing line 8 without the double lines, we are claiming that it follows from our premises. ~A & B does not follow from our premises: ~A was correctly derived, but B was derived by the use of an assumption. The subderivation is terminated and lines 3-6 are no longer accessible.

What we have shown is that if our premises are true then A is false, that is, ~A is true. We showed that by showing that the supposition that A was true (line 3) led us to a contradiction. This is what the method of indirect proof does. So what we can do is the following:

premise	1.	A → B
premise	2.	A → ~B
aip	3.	A
1,3 mp	4.	B
2,3 mp	5.	~B
4,5 conj	6.	B & ~B
3-6 ip	7.	~A

Here we note in line 7 that our subderivation, which occupies lines 3 to 6, has shown that ~A does follow from our premises. At this point our assumption is said to be discharged.

Here is another example of an ip:

premise	1.	~A → A
aip	2.	~A
1,2 mp	3.	A
2,3 conj	4.	A & ~A
2-4 ip	5.	A

This illustrates that you may utilize your aip, as we did at line 4, to obtain a contradiction.

There are two patterns for indirect proofs:

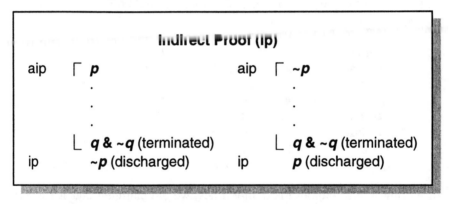

Indirect Proof (ip)

aip	⌐ **p**		aip	⌐ **~p**	
	.			.	
	.			.	
	.			.	
	⌊ **q & ~q** (terminated)			⌊ **q & ~q** (terminated)	
ip	**~p** (discharged)		ip	**p** (discharged)	

Here is a further example of the first pattern:

premise	1.	A ∨ B
aip	2.	~A & ~B
2 simp	3.	~A
1,3 ds	4.	B
2 simp	5.	~B
4,5 conj	6.	B & ~B
2-6 ip	7.	~(~A & ~B)

Notice that it does not matter which contradiction we get. For example, we could have constructed the previous proof in the following way:

premise	1.	A ∨ B
aip	2.	~A & ~B
2 simp	3.	~B
3,1 ds	4.	A
2 simp	5.	~A
4,5 conj	6.	A & ~A
2-6 ip	7.	~(~A & ~B)

Here is yet another example of the first pattern:

premise	1.	A → B
aip	2.	A & ~B
2 simp	3.	A
2 simp	4.	~B
1,3 mp	5.	B
4,5 conj	6.	B & ~B
2-6 ip	7.	~(A & ~B)

Here, finally, is an example of the second pattern:

premise	1.	~A → B
premise	2.	B → A
aip	3.	~A
1,3 mp	4.	B
2,4 mp	5.	A
3,5 conj	6.	A & ~A
3-6 ip	7.	A

Note that if the sentence we wish to derive is a negation ~*p*, the assumption we start off with for an indirect proof will be *p*. If we wish to use indirect proof to derive some sentence *p* that is not a negation, our assumption for an indirect proof will be ~*p*.

2.3 / Strategies, Tips and Tricks

Strategies are based upon the fact that we typically have a goal, namely, the conclusion we wish to reach. They take advantage of the fact that our conclusion will usually be a sentence of a certain sort. As we noted in our discussion of conditional proof, it is often expedient to try to get a conditional sentence by means of a conditional proof. Sometimes our use of a strategy will lead us to add lines to a derivation that could have been avoided, but so long as the extra lines are introduced in accord with our rules, the flaw is an aesthetic one: it does not matter. More advice on strategies will be given to you by your instructor; we list only a few points below, a few tips on what you might try if you cannot otherwise figure out a way to reach the desired conclusion. Following one of these tips never hurts. You may not, of course, reach the conclusion, but if you could not figure out how to do so before, you are now none the worse off. And if you reach the conclusion it does not particularly matter, as we noted above, if you have not constructed as short a derivation as you might otherwise have done. Of course, if you utilize a tip and then suddenly see how to reach your conclusion without following the tip, go ahead and reach the conclusion.

Tip 1: Apply any limited basic rules before applying unlimited rules or using either a cp or an ip.

We have not hitherto spoken of limited or unlimited rules, but if we think a bit the intent of this terminology should be clear. Consider, in particular, addition and double negation. We could go:

> **A**
> **A** $\vee$ **B**
> **A** $\vee$ **C**
> **A** $\vee$ **D**

and so on. Or we could go:

> **A**
> **A** $\vee$ **B**
> **(A** $\vee$ **B)** $\vee$ **C**
> **((A** $\vee$ **B)** $\vee$ **C)** $\vee$ **D**

and so on. This is the sort of situation that we had in mind in speaking of certain rules as unlimited. In a similar vein, we could go:

> **A**
> **~~A**
> **~~~~A**

and so on. But in the cases we will typically consider, we will not need to do so. This is not, of course, to say that we will never use addition or double negation. It is only to say that we should not use them unless we have good reason to believe their use will take us toward our conclusion.

Rules like modus ponens and simplification are, by contrast, limited. If you are stuck but can apply one of the limited rules, it cannot hurt to apply it. You will have a new line or lines to work with, and the way to proceed might become evident to you once you look at the new lines. It may not, of course, but nothing has been lost.

> **Tip 2: If the sentence that you need is a disjunction, keep in mind that both addition and constructive dilemma are rules that introduce disjunctions. Scout around and see if there is any chance of reaching the line you want by means of one of them.**

> **Tip 3: If you have a premise that is a disjunction, see if there is a way of using a constructive dilemma to obtain what you need.**

> **Tip 4: If the sentence you want is a conditional, try setting up a conditional proof. Recall that to do this you add an acp that is the antecedent of the conditional you need. The line you work toward in order to discharge the cp is the consequent of the conditional you want.**

> **Tip 5: If nothing else seems to be working, try setting up an indirect proof. If the sentence you want is some sentence *p* that is not a negation, your aip will be ~*p*; if the sentence you want is some negation ~*q*, your aip will be *q*.**

We wanted our logical system to be complete, that is, to enable us to show any truth-functionally valid argument to be truth-functionally valid. The system you have now is in fact complete, but we are not, at this level, in a position to prove that. We wanted the system to be formal; hence we utilized rules. And we wanted the system to be manageable in the sense of having a reasonably small set of rules. Occasionally, we will find that our limited set of rules does not enable us to make in one step some reasonably obvious move. This is one of the reasons that we shall provide an account of some tricks, some ways in which you can easily get to a certain line.

Trick 1: Getting anything you want from a contradiction

If you have accessible lines, one of which is some sentence p and the other some sentence $\sim p$, there is an easy way to get to any line you want:

	p
	$\sim p$
Use add	$p \vee q$
Use ds	q

Notice that you could get to q by means of an ip as well, but this trick is a bit easier. Remember this trick, as it is one that will frequently prove helpful.

Trick 2: Repeating a line

Some systems have a rule, often called "repetition", that enables us to repeat any accessible line. Such a rule might come in handy in the case where we have q as a line and wish to get to $p \rightarrow q$. Look at the following:

	q
acp	p

If we could get the q below the p we could get the conditional that we desire to get $(p \rightarrow q)$ by means of a cp. That is what a rule of repetition would enable us to do. But we do in fact have two ways of doing what repetition enables us to do. Here is one:

	q
acp	p
add	$q \vee q$
idem	q

We can then get what we want by a cp. The second way takes advantage of a point that we have not yet mentioned. Suppose we have p at some accessible line the number of which is n:

n	p

Our rule conjunction allows us to do the following:

n	p
n,n **conj**	$p \ \& \ p$

Once we have this we can, of course, go on to repeat p by simplification.

2.4 / Multiple Subderivations

Hitherto we have considered cases involving only one subderivation, even though our rules were stated so as to allow us to have as many subderivations as we need. And there are cases in which we will use more than one. There are two such types of situation. The trickier case is where there is more than one subderivation and they are embedded. We shall illustrate this after looking at the simpler case where they are not embedded.

Suppose we wish to derive **B & ~C** from the following premises:

premise	1.	$(\sim B \vee C) \to A$
premise	2.	$A \to \sim A$

Since the sentence we want is a conjunction, we might contemplate deriving it by means of the rule conj. Of course, this requires that we have **B** as a line and **~C** as a line. So let us try to get **B**. We will utilize an ip.

premise	1.	$(\sim B \vee C) \to A$
premise	2.	$A \to \sim A$
aip	3.	$\sim B$
3 add	4.	$\sim B \vee C$
1,4 mp	5.	A
2,5 mp	6.	$\sim A$
5,6 conj	7.	$A \;\&\; \sim A$
3-7 ip	8.	B

Notice that the assumption has been discharged and that lines 3 to 7 are inaccessible. We do have **B**, so let us now try to get **~C**.

premise	1.	$(\sim B \vee C) \to A$
premise	2.	$A \to \sim A$
aip	3.	$\sim B$
3 add	4.	$\sim B \vee C$
1,4 mp	5.	A
2,5 mp	6.	$\sim A$
5,6 conj	7.	$A \;\&\; \sim A$
3-7 ip	8.	B
aip	9.	C
9 add	10.	$C \vee \sim B$
10 comm	11.	$\sim B \vee C$
1,11 mp	12.	A
2,12 mp	13.	$\sim A$
12,13 conj	14.	$A \;\&\; \sim A$
9-14 ip	15.	$\sim C$

Lines 9 to 14, as well as lines 3 to 7, are now inaccessible. But we can enter our conclusion as line 16. It would come from 8 and 15, lines that are accessible, by conj.

premise	**1.**	**(~B ∨ C) → A**
premise	**2.**	**A → ~A**
aip	**3.**	**~B**
3 add	**4.**	**~B ∨ C**
1,4 mp	**5.**	**A**
2,5 mp	**6.**	**~A**
5,6 conj	**7.**	**A & ~A**
3-7 ip	**8.**	**B**
aip	**9.**	**C**
9 add	**10.**	**C ∨ ~B**
10 comm	**11.**	**~B ∨ C**
1,11 mp	**12.**	**A**
2,12 mp	**13.**	**~A**
12,13 conj	**14.**	**A & ~A**
9-14 ip	**15.**	**~C**
8,15 conj	**16.**	**B & ~C**

While this is not an easy derivation, it is a case where we might use our modes of proof more than once.

Let us now consider a case of embedding. Suppose we are given **C** as a premise and are asked to derive **A → (B → C)**. The sentence we are to derive is a conditional, so let us attempt to get it by means of a conditional proof:

premise	**1.**	**C**
acp	**2.**	**A**

Now we wish to get to **B → C**. However, this sentence is itself a conditional, so let us try to get to it by means of a conditional proof:

premise	**1.**	**C**
acp	**2.**	**A**
acp	**3.**	**B**

Now we wish to have **C** below the **B**. We will mobilize one of our tricks.

premise	1.	C
acp	2.	A
acp	3.	B
1 add	4.	C ∨ C
4 idem	5.	C

We are now in a position to utilize a conditional proof:

premise	1.	C
acp	2.	A
acp	3.	B
1 add	4.	C ∨ C
4 idem	5.	C
3-5 cp	6.	B → C

At line 5 the subderivation that began at 3 is terminated. Hence, at this point lines 3 to 5 have become inaccessible; they may not be cited at any subsequent point. In line 6 we have discharged the assumption made at line 3. The "⌊" beside line 6 indicates that it still depends on the assumption we made at line 2, but it indicates as well that we are terminating the subderivation that began at line 2.

premise	1.	C
acp	2.	A
acp	3.	B
1 add	4.	C ∨ C
4 idem	5.	C
3-5 cp	6.	B → C
2-6 cp	7.	A → (B → C)

At line 7 we have discharged the assumption made at line 2. As we have no undischarged assumptions, and have obtained the conclusion we wanted, our derivation is now complete.

Let us go back and illustrate a mistake that you should avoid.

premise	1.	C
acp	2.	A
acp	3.	B
1 add	4.	C ∨ C
4 idem	5.	C
3-5 cp	6.	B → C

Recall that this was a stage in our derivation. Suppose that we had done the following instead:

premise	1.	C
acp	2.	A
acp	3.	B
1 add	4.	C ∨ C
4 idem	5.	C
2-5 cp	6.	A → C	**erroneous**

Line 2 is not the nearest undischarged assumption.

Let us look at another example. Here are our premises:

premise	1.	~(A & B) → (C & D)
premise	2.	~A ∨ ~B

The conclusion we wish to reach is **R → C**. Since this is a conditional, let us try to get it via a conditional proof:

premise	1.	~(A & B) → (C & D)
premise	2.	~A ∨ ~B
acp	3.	R

We know that we need **C**. Note that if we were in a position to use modus ponens on 1 we could get to the **C** we so deeply desire. To use modus ponens, we would need ~(A & B). So let us try to get that.

premise	1.	~(A & B) → (C & D)
premise	2.	~A ∨ ~B
acp	3.	R
aip	4.	A & B
4 simp	5.	A
4 simp	6.	B
2,5 ds	7.	~B
6,7 conj	8.	B & ~B
4-8 ip	9.	~(A & B)

Completing the derivation is now a relatively straightforward task.

premise	1.	~(A & B) → (C & D)
premise	2.	~A ∨ ~B
acp	3.	R
aip	4.	A & B
4 simp	5.	A
4 simp	6.	B
2,5 ds	7.	~B
6,7 conj	8.	B & ~B
4-8 ip	9.	~(A & B)
1,9 mp	10.	(C & D)
10 simp	11.	C
3-11 cp	12.	R → C

2.5 / Using Logical Equivalents

To this point we have used only rules that we applied to whole lines. How-ever, if an argument is valid it remains valid even if a given sentence is re-placed by some sentence that is logically equivalent to it. We can explain this by recalling that an argument is valid if and only if there is no possibil-ity that all the premises are true while the conclusion is false, and that logi-cally equivalent sentences come out true or false under precisely the same conditions. So a valid argument will remain valid if we replace any given sentence by its logical equivalent.

We know, though we have not proved it, that our system is a complete one. Hence we know, even though we may not be able to find a derivation, that if an argument is truth-functionally valid there is a way of deriving its conclusion. Given this, we will now allow the use of certain rules that per-mit us to replace certain sentences, whether they are whole lines or parts of lines, by logically equivalent sentences. We need never use the equivalence rules; our system is complete without them. But having them around will often make the construction of derivations much easier.

Some of the handiest of logical equivalences are those that allow you to alter the form of negations, moving the negation sign in and out of parenthe-ses. These are called the *DeMorgan laws*. They may be stated as follows:

DeMorgan Laws (dem)

~(*p* & *q*) is logically equivalent to ~*p* ∨ ~*q*

~(*p* ∨ *q*) is logically equivalent to ~*p* & ~*q*

You may apply the DeMorgan laws to whole lines, but you may also apply them to parts of lines as follows:

premise	1.	~(A & B) → S
1 dem	2.	(~A ∨ ~B) → S

or as follows:

premise	1.	~(A ∨ B) ∨ C
1 dem	2.	(~A & ~B) ∨ C

Suppose we wish to show that ~(D ∨ C) can be derived from:

premise	1.	R → (~D & ~C)
premise	2.	R

We may proceed in this way:

premise	1.	R → (~D & ~C)
premise	2.	R
1 dem	3.	R → ~(D ∨ C)
2,3 mp	4.	~(D ∨ C)

or we may proceed in this way:

premise	1.	R → (~D & ~C)
premise	2.	R
1,2 mp	3.	~D & ~C
3 dem	4.	~(D ∨ C)

Both derivations are correct. There is little to choose between them.

We have a number of other logical equivalences available. Here is one that is familiar: we will now treat an extended commutation as an equivalence rule.

Commutation (comm)

p ∨ *q* is logically equivalent to *q* ∨ *p*

p & *q* is logically equivalent to *q* & *p*

But here are some quite new logical equivalences:

Association (assn)

$p \lor (q \lor r)$ is logically equivalent to $(p \lor q) \lor r$
$p \;\&\; (q \;\&\; r)$ is logically equivalent to $(p \;\&\; q) \;\&\; r$

These are quite obvious, but they will on occasion be useful for shortening derivations. Here is one small sample:

premise	1.	$(A \;\&\; (B \;\&\; C)) \to D$
premise	2.	$(A \;\&\; B) \;\&\; C$
2 assn	3.	$A \;\&\; (B \;\&\; C)$
1,3 mp	4.	D

Next we will introduce:

Distribution (dist)

$p \;\&\; (q \lor r)$ is logically equivalent to $(p \;\&\; q) \lor (p \;\&\; r)$
$p \lor (q \;\&\; r)$ is logically equivalent to $(p \lor q) \;\&\; (p \lor r)$

Here again is a small sample:

premise	1.	$A \lor (B \;\&\; C)$
premise	2.	$(A \lor B) \to D$
1 dist	3.	$(A \lor B) \;\&\; (A \lor C)$
3 simp	4.	$A \lor B$
2,4 mp	5.	D

There are two other familiar rules that we will now allow to be used as equivalence rules:

Double Negation (dn)

p is logically equivalent to $\sim\sim p$

---

and, in two forms:

Idempotence (idem)

p is logically equivalent to *p* ∨ *p*
p is logically equivalent to *p* & *p*

Recall that we are perfectly free to apply these equivalences to parts of lines. Here is a acceptable argument:

premise	1.	(A ∨ A) → B
1 idem	2.	A → B

Here are more new equivalences that will ease our work with conditionals.

Contraposition (contra)

p → *q* is logically equivalent to ~*q* → ~*p*

Conditional (co)

p → *q* is logically equivalent to ~*p* ∨ *q*

Exportation (exp)

(*p* & *q*) → *r* is logically equivalent to *p* → (*q* → *r*)

Let us look at some short samples of the application of these rules:

premise	1.	A → B
premise	2.	(~~B ∨ ~A) → C
2 co	3.	(~B → ~A) → C
1 contra	4.	~B → ~A
3,4 mp	5.	C

Make sure you see why line 3 involves a genuine application of co. Here is one more example:

premise	1.	A → (B → C)
premise	2.	C → D
1 exp	3.	(A & B) → C
2,3 hs	4.	(A & B) →D

Our final logical equivalences involve biconditionals.

Biconditional (bc)

$p \leftrightarrow q$ is logically equivalent to $(p \rightarrow q)$ & $(q \rightarrow p)$

$p \leftrightarrow q$ is logically equivalent to $(p \& q) \lor (\sim p \& \sim q)$

Here is an example of the use of this:

premise	1.	A ↔ B
premise	2.	(A & B) → Q
premise	3.	(~A & ~B) → Q
1 bc	4.	(A & B) ∨ (~A & ~B)
2,3,4 cd	5.	Q ∨ Q
6 idem	6.	Q

2.6 / Proving Theorems

It may seem strange, but we can construct derivations in which we have no premises. We do this by starting our derivation with an assumption — either for a conditional proof or for an indirect proof. If we discharge any assumptions we have made, we will end up with a genuine derivation, but with one in which our conclusion is not dependent on any premises, or, to be more formal, we will have a derivation from the null or empty set of premises. Do not worry about this terminology; it merely says that we have an argument in which we have employed no premises. The conclusion of such an argument, the sentence that we derive, will be spoken of as a *theorem* of our system. In general, theorems are sentences derivable from the null set of premises.

Although a proof of it would be more difficult than we are now in a position to manage, the following statement is true:

A sentence of our language is a theorem of our language if and only if it is a tautology.

So we now have, at least in principle, a means of establishing in our deductive system that a sentence is a tautology. If the sentence in which we are interested is a conditional, we initially set up a conditional proof. We shall speak in more detail of biconditionals below. But if a sentence is neither a conditional nor a biconditional, then we would attempt the appropriate indirect proof.

Recall that in Chapter 6 we noted that sentences *p* and *q* are logically equivalent if and only if the sentence *p* ↔ *q* is a tautology. So we can, in our system, establish that *p* and *q* are logically equivalent by showing that the sentence *p* ↔ *q* is a theorem. For, as mentioned above, all theorems are tautologies. There is a quite general pattern for derivations in which we wish to establish that *p* ↔ *q* is a theorem: if we have *p* → *q* and *q* → *p* we can form their conjunction and then introduce a biconditional by the rule bc. So what we shall do is to set up two subderivations both of which are conditional proofs:

acp	[	*p*
		q
cp		*p* → *q*
acp	[	*q*
		p
cp		*q* → *p*
conj		(*p* → *q*) & (*q* → *p*)
bc		*p* ↔ *q*

Generally speaking, it is wisest to attempt to obtain a biconditional in this way rather than via an indirect proof. Here is another example of such a proof, where we wish to show that A ↔ ~~A is a tautology:

acp	[	1.	A
dn		2.	~~A
1-2 cp		3.	A → ~~A
acp	[	4.	~~A
dn		5.	A
4-5 cp		6.	~~A → A
3,6 conj		7.	(A → ~~A) & (~~A → A)
7 bc		8.	A ↔ ~~A

Notice that had we stopped at line 3, we would have successfully shown that A → ~~A was a theorem, and hence a tautology. Of course, things are not always this easy. Here is a rather more difficult proof in which we establish that (A → B) ↔ ~(A & ~B) is a theorem:

acp	1.	A → B
aip	2.	A & ~B
2 simp	3.	A
2 simp	4.	~B
1,3 mp	5.	B
4,5 conj	6.	B & ~B
2-6 ip	7.	~(A & ~B)
1-7 cp	8.	(A → B) → ~(A & ~B)
acp	9.	~(A & ~B)
acp	10.	A
aip	11.	~B
10,11 conj	12.	A & ~B
9,12 conj	13.	(A & ~B) & ~(A & ~B)
11-13 ip	14.	B
10-14 cp	15.	A → B
9-15 cp	16.	~(A & ~B) → (A → B)
8,16 conj	17.	((A → B)→~ (A & ~B)) & (~(A & ~B) → (A → B))
17 bc	18.	(A → B) ↔ ~(A & ~B)

This derivation, though long, does not introduce any new principles.

Chapter Summary

In this chapter we introduced a derivation system for sentential logic. In Section 1 we introduced the basic rules for this system.

In 1.1 we introduced *modus ponens* and *modus tollens*.

Modus Ponens (mp)

From:

p → *q* and *p*

To:

q

Modus Tollens (mt)

From:

p → *q* and ~*q*

To:

~*p*

These two rules concerned conditional sentences.

In 1.2 we introduced two rules concerning conjunctions.

Simplification (simp)

From:

p & q

To:

p

From:

p & q

To:

q

Conjunction (conj)

From:

p and *q*

To:

p & q

In 1.3 we turned to some rules concerned with disjunctions.

Disjunctive Syllogism (ds)

From:

p ∨ *q* and ~*p*

To:

q

From:

~*p* ∨ *q* and *p*

To:

q

From:

p ∨ *q* and ~*q*

To:

p

From:

p ∨ ~*q* and *q*

To:

p

Addition (add)

From:

p

To:

p ∨ *q*

From:

p

To:

q ∨ *p*

In 1.4 we turned to:

Hypothetical Syllogism (hs)

From:

$p \rightarrow q$ and $q \rightarrow r$

To:

$p \rightarrow r$

Constructive Dilemma (cd)

From:	From:
$p \rightarrow r$, $q \rightarrow s$, and $p \vee q$	$(p \rightarrow r)$ & $(q \rightarrow s)$ and $p \vee q$
To:	To:
$r \vee s$	$r \vee s$

We then introduced, in 1.5, a rule that enables us to work with biconditionals.

Biconditional (bc)

From:	From:
$p \leftrightarrow q$	$(p \rightarrow q)$ & $(q \rightarrow p)$
To:	To:
$(p \rightarrow q)$ & $(q \rightarrow p)$	$p \leftrightarrow q$

In 1.6 we introduced the final three basic rules:

Commutation (comm)

From:	From:
$p \vee q$	p & q
To:	To:
$q \vee p$	q & p

Idempotence (idem)

From:

$p \lor p$

To:

p

Double Negation (dn)

From:	From:
$\sim\sim p$	p
To:	To:
p	$\sim\sim p$

Our basic rules all introduced lines that followed from preceding lines. However, to complete our system we introduced, in Section 2, *modes of proof*. In 2.1 we introduced *conditional proof*.

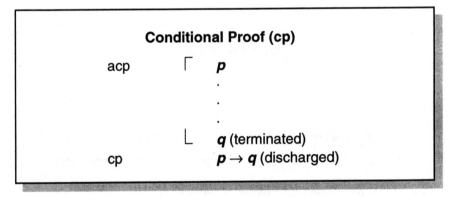

The symbol "$\ulcorner$" indicates that we have made an assumption, that we are beginning what we called a *subderivation*. The lines continue until the assumed premise has been *terminated*. The symbol "$\llcorner$" indicates that this subderivation is terminated. Once we have terminated an assumption, no one of the lines that we have marked off is accessible for later use. These lines depend upon the assumption. The line characterized as discharged is accessible, for we have established that it must be true if what precedes the assumption is true. Notice that the discharged line must be a conditional that has the assumption as an antecedent and the line marked terminated as the consequent.

In 2.2 we introduced our other mode of proof, *indirect proof*.

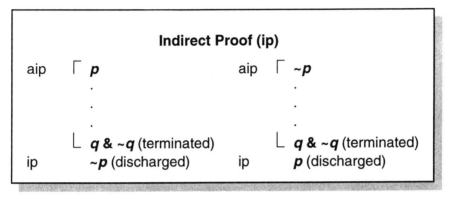

The core idea here is that if an assumption leads to a contradiction then it is not true, or rather is inconsistent with the premises of our argument.

In 2.3 we discussed some strategies, tips and tricks for doing derivations. In 2.4 we turned to proofs using multiple subderviations. Although these are often more complex, they do not introduce any new principles.

In 2.5 we introduced equivalences. These differ in that they may be applied to parts of lines as well as whole lines. They were not necessary for our system to be a complete one. Rather they sometimes make it easier to complete derivations.

Logical Equivalences

DeMorgan Laws (dem)
~(*p* & *q*) is logically equivalent to ~*p* ∨ ~*q*
~(*p* ∨ *q*) is logically equivalent to ~*p* & ~*q*

Commutation (comm)

p ∨ *q* is logically equivalent to *q* ∨ *p*
p & *q* is logically equivalent to *q* & *p*

Association (assn)

p ∨ (*q* ∨ *r*) is logically equivalent to (*p* ∨ *q*) ∨ *r*
p & (*q* & *r*) is logically equivalent to (*p* & *q*) & *r*

Distribution (dist)

p & (*q* ∨ *r*) is logically equivalent to (*p* & *q*) ∨ (*p* & *r*)
p ∨ (*q* & *r*) is logically equivalent to (*p* ∨ *q*) & (*p* ∨ *r*)

Double Negation (dn)

p is logically equivalent to ~~*p*

Idempotence (idem)

p is logically equivalent to *p* ∨ *p*
p is logically equivalent to *p* & *p*

Contraposition (contra)

p → *q* is logically equivalent to ~*q* → ~*p*

Conditional (co)

p → *q* is logically equivalent to ~*p* ∨ *q*

Exportation (exp)

(*p* & *q*) → *r* is logically equivalent to *p* → (*q* → *r*)

Biconditional (bc)

p ↔ *q* is logically equivalent to (*p* → *q*) & (*q* → *p*)
p ↔ *q* is logically equivalent to (*p* & *q*) ∨ (~*p* & ~*q*)

In 2.6 we showed how we can establish theorems. We do so by starting with an assumption. We do not have any premises.

CHAPTER 8

Categorical Logic

We shall now turn to another area of deductive logic, one concerned with a class of arguments involving what we shall call categorical statements. Our intent will be twofold: first, to learn to recognize these statements, and second, to learn how to assess certain arguments involving them.

1 / Categorical Statements

1.1 / The Standard Forms

It is easy enough to specify the kinds of statements with which we are concerned. You will recall that we earlier introduced the notion of a universal generalization, one example of which was:

All *F* are *G*.

This is our first kind of *categorical statement*. We shall speak of it as an *affirmative universal generalization* or, for short, an "A" statement. Another example of a universal generalization was:

No *F* are *G*.

We shall speak of this, for the obvious reason, as a *negative universal generalization* or, for short, an "E" statement. We will also consider two additional kinds of statements, which we will speak of as *particular generalizations*. The first of these has as its standard form:

Some *F* are *G*.

We will call this an *affirmative particular generalization*, or an "I" statement for short. The next, and last, of our basic kinds is:

Some *F* are not *G*.

We will call this one a *negative particular generalization*, or "O" statement. In summary, then, we have as our standard forms:

Standard Forms		
A Statement	All **F** are **G.**	Affirmative Universal Generalization
E Statement	No **F** are **G.**	Negative Universal Generalization
I Statement	Some **F** are **G.**	Affirmative Particular Generalization
O Statement	Some **F** are not **G.**	Negative Particular Generalization

Our choice of labels here is one entrenched in tradition. In medieval times there were few books (and no printed books at all—such books as existed were produced by hand). So, the story goes, labels were chosen that would make distinctions easy to remember. In Latin "affirmo" means "I affirm". The first two vowels in it were used for the two affirmative forms. "Nego" means "I deny", and the two vowels in it were used for the two negative forms.

In many cases it is quite easy to recognize such statements and to put them into one of our standard forms. But there are a number of cases that might be puzzling. We shall consider both some non-puzzling and some puzzling cases:

(1) If it's a whale, it's a mammal.

Notice that while this is not explicitly formulated as a categorical statement, it could be paraphrased by:

(1′) All whales are mammals.

Now consider:

(2) If it's a dog, it does not have gills.

Again the statement is not explicitly formulated as a categorical statement but can be paraphrased by:

(2′) No dogs have gills. (No dogs are things that have gills.)

Let us consider next claims like:

(3) Whales are mammals.
(4) Calgarians have telephones.

Statement (3) seems clearly to amount to:

(3') All whales are mammals.

As you can see, we have various ways of expressing what amounts to an A statement. But it is not plausible to construe statement (4) as a universal generalization. After all, we know that not everyone has a telephone. It is more plausible to take it as a statistical generalization—perhaps as the statement that many or most Calgarians have telephones. Statements using "many" or "most" are not our current concern, but such statements, minimally, contain a claim like the one for this example:

(4') Some Calgarians have telephones.

So we will, when appropriate for our purposes, represent them by the I statement (4'). We do not claim that (4') and (4) mean precisely the same thing; we claim only that (4') is at the very least part of the claim made by (4).

Statements involving "a" or "an" may have various interpretations. Consider, for example:

(5) A whale is a mammal. [said in a biology class]
(6) A car destroyed my car on the way to work.

The first statement is most plausibly construed as our familiar:

(5') All whales are mammals.

whereas the other is quite clearly:

(6') Some car destroyed my car on the way to work (is a car that destroyed mine on the way to work).

There is no problem here that cannot be resolved by the use of common sense. Ask yourself whether the claim is or is not meant to be one about all things of a certain sort. It would be ludicrous to view me as claiming, in the case of (6), that all cars destroyed my car on the way to work.

1.2 / Interpreting Standard Forms

Our next task will be to determine the interpretation we will place upon our categorical statements. There is no problem concerning either I or O statements. An I statement, some *F* are *G*, clearly comes out true if and only if at least one item in the universe is both *F* and *G*. And an O statement, some *F* is not *G*, clearly comes out true if and only if at least one item in the universe is *F* but not *G*. But there has been, historically, a bit of a controversy over A and E statements, sometimes spoken of as a controversy regarding "existential import". The issue can be put in terms of the following question. If one asserts that all *F* are *G*, is the claim that there are things that are *F* part of what one claims? Here is another question that asks much the same sort of thing: is the argument:

All *F* are *G*.
Therefore, some *F* are *G*.

a valid argument? Classically, the answer to this question was taken to be yes. However, we shall adopt instead the standard contemporary approach.

Our A statements **all *F* are *G*** will be counted as true if and only if there is no object in the universe that is *F* but not *G*. If it is true that all cows are brown, then it is not the case that there is a cow that is not brown. If it is false that all cows are brown, then there is at least one cow which is not brown. Notice that a universe devoid of any objects that are *F* is trivially a universe in which it is not the case that there is an object that is *F* but not *G*. Consider the claim that all unicorns are pink. If this is to be false, then there has to be a unicorn that is not pink. If there are no unicorns at all, then it is not the case that there is a unicorn that is not pink. It is then true that all unicorns are pink.

Our E statements **no *F* are *G*** will be counted as true just in case there is no object in the universe that is both *F* and *G*. If no cows are brown, then it is not the case that there is a brown cow. And, again quite trivially, if the universe is devoid of objects that are *F*, then there is no object in the universe that is both *F* and *G*. If there aren't any unicorns at all, then it is not the case that there is a pink unicorn. So it is also true that no unicorns are pink.

This may seen confusing in that we have taken both:

All unicorns are pink.

and

No unicorns are pink.

as true. But this arises only because there are no unicorns. The class or set of unicorns is empty. It will not arise with respect to any set or class of objects that is not empty. Since there are cows it is not the case that both:

All cows are brown.

and

No cows are brown.

are true.

Truth-Conditions

Any statement **All *F* are *G*** is true if and only if **it is not the case that there is an *F* that is not *G*.**

Any statement **No *F* are *G*** is true if and only **if it is not the case that there is an *F* that is *G*.**

Any statement **Some *F* is *G*** is true if and only if **there is an *F* that is *G*.**

Any statement **Some *F* is not *G*** is true if and only if **there is an *F* that is not *G*.**

Let us ask how our approach fits with English. Consider the statement:

All trespassers will be electrocuted. [I once saw this on a sign at a transformer station.]

It seems reasonably clear that one is not committed to the claim that anyone has actually trespassed. On the other hand, consider the statement:

All whales are mammals.

You might think that it does follow from this that some whales are mammals. But more likely you are simply appealing to your background knowledge.

You know independently that there are whales. (Look back at our account of the truth conditions for any statement that **all *F* are *G***. You should remember that on that account it does *not* follow that **some *F* are *G***.) However, there is not really anything to argue about here. Our categorical statements have the truth conditions that we have specified. If a particular claim in English, say:

All the people I met last night were jerks.

seems to require for its truth that there be someone whom I met last night, then you can capture your view with:

There are *F*'s and all *F* are *G*. (There are people whom I met last night and all of the people I met last night were jerks.)

where the **All *F* are *G*** is one of our categorical statements, but where we explicitly make the additional claim that there is an *F*. A similar point can be made about claims like "All unicorns are pink". We counted that as true. If you do not wish to do so, then you are most likely construing the claim as saying that there are unicorns, all of which are pink. Given this construction of the claim, it is indeed a false one. For the remainder of this chapter and in all of our exercises, we will not bother to disentangle the two possible readings; we will take the English universal generalizations that we encounter as categorical statements of our sort.

1.3 / Some Logical Relations

One way to determine whether we understand our categorical statements and what they mean is by seeing whether we are clear about the logical relations between them. Let us adopt the following vocabulary:

Some Logical Relations

A pair of statements *p* and *q* are said to be ***contradictories*** if and only if *q* must be false if *p* is true and *q* must be true if *p* is false.

A pair of statements *p* and *q* are said to be ***contraries*** if and only if *p* and *q* could not both be true, but both *p* and *q* could be false.

> A pair of statements *p* and *q* are said to be *logically equivalent* if and only if it must be the case that either *p* and *q* are both true or are both false.

Keeping these in mind, let us proceed to a survey of the relations among some statements, including our categorical statements.

Note that any A statement **all *F* are *G*** and O statement that **some *F* are not *G*** are contradictories. If it is true that all cows are brown, it is false that some cows are not brown. And if it is false that all cows are brown, it is true that some cows are not brown. As well, any E statement **no *F* are *G*** and I statement **some *F* are *G*** are contradictories. If it is true that no cows are pink, it is false that some cows are pink. And if it is false that no cows are pink, it is true that some cows are pink.

> ### Something to Note
>
> Where statements *p* and *q* are contradictories the statement *p* and the statement ~*q* are logically equivalent.

Thus, the statements **All *F* are *G*** and **It is not the case that some *F* is not *G*** are logically equivalent, as are the statements **It is not the case that all *F* are *G*** and **Some *F* is not *G*.** Similarly the statements **No *F* are *G*** and **It is not the case that some *F* is *G*** are logically equivalent, as are the statements **It is not the case that no *F* are *G*** and **Some *F* is *G*.**

None of our categorical statements are, as such, contraries. Let us make sure that we see why. That **all *F* are *G*** and that **no *F* are *G*** are not contraries can be seen as follows. If there are no objects of the kind *F*, then both of these statements would be true. There are, for instance, human beings, but there *could* be none. Hence, the statement that all humans are tall and the statement that no humans are tall *could* both be true; so they are not contraries. Clearly, both statements could also be false. Next, note that **Some *F* are *G*** and **Some *F* are not *G*** could both be true. For example, that some people are well fed and that some people are not well fed are both true. Given that both can be true, they are not contraries. And both could be false, since there might be no objects that are *F*: there might be no people.

The term on the left in any of our standard form statements (we have typically used *F*) is traditionally called the *subject*. The term on the right in any of our standard form statements (we have typically used *G*) is traditionally called the *predicate*. The operation of switching these in a standard form statement is called *conversion*. Here is a list of these.

Conversions (not all valid)		
A	All *F* are *G*.	All *G* are *F*.
E	No *F* are *G*.	No *G* are *F*.
I	Some *F* are *G*.	Some *G* are *F*.
O	Some *F* are not *G*.	Some *G* are not *F*.

Notice that in some cases conversion yields a logically equivalent statement, whereas in other cases it does not. Here are the ones that are:

Valid Conversions		
E	No *F* are *G*.	No *G* are *F*.
I	Some *F* are *G*.	Some *G* are *F*.

That no humans are reptiles and that no reptiles are human do in that sense make exactly the same claim. That some computers are things with CD-ROM drives and that some things with CD-ROM drives are computers also make exactly the same claim. The other two pairs are *not* generally logically equivalent. That all whales are mammals is true, but it is false that all mammals are whales. That some mammals are not cows is true, but it is false that some cows are not mammals.

We shall be utilizing these relations in the next section, but for now it will be useful to extend our notions of contradictories and contraries so as to apply to terms (our *F*s and *G*s):

Some Relations between Terms

A pair of terms **F** and **G** are:

contradictories if and only if for some particular object **a** the statement **a is an F** and the statement **a is a G** are contradictories.

contraries if and only if for some particular object **a** the statement **a is an F** and the statement **a is a G** are contraries.

logically equivalent if and only if for some particular object **a** the statement **a is an F** and the statement **a is a G** are logically equivalent.

Much care must be exercised in connection with negative terms in English. One problem is that a term may be negative in relation to another term by being a contradictory of it or by being a contrary of it. Consider the terms "happy" and "unhappy". I think you would agree that it would be a mistake to consider these contradictories. They are instead contraries. Taking these terms in general, one could not be both happy and unhappy, but one could fail to be either. "True" and "untrue", by contrast, seem to be contradictory terms. Again, we are in a situation where one has to exercise thought and common sense. But be very careful to note that the presence of either contrary or contradictory terms in a pair of categorical statements does not necessarily make the statements either contrary or contradictory. "Some people are happy" and "Some people are unhappy" are clearly not contrary statements, since both could be true. "All (no) people are happy" and "All (no) people are unhappy" could, given that we allow that there could be no people, both be true.

There do seem to be many terms in English that are contraries, for example, "tall"- "short" and "large"-"small". But considerable caution has to be exercised here. If a person witnessed a crime, most of us would tend to classify a person who was six feet three as a tall person. Such a person is above average height. But in other comparison classes, for example that of National Basketball Association players, he would be short, that is, a short player. He is below the average player height. A 12-ounce goldfish is a large goldfish, but a small fish for all that.

It will be useful for our purposes to have a means of generating contra-dictory terms:

Forming Standard Negative Terms

For any term **F**, the term **F** and the term **non-F** are contradictories.

The term **F** may be taken as picking out the class or set of objects that are **F**. Thus the term "human" may be taken to pick out the class of objects that are human. What the term does is pick out the class or set of objects that are not **F**. So the term "non-human" picks out the class of objects that are not human. This class is often called the *complement*. Note carefully that any statement such as the following:

Some roofing material is non-fireproof.

is an I statement. We are taking the "non" as part of the term. As noted we will call the contradictory term formed in this way a *standard negative term*. You may recall from our consideration of sentential logic that we had a logical equivalence that we called contraposition:

p → q is logically equivalent to ~q → ~p.

Do we have an analog here? Let us call the sentences obtained from a standard form statement by reversing the subject and the predicate while replacing each with its standard negative term its *contrapositive*.

Contrapositive (not all valid)

A	All **F** are **G**.	All non-**G** are non-**F**.
E	No **F** are **G**.	No non-**G** are non-**F**.
I	Some **F** are **G**.	Some non-**G** are non-**F**.
O	Some **F** are not **G**.	Some non-**G** are not non-**F**.

As some of these statements are rather confusing, let us inspect them in turn with an eye to determining which of the pairs are logically equivalent.

A: All *F* are *G*.   **(All non-*G* are non-*F*.)**

Here is one example:

All voters are citizens.   **All non-citizens are non-voters.**

You may be able to see that these are indeed logically equivalent. Or you may think back to our account of the truth conditions for A sentences. For it to be true that all voters are citizens it must be the case that:

(1)   There is not a voter who is not a citizen.

That is equivalent to noting that it must be the the the case that:

(2)   There is no object that is both a voter and a non-citizen.

For it to be true that all non-citizens are non-voters it must be the case that:

(1′)   There is not a non-citizen who is not a non-voter.

But something that is not a non-voter is a voter. So it must be the case that:

(2′)   There is not a non-citizen who is a voter.

Notice that by a conversion that we discussed above, (2) and (2′) are logically equivalent. And we took advantage of the fact that the class of objects that are not **non-*F*** just is the class of objects that are *F*.

What of the others? Next let us look at:

E: No *F* are *G*.   **(No non-*G* are non-*F*.)**

Here is one example:

No birds are mammals.   **No non-mammals are non-birds.**

These are clearly *not* logically equivalent. My current computer is a non-mammal. But it is a non-bird. So while it is true that no birds are mammals it is false that no non-mammals are non-birds. Next:

I: Some *F* are *G*.   **(Some non-*G* are non-*F*.)**

Here is an example:

Some birds are reptiles.   Some non-reptiles are non-birds.

These are also *not* logically equivalent. It is not true that some birds are reptiles. But some non-reptiles (me, for example) are non-birds. Finally let us consider:

O: Some *F* are not *G*.   (Some non-*G* are not non-*F*.)

Here is an example:

**Some dogs are not   Some non-females are not
female.   non-dogs.**

Notice that an item that is not a non-dog is a dog. And items that are not female are non-females. So these are logically equivalent. Thus we come up with:

Valid Contrapositions

A	All *F* are *G*.	All non-*G* are non-*F*.
O	Some *F* are not *G*.	Some non-*G* are not non-*F*

Next let us consider an operation traditionally known as *obversion*. A and I statements are often said to have the *quality* affirmative. E and O statements are then said to have the quality negative. A and E statements are often said to have the *quantity* universal. I and O statements are then said to have the quantity particular. To obvert what we do is change the quality without changing the quantity while replacing the predicate with its standard negative term. Here is the chart:

Valid Obversions

A	All *F* are *G*.	No *F* are non-*G*.
E	No *F* are *G*.	All *F* are non-*G*
I	Some *F* are *G*.	Some *F* are not non-*G*.
O	Some *F* are not *G*.	Some *F* are non-*G*.

Note that not to be a non-*G* is to be a *G*, and not to be a *G* is to be a non-*G* so the last two pairs are logically equivalent. So let us check the first two. The first is:

A: All *F* are *G*.   **(No *F* are non-*G*.)**

Here is one example:

All voters are citizens.   **No voters are non-citizens.**

You may be able to see that these are indeed logically equivalent. Or you may think back to our account of the truth conditions for A sentences. For it to be true that all voters are citizens it must be the case that:

(1) There is not a voter who is not a citizen.

That is equivalent to noting that it must be the the case that:

(2) There is no object that is both a voter and a non-citizen.

For it to be true that no voters are non-citizens it must be the case that:

(1′) There is not a voter who is a non-citizen.

So these are logically equivalent. The last case is:

E: No *F* are *G*.   **(All *F* are non-*G*.)**

Here is one example:

No chickens are mammals. All chickens are non-mammals.

You may be able to see that these are indeed logically equivalent. Or you may think back to our account of the truth conditions for E sentences. For it to be true that no chickens are mammals it must be the case that:

(1) There is not a chicken that is a mammal.

For it to be true that all chickens are non-mammals it must be the case that:

(1′) There is not a chicken that is not a non-mammal.

But, as we know, it must then be the case that

(2′) There is not a chicken that is a mammal.

So these are logically equivalent.

In Section 2 we will develop a means of checking certain arguments involving our standard forms for validity. Consequently we will need to study how to put various English statements into standard form. We will utilize our logical relations in order to do so. Here is a chart summarizing the logical equivalents that we have noted.

Standard Logical Equivalents		
All *F* are *G*.	It is not the case that some *F* are not *G*.	
No *F* are *G*.	It is not the case that some *F* are *G*.	
Some *F* are *G*.	It is not the case that no *F* are *G*.	
Some *F* are not *G*.	It is not the case that all *F* are *G*.	
Some *F* are *G*.	Some *G* are *F*.	Conversion
No *F* are *G*.	No *G* are *F*.	Conversion
All *F* are *G*.	All non-*G* are non-*F*.	Contraposition
Some *F* are not *G*.	Some non-*G* are not non-*F*.	Contraposition
All *F* are *G*.	No *F* are non-*G*.	Obversion
No *F* are *G*.	All *F* are non-*G*.	Obversion
Some *F* are *G*.	Some *F* are not non-*G*.	Obversion
Some *F* are not *G*.	Some *F* are non-*G*.	Obversion

1.4 / Putting Statements into a Standard Form

Many statements we make are already in a standard form:

Some of those invited will not come. [an O statement]

No new comedies are at all funny. [an E statement]
Some of the cop shows are realistic. [an I statement]
All of their friends are my friends. [an A statement]

But there are many statements that are not in standard form. What we shall do is develop means of putting many such statements into a standard form.

There are some statements that cause people problems but should not really do so. Consider the statement:

Only fast cars are fun to drive.

We have not used "only" in our standard forms. What we can do is to see if we can think of a paraphrase of this statement that is in standard form. We can paraphrase this statement by:

All (cars that are) fun to drive are fast cars.

In general, any statement:

Only *G* are *F*.

can be paraphrased as:

All *F* are *G*.

We might keep in mind the slogan that any statement **Only *F* are *G*** is an "all-statement" in reverse order. The mistake that is most frequently made is to construe an "only" statement such as:

Only citizens can vote.

as:

All citizens can vote.

This is clearly incorrect. In most countries it is true that only citizens can vote. However, it is false that all citizens can vote. Children, for example, are citizens but typically they cannot vote. This confirms our claim that:

Only citizens can vote.

is correctly construed as:

All who can vote are citizens.

Look next at:

None but citizens can vote.

This clearly means the same as:

Only citizens can vote.

and should be put into standard form in the same way.

Let us look next at negations such as

It is false that all (D)octors are (H)onest.
It is not true that no (P)erson we invited will (A)ttend.
It is not true that some of my (P)ets are (L)izards
It is false that some of the (D)ogs are not (F)riendly.

None of these, as they stand, are in standard form. However, note that each is the negation of a statement that is essentially in standard form. So we look back to our table of equivalences and come up with the following:

Some D are not H.
Some P are not A.
No P are L.
All D are F.

Some statements that involve negations are a bit problematic. Suppose someone says:

All the (G)uests aren't (D)runk.

This sentence would seem to be ambiguous. Perhaps the most likely interpretation of it is:

It is not the case that all the guests are drunk.

We have already seen how to put this into standard form. But it might be taken as in effect:

All G are not D.

But this is not one of our standard forms. We can, however, put it into standard form by using a standard negative term. We get:

All G are non-D.

This is an A sentence.

We just saw a case in which we introduced a standard negative term. But in many cases we may wish to eliminate negative terms. There are at least two reasons why we might so wish. It is often, though not invariably, true that sentences involving negative terms are rather difficult to understand, particularly when put in sentences that involve negations. Consider:

It is not the case that no (D)ogs are non-(V)icious.

With a statement like this we can choose to work first with the statement that is being negated. In this case it is:

No (D)ogs are non-(V)icious.

Looking back to our table of equivalences we see that this is equivalent to:

All (D)ogs are (V)icious.

So we have:

It is not the case that all (D)ogs are (V)icious.

which comes out as:

Some D are not V.

We could have reached the same result by working from the outside in. You recall that we started with:

It is not the case that no (D)ogs are non-(V)icious.

Notice that this is equivalent to:

Some D are non-V.

which is equivalent to

Some D are not V.

Another reason we might wish to eliminate some terms arises from the technique we will use to check arguments. It will allow a maximum of three terms. Consider the following argument:

> **No (W)hales are non-(M)ammals.**
> **All mammals are (C)reatures with lungs.**
> **So, all whales are creatures with lungs.**

As matters stand this argument contains four terms. But we can remedy that situation once we recall that we can eliminate the negative term from the first premise. So our argument can be restated as:

All W are M.
All M are C.
So, all W are C.

Although many statements that contain negative terms can, via the use of logical equivalents, be replaced by statements that do not contain negative terms, not all can. Consider, though, the statements:

All non-physical objects are mental objects.
No non-physical objects are non-mental objects.

These two statements are logically equivalent, but can you think of any logical equivalent of either that is both categorical and contains no negative terms? You should not be able to, since these statements are not logically equivalent to any categorical statement that contains no negative terms. And be very careful with terms like "unhappy". Consider the statement:

Some persons are unhappy.

We noted above that "unhappy" is a contrary, not a contradictory, of "happy". So it would be a mistake to take this as either:

Some persons are non-happy.

or

Some persons are not happy.

Let us close this section with a small amount of practice in putting English statements into standard form. Consider the statement:

Only citizens are non-voters.

Since this is a sentence involving "only", we know that it is logically equivalent to:

All non-voters are citizens.

This is, as we noted above, a sentence from which the negative term cannot be removed. Consider instead:

Only non-participants are safe.

This comes out as:

All who are safe are non-participants.

We could, if we wish, eliminate the negative term from this statement:

No safe person is a participant.

This, of course, is also equivalent to:

No participant is safe.

Consider now:

It's not the case that some non-citizens are not non-voters.

Working on the negated sentence first, we note that this is logically equivalent to:

It's not the case that some non-citizens are voters.

And this is logically equivalent to:

It's not the case that some voters are not citizens.

Finally, this is logically equivalent to:

All voters are citizens.

What we do is to utilize the handy equivalences that can be applied until we come up with one of our categorical statements.

2 / Venn Diagrams

We shall now introduce a system of diagramming to represent categorical statements. There are various other ways of diagramming that differ visually from the one we will use, but these different systems encode precisely the same information. Once we have seen how to enter the statements into the diagrams, we will see that they can be used to assess the validity of many arguments involving categorical statements.

2.1 / Basic Venn Diagrams

A categorical statement, recall, will contain two terms. Let us begin with an A statement:

All *F* are *G*.

First, we draw two overlapping circles, which we will label the *F* circle and the *G* circle, since those are the terms with which we are now concerned.

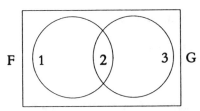

The *F* circle represents the area in which, so to speak, things that are *F* might live. The *G* circle is the area in which things that are *G* might live. Note that there are three distinct sub-areas. Area 1 is the area in which things that are *F* but are not *G* would live. The area of overlap, area 2, is the area in which only things that are both *F* and *G* would live. And area 3 is then the area in which things that are *G* but are not *F* would live. The absence of any entries in the diagram (any shading) indicates that we have no information. What we wish to do is to represent or encode the information contained in our statement. We will use dark shading to indicate that a given area is uninhabited, that is, has no objects in it. Now recall that our A statement in effect says that you will not find any *F* that are not *G*. This is the claim that the area of the *F* circle outside the overlap is uninhabited. So we represent the statement:

All *F* are *G*.

as follows:

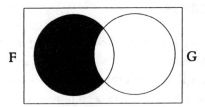

Next we wish to consider the statement:

No *F* are *G*.

This statement, as we have seen, denies that there is anything that is both **F** and **G**. So we represent it as follows:

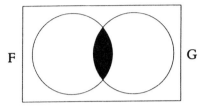

Since dark shading indicates that an area is uninhabited, by shading in area 2 (called the "lune") we indicate that there is nothing that is both F and G.

I and O statements, by contrast, indicate that an area is inhabited, that there is something in it. Consider the statement:

Some F are G.

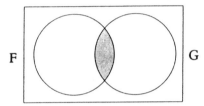

Here we have indicated that an area is inhabited by use of light shading.

Some F are not G.

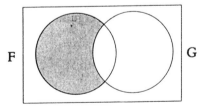

Here we have indicated that there is something inside the **F** circle but outside the **G** circle. Things outside the **G** circle are not **G**.

Once you get a statement into categorical form you should have no problem diagramming it. Diagramming is "mechanical"; it involves merely following the rules. But we can even at this point utilize our system to check certain elementary arguments. Recall that an argument is valid just in case it is impossible that all the premises are true while the conclusion is false. In our system this will be reflected in the following way:

Using Diagrams to Test for Validity

We check for validity by diagramming the premises of the argument. We then inspect this diagram in order to see whether the diagram for the conclusion has already appeared.

So what one does is simply diagram the premises and see whether or not the diagram for the conclusion is already there. If it is already there, then that means that the information contained in the conclusion is already contained in the premise(s). You do not add a diagram for the conclusion: you look and see whether it is already there. Here is a simple example:

No *F* are *G*.
Therefore, no *G* are *F*.

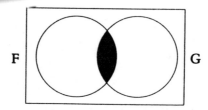

This is a diagram for the premise. But note that this diagram already contains (in fact, in this case just is) a diagram for the conclusion.

Here is an example of an invalid argument:

All *F* are *G*.
Therefore, all *G* are *F*.

Here is the diagram for the premise:

All *F* are *G*.

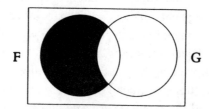

But a diagram for the conclusion would look like this:

All G are F.

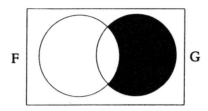

So the information contained in the conclusion is not contained in the premise. Consequently, the argument is not a valid one.

As one last example, consider the argument:

All birds are feathered.
Therefore, some birds are feathered.

You should remember from the discussion above that this is an invalid argument. It moves from a claim that says that an area is empty, devoid of any population, to a claim that an area is populated. Here is the diagram for the premise:

All birds are feathered.

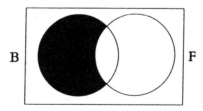

Note that it says that a certain area is empty, whereas the conclusion would be diagrammed as follows:

Some B are F.

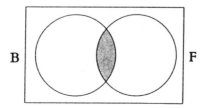

The conclusion does not contain the information contained in the premise. There is a general point to be made here.

Remember:

No argument that contains only premises that are A or E statements and a conclusion that is either an I or O statement is valid. A and E statements make claims that areas are empty; I and O statements make claims that areas are inhabited.

2.2 / More Complex Venn Diagrams

We wish now to consider cases where three terms — say *F*, *G*, and *H* — are involved. The situation is a bit more complex, but does not differ in principle from that discussed above. Our core diagram for three terms will look like the following:

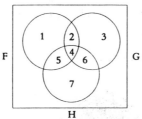

Note that each of the numbered areas is an area in which different kinds of objects might live. Area 2 is, for example, an area for objects that are *F* and *G* but are not *H*. Area 4 is for objects that are *F*, *G*, and *H*. Universal statements (A and E) are entered just as they were before, but a bit of care must be exercised with particular statements (I and O statements). Consider the following case:

Some F are G.

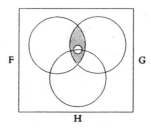

Notice that areas 2 and 4 are shaded, but that a small circle has been drawn. This small circle indicates that while there is at least one *F* that is *G*, we do not know whether it is in area 2 or area 4. In other words, we know that there is an *F* that is *G* but we do not know whether it is also *H*. To rephrase once more, we know that there is at least one object that is both *F* and *G*, but we do not know whether the object (or objects) that is both *F* and *G* is *H* or not *H*. There may be objects of both sorts. That is, there might be objects that are *F* and *G* and *H* and objects that are *F* and *G* and not *H*. That some *F* are *G* tells us that we are in one of these situations, but it does not tell us which one. I may know that some of the students in a class are male, but not know whether or not they are Christians. As noted, there may be male students who are Christians and male students who are not, but our statement does not tell us this. Here is a diagram for the claim that:

Some F are not G.

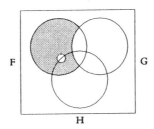

Here again we have light shading, but the circle drawn on the boundary indicates that while we have something that is an *F* and not a *G*, it may fall into either the area for things that are *F*, not *G*, and not *H* or the area for things that are *F*, not *G*, and *H*. Or, of course, there may be things in both of these areas. That some *F* are not *G* leaves open these three possibilities.

Let us now turn to the class of arguments with which we are concerned. The maximum number of terms we can accommodate with our Venn diagrams is three. We will most often be concerned with arguments with two premises. The premises and the conclusion will be categorical statements. One term will occur in both premises, and each of the other terms will occur in only one of the premises. Classically, the conclusion contained the terms that occurred only once in the premises. This restriction is not necessary, but we will typically be concerned only with arguments that meet this condition. These arguments are what we will call *syllogisms*.

We will use this system to check the validity of arguments. Even though we are now considering three terms and two premises, the points made above stand: a valid argument will be one in which the diagram of the premises will give us the diagram of the conclusion; and no argument that moves from premises asserting emptiness (A and E statements) to a conclusion asserting population (I and O statements) will be valid. We will give only a few examples here.

Let us consider the argument:

All F are G.
All G are H.
Therefore, all F are H.

Here is a diagram of the premises:

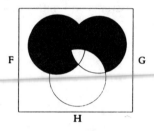

Note that the diagram for the conclusion has already appeared, so the argument is valid.

Now consider the following argument:

All F are G.
Some G are H.
Therefore, some F are H.

Here is a diagram of the premises:

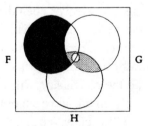

Note that the presence of the circle indicates that although something is in the area for *G* that are *H*, we do not know whether these are in the area for things that are *G* and *H* and *F*, or for things that are *G* and *H* and not *F*, or both. And here is a diagram of the conclusion:

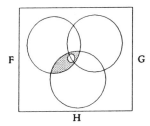

You might be tempted to say that the argument is valid; but it is not. This conclusion requires that there be something that is at least *F* and *H*. If you look back to the preceding diagram, you will note that it does not give us a guarantee that something is in the areas for things that are *F* and *H*. The argument is not valid because we do not have that guarantee. Consider, by contrast:

All *F* are *G*.
Some *F* are *H*.
Therefore, some *G* are *H*.

Let us enter the premises in order. This is a diagram only of the first premise:

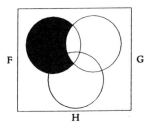

We now wish to enter the second premise. Notice that there is only one place for things that are both *F* and *H*. The area for *F* and *H* and non-*G* items is empty: we will not need one of our small circles. So we now enter the second premise.

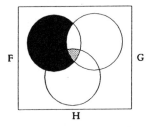

This argument is valid. The conclusion has already appeared, in that we can see that there is something in one of the areas for items that are both *F* and *G*. Now suppose we had done the diagram in a different order:

Some *F* are *H*.
All *F* are *G*.
Therefore, some *G* are *H*.

We shall begin by entering the first premise:

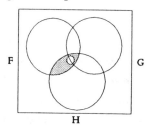

We now enter the second premise into the diagram:

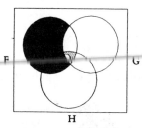

Again, the shading shows us that the area for *F*, *G*, and non-*H* items is empty. Once we entered the second premise, we discovered that it closed off the possibility that there was something that was *F* and *H* but not *G*. We reach precisely the same result, just via a slightly different route.

Chapter Summary

In this chapter we concerned ourselves with categorical logic. In Section 1 we considered *categorical statements*. In 1.1 we introduced:

	Standard Forms	
A Statement	All *F* are *G*.	Affirmative Universal Generalization
E Statement	No *F* are *G*.	Negative Universal Generalization
I Statement	Some *F* are *G*.	Affirmative Particular Generalization
O Statement	Some *F* are not *G*.	Negative Particular Generalization

We examined a number of statements to determine which, if any, of our standard forms they had.

In 1.2 we discussed the interpretation, in terms of truth-conditions, that we would place upon our statements.

Truth-Conditions

Any statement **All *F* are *G*** is true if and only if **it is not the case that there is an *F* that is not *G*.**

Any statement **No *F* are *G*** is true if and only **if it is not the case that there is an *F* that is *G*.**

Any statement **Some *F* is *G*** is true if and only if **there is an *F* that is *G*.**

Any statement **Some *F* is not *G*** is true if and only if **there is an *F* that is not *G*.**

This enabled us, in 1.3, to discuss a number of logical relations between our statements.

Some Logical Relations

A pair of statements *p* and *q* are said to be ***contradictories*** if and only if *q* must be false if *p* is true and *q* must be true if *p* is false.

A pair of statements *p* and *q* are said to be ***contraries*** if and only if *p* and *q* could not both be true, but both *p* and *q* could be false.

A pair of statements *p* and *q* are said to be *logically equivalent* if and only if it must be the case that either *p* and *q* are both true or are both false.

These concepts can be extended so as to apply to terms.

Some Relations between Terms

A pair of terms *F* and *G* are:

contradictories if and only if for some particular object *a* the statement *a* **is an** *F* and the statement *a* **is a** *G* are contradictories.

contraries if and only if for some particular object *a* the statement *a* **is an** *F* and the statement *a* **is a** *G* are contraries.

logically equivalent if and only if for some particular object *a* the statement *a* **is an** *F* and the statement *a* **is a** *G* are logically equivalent.

We decided that we needed *standard negative terms*.

Forming Standard Negative Terms

For any term *F*, the term *F* and the term ***non-F*** are contradictories.

We introduced certain classical notions, that of the *subject* — the term on the left in a standard form — and that of the *predicate* — the term on the right in a standard form. We noted that the operation of *conversion* involves switching the subject and the predicate. We then introduced the operation of *contraposition*. This involved switching the subject and the predicate, while replacing each term by a standard negative term. We then considered an operation traditionally known as *obversion*. A and I statements are often said to have the *quality* affirmative. E and O statements are then said to have the quality negative. A and E statements are often said to have the *quantity* universal. I and O statements are then said to have the quantity particular. We obvert a statement by changing the quality but not changing the quantity and replacing the predicate by a standard negative term. The following chart contains all the results of such operations that yield a logical equivalent.

Standard Logical Equivalents		
All **F** are **G**.	It is not the case that some **F** are not **G**.	
No **F** are **G**.	It is not the case that some **F** are **G**.	
Some **F** are **G**.	It is not the case that no **F** are **G**.	
Some **F** are not **G**.	It is not the case that all **F** are **G**.	
Some **F** are **G**.	Some **G** are **F**.	Conversion
No **F** are **G**.	No **G** are **F**.	Conversion
All **F** are **G**.	All non-**G** are non-**F**.	Contraposition
Some **F** are not **G**.	Some non-**G** are not non-**F**.	Contraposition
All **F** are **G**.	No **F** are non-**G**.	Obversion
No **F** are **G**.	All **F** are non-**G**.	Obversion
Some **F** are **G**.	Some **F** are not non-**G**.	Obversion
Some **F** are not **G**.	Some **F** are non-**G**.	Obversion

In 1.4 we studied how to put statements into standard form. This involved heavy use of our logical equivalents.

In Section 2 we turned to Venn diagrams. In 2.1 we looked at some basic diagrams, noting that we would use dark shading to indicate that an area was empty and light shading to indicate that an area was inhabited. In 2.2 we saw how to use Venn diagrams to check more complex arguments for validity. We called some of these arguments *syllogisms*. In valid arguments the entry for the conclusion will already have appeared once we enter the premises.

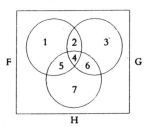

We enter an A statement "All *F* are *G*" by dark-shading areas 1 and 5, thereby indicating that the areas for objects that are *F* but not *G* are empty.

We enter an E statement "No *F* are *G*" by dark-shading areas 2 and 4, thereby indicating that the areas for objects that are both *F* and *G* are empty.

We enter an I statement "Some *F* are *G*" by light-shading areas 2 and 4, thereby indicating that there is something that is *F* and *G*, but we place a small circle on the boundary between the areas to indicate that we lack information as to whether those objects are or are not *H*.

We enter an O statement "Some *F* are not *G*" by light-shading areas 1 and 5, thereby indicating that there is an *F* that is not a *G*. We put a circle on the boundary for the same reason as in the preceding case.

CHAPTER 9

Quantification Theory

In our study of sentential logic we learned how to symbolize some sentences so as to be able to check certain arguments for validity. But sentential logic is limited to the structures or forms generated by the presence of truth-functional connectives. Consider, for example, the following very simple argument:

> **Every whale is a mammal.**
> **Willy is a whale.**
> **So, Willy is a mammal.**

This is clearly a valid argument but, as we have noted before, operating within a system of sentential logic we could only symbolize such arguments in the following way:

> **A**
> **B**
> **So, C**

We do not, in sentential logic, have any means of representing the common elements in the internal structure of these sentences. This does not show that there is something wrong with sentential logic; it merely indicates something we have already noted, that sentential logic is limited. The above argument regarding Willy, although valid, is not truth-functionally valid. When we looked at categorical logic we did indeed "look inside" some sentences, but the techniques we developed there were very limited.

What we will here do is develop a more advanced branch of logic, often called either "predicate logic" or "quantification theory", terms which we shall use interchangeably. Our goal will be to present a complete system of quantification theory, but one that will be restricted in certain ways. We will emphasize only the more elementary parts of the system. Nonetheless we will, with this system, be able to assess the validity of a much broader range of arguments than we could before.

1 / The Basics

1.1 / Our Language: An Informal Approach

The structure of the language we will develop in this chapter will be much more complex than that of the language used for sentential logic. This is to be expected, since we are now concerning ourselves with the internal complexity of the sentences we will be symbolizing. We will first present our language informally and then provide a more rigorous definition.

Consider the following claim:

Everything is physical.

As we did when we considered categorical sentences, we shall utilize capital letters as our predicate letters. Let us use "P" to stand in for what we shall call the predicate "___ is physical". (The choice of "P" is only made for the sake of convenience — any other capital letter could have been chosen.) Notice that when we fill the gap in a predicate with a particular, singular term, for example, a name, we have a respectable English sentence. This predicate has one gap, and so we shall call it a one-place predicate. As we shall see, there are predicates with more than one place. For example, "___ loves ..." is a two-place predicate. We can form a sentence by placing singular terms in each of the gaps. We will look at multi-place predicates at a later point.

We shall read "Px" as saying "x is physical". We shall speak of "x", which in this context functions very much like a pronoun, as an individual variable. We will utilize "(x)" as our means of saying "For all x" or "Everything x is such that". In other words, when we encounter an individual variable enclosed in parentheses we shall call it a universal quantifier. We can now symbolize our sentence as:

(x)Px

which in this case we can read as "For all x, x is physical", or as "Everything x is such that x is physical". Notice that in the latter case we might well have said "Everything x is such that it is physical".

Let us look back at the argument with which we began this chapter. We can paraphrase it in the following way:

Everything x is such that if it is a whale then it is a mammal.
Willy is a whale.
So, Willy is a mammal.

We will utilize the predicate letter "W" to symbolize the predicate "___ is a whale" and the predicate letter "M" to symbolize the predicate "___ is a mammal". We now have a need for singular terms. We shall use lowercase letters as our particular terms, and shall speak of these letters as *individual constants*. Let us now use the individual constant "a" to symbolize the singular term "Willy". We can now symbolize the whole argument as follows:

(x)(Wx→Mx)
Wa
Ma
(Everything x is such that if it is a whale then it is a mammal.
Willy is a whale.
So, Willy is a mammal.)

English also contains sentences like these:

There are whales.
Something is a whale.

These we call existential sentences. We will view both as claiming that there is at least one whale. In order to symbolize these, we shall utilize what we will speak of as an existential quantifier, which we will form by placing the symbol "∃" before an individual variable and enclosing the result in parentheses. Thus, at this point we have available the existential quantifier "(∃x)" as well as the universal quantifier "(x)". We will read "(∃x)" as "There is an x such that" or "At least one x is such that". We can thus symbolize the sentence "There is at least one whale" by:

(∃x)Wx
(There are whales, or something is a whale. Remember that we are taking both to say only that there is at least one whale.)

which we may read as "There is an x such that x is a whale" or "There is an x such that it is a whale".

Consider now the statement that there are students who will find this material easy. This statement may be analysed as containing the one complex predicate "___ is a student who will find this material easy". However, since we will generally be concerned with revealing the structure of sentences, we will take this complex predicate as being a conjunction of two predicates: the predicate "___ is a student" and the predicate "___ will find this material easy". We can symbolize this statement by the sentence:

(∃x)(Sx & Ex)

which we may read as "There is an x such that x is a student and x will find this material easy".

Suppose we wish to symbolize the statement "There are birds that do not fly". We could utilize the predicates "___ is a bird" and "___ is a non-flyer". You will recognize here the presence of what we earlier called a negative term. Since our general preference is to reveal as much sentential structure as possible, we prefer to utilize the predicates "___ is a bird" and "___ is a flyer", symbolizing the statement as follows:

(∃x)(Bx & ~Fx)
(There are birds that don't fly, or there is a bird that doesn't fly.)

We may read this as "There is an x such that x is a bird and x is not a flyer". As you may have guessed, we are making structure explicit in this way so that later on we will be able to take advantage of the rules of sentential logic.

1.2 / Our Language: A More Formal Approach

We will now present our quantification language in a more formal way, using certain special symbols. All of these will be explained as we proceed.

We first need predicate letters. These will be capital letters **A ... Z**. In a more advanced treatment we would want an unlimited supply of these, that we would form by using numeric subscripts or some similar device; but the current lot will be quite sufficient for our purposes here. We will, of course, use parentheses. And we will have individual variables **w, x, y,** and **z**. Again, in a more advanced treatment we would need an unlimited supply of variables, but here we can get by with only these. We also need individual constants. These will be lowercase letters **a ... t**. Again, these will suffice for our purposes. We will also utilize all the connectives that we introduced in sentential logic.

We form universal quantifiers by enclosing an individual variable in parentheses. Each of the following will then be called a universal quantifier:

(x) (y) (z)

And we form existential quantifiers by putting an "∃" before an individual variable and enclosing the result in parentheses. Each of the following will be an existential quantifier:

(∃x) (∃y) (∃z)

We will now define what counts as a formula of our language. You may prefer to skim the boxes you will encounter as you work through this chapter, but you should carefully attend to the discussions that follow them.

Formula of Our Language

(Notice that we are using Σ when we wish to talk about any predicate letter of our language.)

1. If Σ is any predicate letter and *a* and *b* are any individual variables or individual constants (not necessarily different), then each of
   Σa
   Σab
   is a basic formula of our language.

2. Every basic formula of our language is a formula of our language.

3. Where *p* and *q* are formulas of our language (not necessarily different), then where *a* is any individual variable each of:
   (a) p
   (∃a) p
   (p & q)
   (p ∨ q)
   (p → q)
   (p ↔ q)
   ~p
   is a formula of our language.

All of these formulas will be utilized in the construction of derivations, but only certain ones will count as sentences. Before we turn to the definition of a sentence, note that we have all the kinds of formulas that we had as non-basic sentences in sentential logic, that is, we have conjunctions, conditionals, and so on. But we also have two new kinds. One, which has the form (*a*)*p*, will be spoken of as a ***universally quantified formula*** or ***universal generalization***. The other, which has the form (∃*a*)*p*, will be spoken of as an ***existentially quantified formula*** or ***existential generalization***.

In order to define which formulas count as sentences, we need the following concepts:

Scope

In (***a***)***p*** every individual variable is said to be in the scope of the quantifier (***a***).

In (∃***a***)***p*** every individual variable is said to be in the scope of the quantifier (∃***a***).

Bound vs. Free

An occurrence of an individual variable in a formula is bound if and only if it occurs within the scope of a quantifier formed from that variable.

An occurrence of an individual variable in a formula is free if and only if it is not bound.

A Sentence of Our Language

A formula is a sentence if and only if it contains no free occurrences of an individual variable.

We need one more notion before we present some examples that will show that this language is not nearly as difficult as it looks.

Bound By

Given a formula (***a***)***p***, a free occurrence of ***a*** in ***p*** is said to be bound by that occurrence of (*a*).

Given a formula (∃***a***)***p***, a free occurrence of ***a*** in ***p*** is said to be bound by that occurrence of (∃***a***).

These notions will be utilized in our statement of the derivation rules for quantification theory. Here are a few sample sentences of our language; we shall talk a bit about them as we proceed:

(x)Fx   **(x)Fxx**
(∃x)Fx   **(∃x)Fxx**

In the first pair of sentences the predicate letter "F" is functioning as a one-place predicate letter. We would utilize it to symbolize a one-place predicate such as "___ is a physical object", in which case our first sentence would say that everything is a physical object, and the second sentence would say that something is a physical object. In the second pair of sentences, "F" is functioning as a two-place predicate letter. We would utilize it to symbolize a two-place predicate such as "___ is in the same place as ...". In this case, the first sentence would say that everything x is such that x is in the same place as x. (We could put this more idiomatically as the statement that everything is in the same place as itself.) The second sentence in the pair then says that something is in the same place as itself.

Next let us look at the sentences:

(x)Fx ∨ (x)Gx
(x)(Fx ∨ Gx)

These two sentences may look similar, but they are quite different. The first is a disjunction. It is *not* a universal sentence even though both of its disjuncts are. It says that either everything is F or everything is G. The second, however, is a universally quantified sentence: both occurrences of "x" that follow the universal quantifier are bound by that quantifier. This sentence says that everything x is such that either it, x, is F, or it, x, is G. More idiomatically, we would say that everything is either F or G. Think of the difference between the statement that every number is odd or every number is even and the statement that every number is odd or even. In this case the former statement is false, while the latter statement is true. So you must always pay attention to the kind of sentence you have in front of you; if you do not, you will have trouble both with symbolizing and with derivations.

Now consider the sentences:

(x)Fx ∨ (y)Gy
(x)Fx ∨ (x)Gx

These are, of course, different sentences, but if you understood the preceding example you should be able to see that these two say the very same thing: both say that either everything is F or everything is G. But consider:

(x)(Fx ∨ Gy)

Notice that this is not a sentence of our language, as it contains a free variable. However:

(x)(Fx ∨ Gx)
(y)(Fy ∨ Gy)

are both sentences, and they do both say the same thing.

Now let us take a look at some sentences involving negation signs:

~(x)Fx
(x)~Fx

It is very important to keep these two distinct. Let us use the predicate letter "F" to symbolize "___ is a living creature". The first sentence is not a universal generalization; it is the negation of one. It says that it is not the case that everything is a living creature, which is true. The second sentence is a universal generalization. It says that everything x is such that it is not a living creature, or that everything is not a living creature. This clearly is a different claim, and a false one. You, for example, are a living creature.

Here are three sentences that utilize two-place predicates:

(x)Rxx
(x)(y)Rxy
(x)(∃y)Rxy

Hitherto we have, in effect, supposed that we were speaking of any objects whatsoever: we supposed what we shall call an ***unrestricted domain of interpretation***. On occasion it is more convenient to utilize a ***restricted domain of interpretation***. Here we will suppose that, for example, we are talking only about persons. Our domain of interpretation will be restricted to persons. Our two-place predicate letter "R" will symbolize the two-place predicate "___ loves ...". Given this, our first sentence now says that everyone x (every person x) is such that x loves x or, more idiomatically, everyone loves him or herself.

Restricted Domains: A Note

When we restrict our domain to, as in this case, persons, we shall typically read the universal quantifier "(x)" as "all persons x are such that" and the existential quantifier "(∃x)" as "there is a person x such that". Similarly, were we to restrict our domain to numbers we would read "(x)" as "all numbers x are such that", and would read "∃x" as "there is a number x such that".

The second sentence, "(x)(y)Rxy", says that everyone x and everyone y are such that x loves y, or everyone loves everyone. (Note that if this sentence is true then the first sentence must be true, for "everyone" includes oneself. Do not let our use of different variables lead you to interpret the second sentence as saying that everyone loves everyone other than him or herself.) Our third sentence, "(x)(∃y)Rxy", says that everyone loves someone or another. Here again, our use of different variables does not force the reading that everyone loves someone other than him or herself. Thus, a world in which everyone loved him or herself would be a world in which everyone loves someone. But, of course, our sentence would also be true in a world in which the first person loved the second, the second loved the third, and so on down the line. Let us exhibit these by looking at some small worlds:

World 1

a loves a.　a does not love b or c.
b loves b.　b does not love a or c.
c loves c.　c does not love a or b.

This world is, we are supposing, inhabited only by three persons. Is this a world in which "(x)(∃y)Rxy" (the statement that everyone loves someone) is true? Sure. **a** loves someone, namely **a**. So do **b** and **c**. It is also a world in which "(x)Rxx" is true. But it is not a world in which "(x)(y)Rxy" is true. **a**, for example, does not love **b**. So it is false that everyone loves everyone. Let us now look at another world.

World 2

a loves a, b, and c.
b loves a and c but does not love b.
c loves a and c but does not love b.

In this world "(x)(∃y)Rxy" is true. But "(x)(y)Rxy" and "(x)Rxx" are both false. Now let us look at one more world.

World 3

a loves a, b, and c.
b loves a, b, and c.
c loves a, b, and c.

In this world all three of the statements we have been considering are true.

1.3 / Symbolizing Sentences: One-Place Predicates

Quantification theory is more complex than sentential logic, but symbolizing, at least at the level we shall attempt, should not prove too difficult if you master certain basic principles. Recall that we have studied some basic kinds of sentences that we called A, E, I, and O sentences. You will find that symbolizing proceeds much more easily if you learn how to symbolize these sentences. We will turn to them after considering some other sentences.

When we are symbolizing sentences we need to specify what we shall call a symbolization key. This key will consist of the following:

Symbolization Key

Will specify:
(1) the domain of interpretation; if not specified, it will be taken as unrestricted.
(2) which objects the individual constants are taken as designating.
(3) which predicates the predicate letters are taken to symbolize.

In each given context, a predicate letter will only be used to symbolize some one predicate, and an individual constant will only be used to designate some one object. Consider the claim that Hume is a philosopher. Here we would proceed as follows:

"h" is to designate Hume.
"P_" is to symbolize "_ is a philosopher".

We would then symbolize the sentence in question as:

Ph
(Hume is a philosopher.)

Let us add to our key:

"g" designates Gretzky.
"H_" symbolizes "_ is a hockey player".

We will not normally use the same letter as both an individual constant and a predicate letter; here we do so only for the sake of visual convenience. A predicate letter is a capital letter, an individual constant a lowercase letter, and the two play quite different roles in our language. With this in mind, let us go on to symbolize some sentences.

Ph & ~Pg
(Hume is a philosopher but Gretzky is not.)
~Hh & Hg
(Hume is not a hockey player, but Gretzky is.)
Ph ∨ Pg
(Hume or Gretzky is a philosopher.)
(Pg & Ph) ∨ ~(Pg ∨ Ph)
(Both Gretzky and Hume are philosophers, or neither is.)

We already know how to symbolize the following three statements:

Everything is a living creature.
It is not the case that everything is a living creature.
Everything is not a living creature.

Using "L_" for "_ is a living creature", these come out, respectively, as:

(x)Lx
~(x)Lx
(x)~Lx

And you should see how to symbolize the following three statements:

> **Something is a living creature.**
> **It is not the case that something is a living creature.**
> **Something is not a living creature.**

Respectively, these come out, with an unrestricted domain and with "L_" still taken to symbolize "_ is a living creature", as:

> **(∃x)Lx**
> **~(∃x)Lx**
> **(∃x)~Lx**

Using "M_" to symbolize "_ is a mental item" and "P_" to symbolize "_ is a physical item", let us consider the following sentences.

> **Something is both mental and physical.**
> **Something is mental and something is physical.**

The first comes out as:

> **(∃x)(Mx & Px)**

and the second as:

> **(∃x)Mx & (∃x)Px**

The second sentence, which is a conjunction, not an existential statement, could equally well have been symbolized as:

> **(∃x)Mx & (∃y)Py**

which would say exactly the same thing. This point was discussed in the preceding section. We will typically restrict ourselves to as few variables as possible, simply to facilitate the exercises on symbolizing.

Here, too, you must be careful regarding negations. Consider the statements:

> **It's not the case that something is both mental and**
> **physical.**
> **Something is not both mental and physical.**

The first sentence is a negation, and is symbolized as:

> **~(∃x)(Mx & Px)**

The second is an existential statement, symbolized as:

(∃x)~(Mx & Px)

The first sentence, the negation, does not say the same thing as the second sentence, the existential. These cautionary remarks apply equally to statements involving universal quantifiers. For example, recall that the two sentences:

Everything is mental or physical.
Everything is mental or everything is physical.

are quite distinct. The first sentence is a universal one and is symbolized as:

(x)(Mx ∨ Px)

whereas the second is a disjunction that may be symbolized as:

(x)Mx ∨ (x)Px

Remember that the first sentence does not say the same thing as the second sentence.

It is now time to turn to the following four kinds of sentences, ones we encountered in Chapter 8:

Categorical Sentences:

A:	All F are G
E:	No F are G
I:	Some F are G
O:	Some F are not G

We have in fact already seen how to symbolize both I and O sentences:

I: (∃x)(Fx & Gx)
O:(∃x)(Fx & ~Gx)

And our A sentences come out as:

A: (x)(Fx → Gx)

Warning:

Do *not* symbolize "All F are G" as:

   (x)(Fx & Gx)

This symbolic sentence makes the different claim that everything is both F and G.

   As well, do *not* symbolize "Some F are G" as:

   (∃x)(Fx → Gx)

This makes the different claim that there is something that, if it is an F, is also a G.

But what of our E sentences? Let us consider the following:

No birds are mammals.

says the same thing as:

Everything, if it is a bird, is then not a mammal.

It is this latter we shall utilize as a standard means of symbolizing an E sentence. So:

No F are G

comes out as:

E: (x)(Fx → ~Gx)

Again, symbolizing will proceed much more smoothly if you keep the standard symbolizations in mind.

As we have noted at several points, you must pay careful attention to the placement of negations:

It's false that all F are G

comes out as:

~(x)(Fx → Gx)

whereas:

Every F is not a G

comes out as:

(x)(Fx → ~Gx)

Finally, there are certain sentences that are not, strictly speaking, A, E, I, or O sentences but that are symbolized in much the same kind of way:

Everything that is not an F is G.
Something that is not an F is G.

can be symbolized as, respectively:

(x)(~Fx → Gx)
(∃x)(~Fx & Gx)

These sorts of sentences should not cause much of a problem.

1.4 / Symbolizing Sentences: Multi-Place Predicates

To this point our primary interest has been in one-place predicates. We will now expand our focus and turn to some multi-place predicates. There are English predicates with more than two places (for example, "... is between ___ and ,,,"), but we shall not concern ourselves with them. We shall confine ourselves to two-place predicates.

In the discussion below we shall use the following symbolization key:

Domain: Persons
"s" will designate Steven
"a" will designate Ann
"T_..." will symbolize "_ is taller than ..."

Let us now symbolize:

Steven is taller than Ann.
Ann is taller than Steven.

These are, respectively:

Tsa
Tas

Note that these two do not say the same thing. Now let us consider:

Steven is taller than someone.

Someone is taller than Steven.

The first of these comes out as:

(∃x)Tsx

We may read this as the statement that there is someone x such that Steven is taller than x. This does indeed say what we wanted to say. The second comes out as:

(∃x)Txs

We may read this as the statement that there is someone x such that x is taller than Steven. Again, this says what we want it to say.

As usual, we must be very careful with negations. Consider:

Someone is not taller than Steven.
It's not the case that someone is taller than Steven.

The first is an existential sentence:

(∃x)~Txs

whereas the second is a negation:

~(∃x)Txs

And you must watch out for the following as well:

Someone is taller than Ann or Steven.
Someone is taller that Ann or someone is taller than Steven.

The first is an existential sentence:

(∃x)(Txa ∨ Txs)

The second is a disjunction:

(∃x)Txa ∨ (∃x)Txs

Mastering all of this is, of course, a matter of practice and thought. It will be difficult unless you pay careful attention to the kinds of sentences you are working with.

Let us now turn to some sentences in which we have no singular terms. Here we will often need more than one variable. And as we will see, the order of quantifiers is often of considerable importance.

The sentence:

Everyone is taller than someone.

comes out as:

(x)(∃y)Txy

Let us retranslate this into near-English. It says that for every person x there is some person y such that person x is taller than person y. This is near enough to English to enable us to see that our sentence does say what we want it to say.

We will now use "T_ ..." for the predicate "_ is at least as tall as ...". (I am at least as tall as someone if I am the same height or taller.) Our domain will remain the same. The sentence "(x)(∃y)Txy" says that for every person x there is some person y such that x is at least as tall as y. Consider the sentence:

(∃y)(x)Txy

Note that the change here is a change in the order of the existential and the universal quantifier. What does this sentence say? Let us read it very carefully. It says that there is some person y such that for every person x, x is at least as tall as y. Put in slightly less stiff English, it says that there is a person who is equalled or exceeded in height by everyone. We may safely suppose such a person is very short.

It should be clear that the sentences

(x)(∃y)Txy

and

(∃y)(x)Txy

do not say the same thing. Let us use "T_..." for the predicate "_was born on day...". Consider the claim that every person was born on some day. As symbolized by the first sentence, this claim is the true one that everyone has a day on which they were born. However, the second sentence yields the false claim that there is some one day everyone was born on. In order to make sure that we see this, let us look at two worlds.

It is not always easy, if one hears or reads claims like these, to tell exactly what was meant. Consider the claim that everyone is loved by someone. This might mean that everyone is loved by someone or another. This is the first type of symbolization. But it could also mean there is some being such that everyone is loved by that being. This is the interpretation captured by the second type of symbolization. Typically we appeal to the context and our background knowledge in order to decide precisely what is meant. The second symbolization might, for example, be the most plausible interpretation if someone argued that since God exists, everyone is loved by someone.

One of our constant themes has been that we must be very careful with sentences involving negations. That obtains here as well. Consider the statement:

It is false that every number is larger than some number.

Here we should see that the statement is a negation. But we still have two ways of construing the sentence being negated. The statement might be taken as either:

~(x)(∃y)Lxy
(It is false that for every number x there is some number or another y such that x is larger than y.)

or:

~(∃y)(x)Lxy
(It is false that there is a number y such that every number x is larger than it, y, is.)

Here, the first seems to be the most natural interpretation, but the second interpretation is also possible. Or consider the claim that it is false that everyone in your logic classroom speaks some language. This sentence seems to admit of both interpretations. Certainly if we said explicitly that it is false that there is some language that everyone in that room speaks, we would have an example of a statement with a structure like that of the second sentence.

Let us now look at a few statements that have a more complex structure. We shall use the following symbolization key.

Domain: Persons
"s" will designate Steven
"M_" will symbolize "_ is a male"
"P_..." will symbolize "_ is a parent of ..."
"F_..." will symbolize "_ is a father of ..."

Notice that it is quite legitimate to take "father" as a two-place as well as a one-place predicate: a father is always a father of someone. We will, then, symbolize the statement that Steven is a father as:

(∃x)Fsx
(There is a person x such that Steven is the father of x.)

How should we symbolize the following?

Some males are parents.

This is, in effect, an I sentence. It would be symbolized as:

(∃x)(Mx & (∃y)Pxy)

We can read this as the statement that someone x is such that x is a male and, for someone or another y, x is a parent of y. What we are doing is using "(∃y)Pxy" to express that "x is a parent". This is the statement we wanted. Suppose now we wanted to symbolize:

Every male is a parent.

This is an A sentence. It comes out as:

(x)(Mx→(∃y)Pxy)

We can read this as the statement that for everyone x, if x is a male then there is some y or other such that x is the parent of y. Trickier yet is the statement:

Every father is a parent.

Recall that we already know how to symbolize A statements and already know how to symbolize both "x is a father" and "x is a parent". So our statement is symbolized in the following way:

(x)((∃y)Fxy → (∃y)Pxy)

Here we said that everything x is such that, if x is a father, then x is a parent. Finally, let us symbolize:

Some male parent is a father.
Every male parent is a father.

These come out as, respectively:

(∃x)((Mx & (∃y)Pxy) & (∃y)Fxy) (This is still an I sentence.)
(x)((Mx & (∃y)Pxy) → (∃y)Fxy) (This is still an A sentence.)

What we have done is utilized "(∃x)(Mx & (∃y)Pxy)" as our means of symbolizing "x is a male parent".

1.5 / Relational Predicates

The predicates that we have spoken of as two-place predicates are often called relational predicates. In using these, we speak of relations between objects. Relations may have certain important features that, if we learn to recognize them, can help considerably in assessing certain arguments.

Symmetry

A relation **R** is **symmetric** if and only if **(x)(y)(Rxy → Ryx)**.

Let us think about what this says, taking the predicate "_is a sibling of ..." as symbolized by "R_...". (To be a sibling of is to be a brother or sister of.) The symbolic sentence in the box now says that for everyone x and for everyone y, if x is a sibling of y then y is a sibling of x. This seems clearly true. Given that it is true, we will characterize the relation "being a sibling" as a symmetric relation. Hence we know that, for example, if I am a sibling of Barbara then Barbara is a sibling of me.

Some other relations, such as "being in love with", are not symmetric. Many of us have learned this through painful experience. To say that a relation R is not symmetric is simply to say that it is not the case that (x)(y)(Rxy → Ryx). Do not confuse this with the following property:

Asymmetry

A relation **R** is **asymmetric** if and only if **(x)(y)(Rxy → ~Ryx)**.

Our relation of being taller than is an asymmetric relation: if I am taller than you, then you are not taller than me.

Relations may also be *reflexive*:

Reflexivity

A relation **R** is *reflexive* if and only if **(x)Rxx**.

Consider the relation "being of the same height". Clearly, I am the same height as myself. We would never bother saying this simply because we all know this relation is a reflexive one. "Being in love with" is a relation that is not reflexive: some people are in love with themselves, but not everyone is. Be careful not to confuse the claim that a relation is not reflexive with the claim that it is *irreflexive*:

Irreflexivity

A relation **R** is *irreflexive* if and only if **(x)~Rxx**.

The relation of being taller than, as well as being asymmetric, is irreflexive. The relation of being in love with is not irreflexive; it is only not reflexive.

The final property we shall consider is *transitivity*:

Transitivity

A relation **R** is *transitive* if and only if
(x)(y)(z)((Rxy & Ryz) → Rxz).

We can most easily grasp the point of this by considering an example:

> **If a person x is an ancestor of a person y, and that person y is an ancestor of a person z, then x is an ancestor of z (and this holds for any persons x, y, and z).**

"Being an ancestor of" is a transitive relation. Again, note that some relations are not transitive: "being a friend of" is a familiar one. We can, of course, now introduce *intransitivity*:

Intransitivity

A relation **R** is *intransitive* if and only if
(x)(y)(z)((Rxy & Ryz) → ~Rxz).

Many kinship terms are intransitive. Consider the relation of being a father of. If Howard is a father of Max, and Max is a father of me, then Howard is of course not a father of me—a grandfather of me is not a father of me.

Suppose someone presented the following argument:

> **a is a brother of b.**
> **b is a brother of c.**
> **So, a is a brother of c.**

As it stands, this argument is invalid. But clearly a person who presents it is supposing that "being a brother of" is a transitive relation. If we add a premise specifying this, then we do have a valid argument.

The properties of relations that we are looking at are themselves related in certain ways. Suppose we have, for example, a relation that is both transitive and symmetric. Does it remain an open question as to whether that relation is reflexive? If you consider this for a bit you should see that the answer is no. Let us briefly see why by means of an example. Let us introduce three terms: "a", "b", and a relational predicate "R_...". Since by supposition we have transitivity we know that:

> **If Rab and Rba, then Raa**

But since we have symmetry we also know that:

> **If Rab, then Rba**

From these we can conclude that:

> **If Rab then Raa**

This is not, strictly speaking, a proof of our claim, but if you think about it you should see that any relation that is transitive and symmetric is also reflexive.

1.6 / Identity

There are many relations that are transitive and symmetric and thereby, as we just saw, reflexive. Being of the same height is one. But one such relation is typically singled out for special attention. This is the relation of identity. In math this relation is often spoken of as equality. But, with numbers for example, equality is just identity. We shall reserve the letter "I" for identity. Since identity is transitive, symmetric, and reflexive we know that all the following are true:

> **(x)(y)(z)((Ixy & Iyz) → Ixz)**
> **(x)(y)(Ixy → Iyx)**
> **(x)Ixx**

We frequently utilize identity, appealing to these properties, in our reasoning.

Consider the following simple case. I find out that this gun is the murder weapon. I conclude that since I have handled this gun, I have handled the murder weapon. Here I am utilizing the properties of identity. And of course in mathematics we appeal to identity all the time though as noted we typically use an "=" sign. Here is a trivial example:

> **$8 = 2^3$**
> **$8 + 8 = 16$**
> **So, $2^3 + 8 = 16$**

Again we are appealing to the properties of identity.

2 / Further Questions of Interpretation

2.1 / Understanding Quantificational Sentences

Due to the complexity of the sentences of quantification theory it is often difficult to see quite what they mean. One of the best ways to understand them is to consider one or more interpretations of a given sentence. Each symbolization key specified a particular interpretation. And, in certain cases, we could provide a specification of a "world". In many cases we could see that two sentences did not say the same thing by way of constructing a world in which one was true but the other was false. Consider the following two sentences:

> (∃x)(Fx → Gx)
> (∃x)(Fx & Gx)

Let us look at a very small world:

World 1

a is not F. a is G.
b is not F. b is not G.
c is F. c is not G.

For it to be true that:

> (∃x)(Fx → Gx)

there must be at least at least one object x such that if it is an F then it is a G. There is one such object; in fact in this world there are two. Consider the object **a:**

> **If a is an F, then a is a G.**

This statement is true, so there is an object, namely **a,** such that it is if an F then it is a G. **b** is also an object such that:

> **If b is an F, then b is a G.**

is also true. But in this world there is no object that is both F and G. So the claim that:

> (∃x)(Fx & Gx)

is not true. This world exhibits the fact that these claims are not logically equivalent.

Next consider the following two sentences:

> (x)((Fx ∨ Gx) → Hx)
> (x)(Fx → Hx) & (x)(Gx → Hx)

Note that the first sentence is universally quantified while the second sentence is a conjunction.

> ## World 2
>
> **a is not F. a is G and a is H.**
> **b is not F. b is not G. b is not H.**
> **c is F. c is not G. c is H.**

Notice that for each of the three objects in our universe it is true that if it is either F or G then it is H. **b** is not H, but that does not matter since it is neither F nor G. Now let us look at the second sentence. Since it is a conjunction it will be true just in case both the left conjunct and the right conjunct are true. The left is true, that is, every object which is F is also H. And the right is true since every object which is G is also H. So both sentences come out true in this world. Can we infer that they are logically equivalent on the basis of our examination of this world? The answer is no. We are considering only one world, only one interpretation. As it happens these are logically equivalent but we have *not* proven this claim.

In some cases we will not wish to, or will not be able to, provide a picture of the world in question. For example, if I wish to speak of all natural numbers I am hardly in a position to write down an infinite set of statements. Here what we might do is to specify our symbolization key. Consider the

> **Domain: Natural Numbers Including 0**
> **"L_..." will symbolize "_ is less than ..."**
> **"S_..." will symbolize "_ is a successor of ..."**

Let us look at the following two sentences:

> **(x)(∃y)Syx**
> **(x)(y)(Syx → Lxy)**

If you consider both of these for a moment you should see that they are true in this interpretation. Now consider this sentence.

> **(x)(∃y)Sxy**

This looks rather like the first sentence above, but it is not the same. It says something holds of everything. So it should hold of 0.

> **(∃y)S0y**

This says that there is a number such that 0 is a successor of that number. But in this domain there is no such number. So the statement is false in this domain. You must be very careful about the order of quantifiers and the variables that they bind.

2.2 / Logical Truth in Quantification Theory

We saw in sentential logic that certain sentences were tautologies. Those sentences came out true in every interpretation. There are sentences in quantification theory that have a similar feature. They can be counted on to come out true in every interpretation in a non-empty domain, that is, a domain in which there is at least one object. We shall call such sentences *quantificational logical truths*. And argument validity is the same in quantification theory as it was before. That is, an argument is quantificationally valid just in case there is no interpretation in a non-empty domain in which all the premises are true while the conclusion is false. We will not, due to the complexities of quantification theory, undertake to provide a detailed account of quantificational logical truth. Suffice it to say that such accounts can be provided and are provided in more advanced texts.

That portion of quantification theory that involves only one-place predicates is similar to sentential logic in one respect. In sentential logic we saw that truth tables provided us with a finite, mechanical means of determining whether a given sentence was or was not a tautology. It can be shown, though we shall not do so, that a quantificational sentence that uses only n one-place predicates is a quantificational logical truth if and only if it is true in every interpretation in a domain with 2^n objects. Notice that this also gives us a means of determining whether a given sentence is a contradiction. If it is, its negation will be a logical truth. Given this we could in principle "write down" all those worlds and determine in a finite amount of time whether or not the sentence we were considering was a logical truth or a contradiction. However, the same is not true in full quantification theory. There are sentences, for example, that are false in every finite domain but true in some infinite domains.

We can characterize a system as *decidable* if and only if there is a procedure whereby we can in a finite number of steps determine that a sentence is a logical truth if it is and that it is not a logical truth if it is not. Sentential logic was decidable in this sense. Full quantification theory is *not* decidable in this sense. We can construct a device that will generate logical truths.

But at any particular finite point we cannot say that a sentence that has not yet been generated is not a logical truth. For all we know it may be generated at some later point. We did not "need" derivations in sentential logic because in principle truth tables provided us with a means of answering any question that we had. But since quantification theory is not decidable derivations or some equivalent of them are essential. So in the next chapter we will turn to derivations.

Chapter Summary

In this chapter we introduced quantification theory, turning in Section 1 to the basics. In 1.1 we discussed informally our quantificational language, turning in 1.2 to a more rigorous description of the language.

Formula of Our Language

(Notice that we are using Σ when we wish to talk about any predicate letter of our language.)

1. If Σ is any predicate letter and **a** and **b** are any individual variables or individual constants (not necessarily different), then each of

   Σ**a**
   Σ**ab**

   is a basic formula of our language.
2. Every basic formula of our language is a formula of our language.
3. Where **p** and **q** are formulas of our language (not necessarily different), then where **a** is any individual variable each of:

   (a) p
   (∃a) p
   (p & q)
   (p ∨ q)
   (p → q)
   (p ↔ q)
   ~p

   is a formula of our language.

Only certain formulas of this language were sentences. But in order to define a sentence we needed two preliminary concepts.

Scope

In (**a**)**p** every individual variable is said to be in the scope of the quantifier (**a**).

In (∃**a**)**p** every individual variable is said to be in the scope of the quantifier (∃**a**).

Bound vs. Free

An occurrence of an individual variable in a formula is bound if and only if it occurs within the scope of a quantifier formed from that variable.

An occurrence of an individual variable in a formula is free if and only if it is not bound.

Using these a sentence could be simply defined by:

A Sentence of Our Language

A formula is a sentence if and only if it contains no free occurrences of an individual variable.

Then we introduced one more concept:

Bound By

Given a formula (**a**)**p**, a free occurrence of **a** in **p** is said to be bound by that occurrence of (**a**).

Given a formula (∃**a**)**p**, a free occurrence of **a** in **p** is said to be bound by that occurrence of (∃**a**).

We spoke of *restricted* and *unrestricted domains of interpretation*, noting that:

Restricted Domains: A Note

When we restrict our domain to, as in this case, persons, we shall typically read the universal quantifier "(x)" as "all persons x are such that" and the existential quantifier "(∃x)" as "there is a person x such that". Similarly, were we to restrict our domain to numbers we would read "(x)" as "all numbers x are such that", and would read "∃x" as "there is a number x such that".

In 1.3 and 1.4 we studied how to symbolize various ordinary statements in our new formal language. We will always utilize a *symbolization key*:

Symbolization Key

Will specify:
(1) the domain of interpretation; if not specified, it will be taken as unrestricted.
(2) which objects the individual constants are taken as designating.
(3) which predicates the predicate letters are taken to symbolize.

In 1.5 we studied various properties of relational predicates:

Symmetry

A relation R is *symmetric* if and only if $(x)(y)(Rxy \rightarrow Ryx)$.

Asymmetry

A relation R is *asymmetric* if and only if $(x)(y)(Rxy \rightarrow {\sim}Ryx)$.

Reflexivity

A relation **R** is *reflexive* if and only if **(x)Rxx**.

Irreflexivity

A relation **R** is *irreflexive* if and only if **(x)~Rxx**.

Transitivity

A relation **R** is *transitive* if and only if **(x)(y)(z)((Rxy & Ryz) → Rxz)**.

Intransitivity

A relation **R** is *intransitive* if and only if **(x)(y)(z)((Rxy & Ryz) → ~Rxz)**.

In 1.6 we briefly glanced at the very special relation *identity*, for which we use "I". We noted that the following are true:

$$(x)(y)(z)((Ixy \ \& \ Iyz) \to Ixz)$$
$$(x)(y)(Ixy \to Iyx)$$
$$(x)Ixx$$

That is, identity is a relation that is symmetric, reflexive, and transitive. These properties play an important role in the use of identity in reasoning.

In Section 2 we turned to further questions of interpretation. In 2.1 we gave some detailed examples illustrating the meaning of our quantificational sentences. In 2.2 we introduced the notion of a *quantificational logical truth*. Such sentences can be counted on to come out true in any non-empty domain of interpretation. We noted that quantification theory was not *decidable*. That is we have no 'mechanical' means of determining which sentences are logical truths and which are not.

CHAPTER 10

Quantificational Derivations

In the previous chapter we looked at the basics of quantification theory. In this chapter we will introduce a derivation system that we will be able to use in order to show quantificationally valid arguments to be valid.

1 / The Basics

1.1 / Some Basic Derivations

We will begin by developing some rules for the construction of derivations in predicate logic. As we proceed, keep in mind the following:

Use of Sentential Logic

All rules of sentential logic may be used, and both indirect and conditional proof may be used.

Each quantificational formula works from our new vantage point much the same as an atomic sentence insofar as the rules of sentential logic are concerned. Consider the following argument:

> **Either all the (P)eople invited will (C)ome or I will be very (D)isappointed. They will not all come. So, I will be very disappointed.**

From the standpoint of sentential logic we have as premises:

> **P ∨ Q**
> **~P**

Put in quantification form we have, taking 's' to designate me:

> **(x)(Px → Cx) ∨ Ds**
> **~(x)(Px → Cx)**

Notice that the first sentence is a disjunction and the second sentence is the negation of the left disjunct. So we can use disjunctive syllogism to move to:

Ds

Similarly, given:

(x)Fx → (x)Gx
(x)Fx

you can use modus ponens to move to:

(x)Gx

But considerable care must be exercised. Given:

(x)(Fx → Gx)
(x)Fx

you cannot move directly to:

(x)Gx

by modus ponens. The first sentence is a universal generalization, not a conditional.

1.2 / Two Basic Rules

Recall that in sentential logic we applied our basic rules only to whole lines, never to parts of lines. The rules we shall now introduce also apply only to whole lines.

The first rule we shall introduce (in a limited version) is one we will call *universal instantiation* (or *ui* for short).

Limited Universal Instantiation (ui)

From: $(a)\Sigma a$
To: Σb

where **b** is any individual constant, and **b** replaces all occurrences of **a** in Σa that were bound by **(a)**.

Recall that this rule applies only to whole lines. It does allow us to move from, for example:

(x)(Fx & Gx)

to:

Fa & Ga

The sentence to which we applied the rule was a universal generalization. But it does not allow us to move directly from:

(x)Fx & (y)Gy

to:

Fa & (y)Gy

or to

Fa & Ga

The sentence "(x)Fx & (y)Gy" is not a universal generalization; it is a conjunction. However, we are allowed to utilize the rules of sentential logic. So we could do the following:

premise	1.	**(x)Fx & (y)Gy**
1 simp	2.	**(x)Fx**
2 ui	3.	**Fa**
1 simp	4.	**(y)Gy**
3,4 conj	5.	**Fa & (y)Gy**

Here is another example of the use of universal instantiation:

premise	1.	**(x)Fx & (y)Gy**
1 simp	2.	**(x)Fx**
2 ui	3.	**Fa**
1 simp	4.	**(y)Gy**
4 ui	5.	**Ga**
3,5 conj	6.	**Fa & Ga**

As we noted above, we could not go directly from line 1 to line 6 by ui since line 1 is not a universal generalization. A similar point obtains with respect to the following argument:

premise	1.	(x)(y)(Fxy → Fyx)
1 ui	2.	(y)(Fay → Fya)
2 ui	3.	Faa → Faa

We could not do the following:

premise	1.	(x)(y)(Fxy → Fyx)	
1 ui	2.	(x)(Fxa → Fax)	**erroneous**
2 ui	3.	Faa → Faa	

You should not have any difficulty with universal instantiation provided you remember to apply it only to whole lines that are universal generalizations.

Universal instantiation, which allowed us to eliminate universal generalizations, is essentially the principle that what holds true of everything holds true of any particular thing. Our next basic rule essentially says that if something holds true of a particular thing then it holds true of something or another. This rule allows us to introduce existential quantifiers. We shall call this rule *existential generalization*:

Existential Generalization (eg)

From: Σb

To: $(\exists a)\Sigma a$

where **b** is any individual constant and **a** replaces some or all occurrences of **b** in Σb, provided those occurrences of **b** are not in the scope of a quantifier **(a)** or **(∃a)** already occurring in Σb.

Let us look at some of the moves that existential generalization enables us to make. We shall utilize "L_…" for the predicate "_ loves …" and shall restrict our domain to persons. "c" and "d" will designate two distinct individuals.

Suppose we have the following as a premise:

c loves c.

From this we can get to any of the following:

(1)   Someone loves themself.
(2)   c loves someone.

(3) Someone loves c.
(4) Someone loves someone.

Here is the move to the first:

premise	1.	Lcc
1 eg	2.	(∃x)Lxx

Here is the move to the second:

premise	1.	Lcc
1 eg	2.	(∃x)Lcx

Here is the move to the third:

premise	1.	Lcc
1 eg	2.	(∃x)Lxc

And finally, here is the slightly more complex move to the fourth:

premise	1.	Lcc
1 eg	2.	(∃x)Lxc
2 eg	3.	(∃y)(∃x)Lxy

Notice that we could not do the following:

premise	1.	Lcc	
1 eg	2.	(∃x)Lxc	
2 eg	3.	(∃x)(∃y)Lxy	**erroneous**

Our rule only allows us to put an existential quantifier in front of a whole line. There is, however, a way to get to line 3 in accord with our rules:

premise	1.	Lcc
1 eg	2.	(∃y)Lcy
2 eg	3.	(∃x)(∃y)Lxy

Here is another mistake you should avoid making:

premise	1.	Lcd	
1 eg	2.	(∃x)Lxx	**erroneous**

There is no way to repair this, for it does not follow from line one that someone loves him or herself.

Let us now look at some derivations that involve the use of both of our rules. Suppose we want to move from:

c loves everyone.

to:

Someone loves d.

Here is one way we could do that:

premise	1.	**(x)Lcx**
1 ui	2.	**Lcd**
2 eg	3.	**(∃x)Lxd**

Note that if c loves everyone, then someone does love him or herself. Here is a way we can derive that:

premise	1.	**(x)Lcx**
1 ui	2.	**Lcc**
2 eg	3.	**(∃x)Lxx**

Recall that ui allows us to introduce any individual constant we wish. Line 3 is, of course, a standard use of existential generalization.

1.3 / Quantifier Exchange

The rules we shall now introduce will, like the preceding ones, be restricted to whole lines. Suppose I say that it is not the case that everything is a living creature. You should see that from this we can move to the claim that something is not a living creature. And from the claim that something is not a living creature I should be able to derive the claim that not everything is a living creature. These lead to the first two of our four *quantifier exchange* (*qe*) rules.

Quantifier Exchange (qe)

From: ~(*a*)*p*   From: (∃*a*)~*p*
To: (∃*a*)~*p*   To: ~(*a*)*p*

So long as you pay attention to the form of sentences, there should be few problems in applying this rule. The following is one application:

premise	1.	(∃x)~(Fx ∨ Gx)
1 qe	2.	~(x)(Fx ∨ Gx)

But this is not an application:

premise	1.	(∃x)(~Fx ∨ Gx)	
1 qe	2.	~(x)(Fx ∨ Gx)	**erroneous**

In premise 1 here we do not have an existential quantifier followed by a negation. Instead, we have an existential quantifier preceding a disjunction. Here is a legitimate application of qe:

premise	1.	~(∃x)(Fx ∨ Gx)
1 qe	2.	(x)~(Fx ∨ Gx)

And here is an application that is not legitimate:

premise	1.	~((∃x)Fx ∨ (∃x)Gx)	
1 qe	2.	(x)~(Fx ∨ Gx)	**erroneous**

Line 1 is not the negation of an existentially quantified sentence; it is the negation of a disjunction.

There are two more cases of the rule we have called "qe":

Quantifier Exchange (qe)

From: (*a*)~*p*   From: ~(∃*a*)*p*

To: ~(∃*a*)*p*   To: (*a*)~*p*

The first says, for example, that given the premise that everything is not a unicorn, we can conclude that it is not the case that something is a unicorn. The second says that given that it is not the case that something is a unicorn, we can conclude that everything is not a unicorn. If one has as a line that everything is not either F or G, we can add the line that there is not something that is F or G:

premise	1.	(x)~(Fx ∨ Gx)
1 qe	2.	~(∃x)(Fx ∨ Gx)

But the following move is not legitimate:

premise	1.	(x)(~Fx ∨ Gx)	
---------	----	--------------	
1 qe	2.	~(∃x)(Fx ∨ Gx)	**erroneous**

In this case, the sentence does not contain a universal quantifier followed by a negation sign; it is a universal quantification of a disjunction.

2 / Extending the System

Our current set of rules enables us to do a great deal, but not everything we might want to do. Here are two arguments that we cannot as yet show to be valid:

> **Everything is F and everything is G.**
> **So, everything is both F and G.**

> **Every F is G.**
> **Something is an F**
> **So, something is a G.**

We will now extend our system to allow us to show these arguments to be valid.

2.1 / Universal Instantiation and Generalization

In the previous section we introduced a limited version of universal instantiation. In order to complete our system we will need to extend it.

Extended Universal Instantiation (ui)

From: *(a)Σa*
To: *Σb*

where:

(1) if *b* is a constant then it replaces all occurrences of *a* bound by *(a)*.

(2) if *b* is a variable and *a* does not occur in *Σa* in the scope of any quantifier *(b)* or ∃*b*, then it replaces all occurrences of *a* bound by *(a)*.

We will now state our rule of *universal generalization*.

Universal Generalization (ug)

From: Σa

where Σa is not an assumption and *a* is a variable that does not occur free in any earlier undischarged assumption,

To: $(b)\Sigma b$

where *b* is an individual variable that does not occur in Σa and *b* replaces all occurrences of *a* in Σa.

Keep in mind that this rule applies only to whole lines. We are now in a position to show valid one of the above arguments:

premise	1.	(x)Fx & (x)Gx
1 simp	2.	(x)Fx
2 ui	3.	Fy
1 simp	4.	(x)Gx
4 ui	5.	Gy
3,5 conj	6.	Fy & Gy
6 ug	7.	(x)(Fx & Gx)

2.2 / Existential Instantiation

Let us now introduce a mode of proof that we will call *existential instantiation*: Suppose we had the following two premises:

premise	1.	($\exists$x) Fx
premise	2.	(y) Gy

We should be able to get from these two premises to:

($\exists$x) (Fx & Gx)

But we have no way of showing this argument to be valid with the rules that we have so far introduced. What we shall do is to introduce a new mode of proof that we shall call *existential instantiation.* You will recall that modes of proof involve the introduction of assumptions. Here is the bare statement of the mode of proof:

Existential Instantiation (ei)

$$(\exists a) \, \Sigma a$$

aei $\quad\lceil \quad \Sigma b$

.

.

.

$\lfloor \quad$ *q* (terminated)

ei $\qquad$ *q* (discharged)

where *b* is a constant that does not occur in any accessible line and *q* does not contain any occurrence of *b*.

This mode of proof differs from those introduced earlier by way of being more complex. But, more important, its use requires the presence of an accessible existential statement prior to the introduction of the assumption for an existential instantiation. We mention this line when we state the justification that assumption must bear the specified relation to the existential statement.

The idea behind this mode of proof is that if it is true that $(\exists x)Fx$, then there is at least one object that is F, but we don't know which object (or objects) this might be. In using existential instantiation and moving to Fb, I am in effect pretending that I know that "b" picks out an object that is F. "Fb" does not actually follow from my premises; it is an assumption. Let us see how we can now show the argument that we mentioned at the outset to be valid.

premise	1.	$(\exists x)\ Fx$
premise	2.	$(y)\ Gy$
aei	3.	Fa
2 ui	4.	Ga
3,4 conj	5.	Fa & Ga
5 eg	6.	$(\exists x)(Fx\ \&\ Gx)$
1, 3-6 ei	7.	$(\exists x)(Fx\ \&\ Gx)$

Here is another of the derivations that we could not have done without the recently introduced rules:

premise	1.	(x)(Fx → Gx)
premise	2.	(∃x)Fx
aei	3.	Fb
1 ui	4.	Fb → Gb
3,4 mp	5.	Gb
5 eg	6.	(∃x)Gx
2, 3-6 ei	7.	(∃x)Gx

Our ei rule contains a number of restrictions. Let us look at an example which show why those restrictions are necessary.

premise	1.	Bp	
premise	2.	(∃x)Dx	
aei	3.	Dp	**erroneous**
1,3 conj	4.	Bp & Dp	
5 eg	5.	(∃x)(Fx & Gx)	
2, 3-6 ei	6.	(∃x)(Fx & Gx)	

Here at line 3 we violated the restriction which required that we use a new individual constant. It should be clear that this conclusion does not follow from the premises. Suppose "Bp" is the statement that my pet is a bird, while the second premise is that statement that there are dogs. These are both true, but it is false that there is something which is both a bird and a dog.

Let us consider a rather tricky argument in which we wish to get to "(x)Gx" from these premises:

premise	1.	(x)Fx ∨ (x)Gx
premise	2.	(∃x)(~Fx ∨ Hx)
premise	3.	(x)~Hx

Notice that we could get to "(x)Gx" by disjunctive syllogism if we had "~(x)Fx" as a line. Let us try to get the latter using an indirect proof.

premise	1.	(x)Fx ∨ (x)Gx
premise	2.	(∃x)(~Fx ∨ Hx)
premise	3.	(x)~Hx
aip	4.	(x)Fx
aei	5.	~Fa ∨ Ha
4 ui	6.	Fa
5,6 ds	7.	Ha
7 eg	8.	(∃x)Hx
2, 5-8 ei	9.	(∃x)Hx
3 qe	10.	~(∃x)Hx
9,10 conj	11.	(∃x)Hx & ~(∃x)Hx
4-11 ip	12.	~(x)Fx
1,12 ds	13.	(x)Gx

Both indirect and conditional proof work in the same way as they did in sentential logic.

2.3 / More on Derivations

You must always be careful to attend to what kind of sentence you have. Suppose you are given the following two premises:

premise	1.	(x)(Fx → Gx)
premise	2.	(x)(Gx → Hx)

and are asked to derive "(x)(Fx → Hx)". The following is a mistake:

premise	1.	(x)(Fx → Gx)	
premise	2.	(x)(Gx → Hx)	
1,2 hs	3.	(x)(Fx → Hx)	erroneous

None of lines 1 through 3 are conditional sentences; they are all universal generalizations. Here is another mistake:

premise	1.	(x)(Fx → Gx)
premise	2.	(x)(Gx → Hx)
acp	3.	(x)Fx
1 ui	4.	Fx → Gx
2 ui	5.	Gx → Hx
4,5 hs	6.	Fx → Hx
3 ui	7.	Fx
6,7 mp	8.	Hx
8 ug	9.	(x)Hx
3-9 cp	10.	(x)Fx → (x)Hx

This is a legitimate derivation, but it was doomed at the start in that the sentence we wished to establish is not a conditional. All we will obtain with this acp is a conditional with "(x)Fx" as the antecedent. How then are we to obtain the conclusion that we wish? Well, it is a universal sentence and one way to establish a universal sentence is by an application of ug. To do this we would need "Fx → Gx" in the main column. Since this is a conditional we should try to establish it by a conditional proof.

premise	1.	$(x)(Fx \rightarrow Gx)$
premise	2.	$(x)(Gx \rightarrow Hx)$
acp	3.	Fx
1 ui	4.	$Fx \rightarrow Gx$
2 ui	5.	$Gx \rightarrow Hx$
3,4 hs	6.	$Fx \rightarrow Hx$
3,6 mp	7.	Hx
3-7 cp	8.	$Fx \rightarrow Hx$
8 ug	9.	$(x)(Fx \rightarrow Hx)$

While we have introduced a number of new rules, doing derivations in quantification theory still involves exercising care and thinking carefully about how you might get to the conclusion that you need.

2.4 / Identity

In the previous chapter we noted that identity is a relation that is very important for reasoning. It is transitive, reflexive, and symmetric, so all the following are true ("I" remains reserved for identity):

$(x)(y)(z)((Ixy \ \& \ Iyz) \rightarrow Ixz)$
$(x)(y)(Ixy \rightarrow Iyx)$
$(x)Ixx$

In order to enable our derivation system to cope with reasoning involving identity, we will introduce our two final rules. The first is:

> ### Reflexive Introduction (ri)
>
> At any point
> **(a)Iaa**
> may be introduced as a line.

None of our previous rules has taken quite this form. But suppose we were given "Fa" as our premise and asked to derive "$(\exists x)(Ixa \ \& \ Fx)$". Notice that given that we are taking "I" as identity this does follow. We could derive this as follows:

premise	1.	Fa
ri	2.	(x)Ixx
2 ui	3.	Iaa
1,2 conj	4.	Iaa & Fa
3 eg	5.	(∃x)(Ixa & Fx)

But we also need a rule that would enable us to utilize the symmetric and transitive character of identity.

Identity (=)

From:
Σa and **I**ab

From
Σa and **I**ba

To:
Σb

To:
Σb

where **a** and **b** are constants.

This rule enables us to complete a number of useful derivations.

premise	1.	Fa
premise	2.	Iba
1,2 =	3.	Fb

or

premise	1.	Fa
premise	2.	Iab
1,2 =	3.	Fb

2.5 / Theorems

We noted in Chapter 7 that we could utilize our system in order to prove theorems. The same is true of our quantificational system. Let us show that it is a theorem that identity is transitive. Recall that this would involve establishing:

$$(x)(y)(z)((Ixy \ \& \ Iyz) \rightarrow Ixz)$$

This is a sequence of universal quantifications. So we could obtain it if we had in our main column, where we have no undischarged assumptions:

(Ixy & Iyz) → Ixz

Notice that if we tried to utilize a conditional proof we might get into trouble. That would introduce free variables and our rule = only allows us to work directly on constants. However, showing this to be a theorem involves a rather long derivation so let us instead show how to establish a special case:

(Icd & Ide) → Ice

This is a conditional on which we can use our rule = since it contains constants.

acp	1.	Icd & Ide
1 simp	2.	Icd
1 simp	3.	Ide
2,3 =	4.	Ice
1-4 cp	5.	(Icd & Ide) → Ice

Notice that here we are taking "**d**" as being the *a* and "**c**" as being the *b* from the standpoint of our rule =. And "**Ide**" is our *Iab*.

This completes our study of quantification theory, although there is much more to be studied. We could go on to prove certain theorems in just the way that we did here and in sentential logic. And we might want to know whether we have enough rules to enable us to show that quantificationally valid arguments are valid. How do we know that the last line of a completed derivation does indeed follow from the premises of that argument? Again, these and other topics belong to a more advanced course of study.

Chapter Summary

In Section 1 of this chapter we introduced our derivation system for quantification theory. In 1.1 we noted that:

Use of Sentential Logic

All rules of sentential logic may be used, and both indirect and conditional proof may be used.

In section 1.2 we introduced two rules that appeal to the 'meaning' of the internal structure of our quantificational sentences. The first was a limited version of *universal instantiation*.

Limited Universal Instantiation (ui)

From: $(a)\Sigma a$
To: Σb

where *b* is any individual constant, and *b* replaces all occurrences of *a* in Σa that were bound by (*a*).

Universal instantiation appeals to the fact that what is true of everything is true of any particular thing. We then introduced *existential generalization*:

Existential Generalization (eg)

From: Σb
To: $(\exists a)\Sigma a$

where *b* is any individual constant and *a* replaces some or all occurrences of *b* in Σb, provided those occurrences of *b* are not in the scope of a quantifier (*a*) or ($\exists a$) already occurring in Σb.

This appeals to the fact that if a particular thing has some feature then there is something with that feature.

In 1.3 we introduced our *quantifier exchange* rules.

Quantifier Exchange (qe)

From: $\sim(a)p$ From: $(\exists a)\sim p$
To: $(\exists a)\sim p$ To: $\sim(a)p$

From: $(a)\sim p$ From: $\sim(\exists a)p$
To: $\sim(\exists a)p$ To: $(a)\sim p$

In Section 2 we extended our system in order to enable us to show a broader class of arguments to be valid. In 2.1 we extended universal instantiation and introduced universal generalization.

Extended Universal Instantiation (ui)

From: **(a)Σa**
To: **Σb**

where:
(1) if **b** is a constant then it replaces all occurrences of **a** bound by **(a)**.
(2) if **b** is a variable and **a** does not occur in Σ**a** in the scope of any quantifier **(b)** or ∃**b**, then it replaces all occurrences of **a** bound by **(a)**.

This version, as opposed to our initial one, allows us to introduce free variables. We then turned to *universal generalization*:

Universal Generalization (ug)

From: **Σa**
where Σ**a** is not an assumption and **a** is a variable that does not occur free in any earlier undischarged assumption,

To: **(b)Σb**
where **b** is an individual variable that does not occur in Σ**a** and **b** replaces all occurrences of **a** in Σ**a**.

We then turned, in 2.2, to a new mode of proof, one which we called *existential instantiation*:

Existential Instantiation (ei)

$$(\exists a)\, \Sigma a$$

aei   ⌐ Σb
             .
             .
             .

         ⌊   *q* (terminated)

ei   *q* (discharged)

where **b** is a constant that does not occur in any accessible line and **q** does not contain any occurrence of **b.**

We noted that it was extremely important to observe the restrictions placed on the use of this rule.

In 2.3 we provided some examples of derivations along with some further warnings regarding mistakes to avoid. In 2.4 we turned to identity, introducing the rules necessary to complete derivations that rely upon its special features:

Reflexive Introduction (ri)

At any point
(a)Iaa
may be introduced as a line.

Identity (=)

From: From
Σa and **Iab** Σa and **Iba**
To: To:
Σb Σb

In 2.5 we noted that we could prove theorems using this system.

CHAPTER 11

Probabilities

In this chapter we will be concerned with reasoning that involves numerical probabilities. Consider the following very simple question: if the probability that Jones will go through a given door is 50% and the probability that Wong will go through the same door is 50%, what is the probability that both will go through that door? Though reasoning with probabilities is quite common, we will find that it is something we do not necessarily do well.

1 / The Primary System

1.1 / Concepts of Probability

Suppose you randomly pick a card from a standard deck of cards. To say you randomly pick a card is simply to say that each card has an equal chance of being drawn. Here it is natural to suppose, since there are 52 cards, that there are 52 possible results of your pick. Exactly one of those cards is an ace of spades so, given that we are picking randomly, the probability of picking the ace of spades is 1/52. Assuming as we did that all outcomes are equally likely, our probability claim is, in effect, a claim about the ratio of favorable outcomes to possible outcomes. There are 4 aces, so we would say that there is a 4/52 chance of drawing an ace. Let us call this the concept of probability as *mathematical odds*.

Consider a typical coin. Suppose I asked you what the probability of getting two heads in a row was. You would likely answer 1/4. After all, there are four possible outcomes: head/head, head/tail, tail/head, and tail/ tail. Note that you are taking for granted that the coin is a fair one, that is, for any toss there is a 50% chance of landing heads and a 50% chance of landing tails. Mathematics does *not* tell us that this is so; actual coins may or may not be fair. Whether they are is a matter for investigation. The rules we shall introduce below will generally only tell us how to compute the probability of a complex statement such as "*p* and *q*" given that we already know the probabilities of *p* and of *q*. They will typically not give us any information about the probability of *p* or of *q,* but will instead tell us how to use such information to compute other probabilities.

Our second concept of probability is one based upon *relative frequency,* or what proportion of the members of one class or group are members of another class or group. Statistical generalizations typically are reports of relative frequencies. Suppose a bag contains 100 marbles, 40 of which are red. Then 40/100, or 40%, of the members of the group of marbles in the bag are red marbles. Probability statements based on relative frequency are the sort insurance companies use when they set their rates. For example, insurance companies keep track of the number of male drivers between 18 and 25 who have accidents. Let us say that 10% of male drivers between those ages are members of the group of drivers who have accidents. If far fewer female drivers in that age group have accidents, then the rates charged for insurance are, in many places, set higher for male drivers. For similar reasons I, who smoke, pay more for life insurance than my friends of the same age who do not smoke. Probability statements of this sort are also made by weather forecasters, who, when they say there is a 9/10 chance of rain, are really saying that 90% of the time when the current conditions prevail, it rains.

Finally, we sometimes use probability statements to characterize the degree to which it is rational to believe something. For example, as I write this in the morning I judge that it is overwhelmingly likely — that there is something like a 99% chance — that I will go to my office this afternoon. My judgment here is based upon my knowledge of my intentions. I am not claiming that 99 out of 100 afternoons I have gone or will go to my office; this is not a judgment of relative frequency.

To cite another kind of example, I may judge it likely that the Supreme Court will uphold a certain law, a law that has not hitherto been subjected to their review. I would not typically base such a judgment on relative frequencies or some sort of ratio of favorable to unfavorable outcomes. I may be taking into account, for example, the general temperament of the justices as manifested in rulings on cases of a quite different sort. We shall call this third concept of probability *credibility* (the degree to which it is rational to believe something). Probability in this sense is much less often expressed numerically than are probabilities in the preceding two senses.

1.2 / The Probability Calculus

We want here to specify the rules whereby we calculate probabilities of certain complex statements given information regarding the probability of certain other statements. For example, we asked at the outset what the probability was that both Jones and Wong would go through a given door given that there is a 50% chance that each will go through that door.

We now need to standardize our vocabulary. Our standard form for a report of a probability will be "Pr(...) = n". The "..." will be replaced by the sentence in which we are interested, and the "n" by a term picking out a real number between (and including) 0 and 1. Sometimes we will use decimal notation, sometimes percentages, and sometimes fractions, but for the sake of simplicity we will typically stick with fractions. Nothing much is at stake here: .5, 50%, and 1/2 are different ways of expressing the same thing.

In the preceding chapters we noted that certain statements are logically true (can be counted on to come out true regardless of how the world turns out). Tautologies were one sort of logically true statement that we have encountered. Other statements are logically false (can be counted on to come out false regardless of how the world turns out); contradictions are one such type of statement. "Either x will happen or x will not happen" is an example of a logically true statement; "x both will happen and will not happen" is an example of a logically false statement. We can now note:

Rules 1.1 and 1.2

R1.1:   Where p is a logically true statement, Pr(p) = 1
R1.2:   Where p is a logically false statement, Pr(p) = 0

These rules should occasion no difficulty. We can also say something about the probability of logically equivalent statements (ones that can be counted on to be either both true or both false: for instance, the statement that it is not the case that either John or Mary will come is logically equivalent to the statement that John will not come and Mary will not come).

Rule 1.3

R1.3: Where p and q are logically equivalent, Pr(p) = Pr(q)

Intuitively, we may put the point as follows. Logically equivalent statements are, in one sense, merely different ways of saying the same things, and so their probabilities will be the same. Here is an example of this rule. Let *p* be the statement that Hans will come, and *q* the complex statement that (either Hans will come and Mary will come, or Hans will come and Mary will not come). We have studied the question in more detail elsewhere, but here you should be able to see that these two statements are logically equivalent. Hence the probability of the one is equal to the probability of the other.

Suppose we know the likelihood of drawing an ace of spades and the likelihood of drawing a king of spades from a deck of cards. How could one determine the likelihood of drawing either the ace of spades or the king of spades? We are here asking about the probability of a disjunction, the rule for calculating which is:

Rule 2: General Disjunction

R2. Pr(*p* or *q*) = [Pr(*p*) + Pr(*q*)] - Pr(*p* and *q*)

R2 is often spoken of as the ***general disjunction rule***. Let us begin our discussion by considering a special case. In certain cases statements are what we call mutually exclusive:

Definition of *Mutually Exclusive*

p and *q* are ***mutually exclusive*** if and only if Pr(*p* and *q*) = 0

In the above case, you cannot draw a card that is both an ace of of spades and a king of spades; hence Pr(drawing an ace on the draw and drawing a king on the draw) = 0. Now, if you look at R2 you should see that it has the following special case:

Rule 2.1: Special Disjunction

R2.1: Where *p* and *q* are mutually exclusive Pr(*p* or *q*) = [Pr(*p*) + Pr(*q*)]

Sometimes this special case is spoken of as the ***special disjunction rule***. The example of cards involved statements that were mutually exclusive, so we can conclude, given that the deck is fair, that each card has an equal chance of being drawn: that the probability of drawing a card that is either an ace of spades or a king of spades is 2/52.

Why do we need the general disjunction rule? Well, suppose you wonder about the chance of drawing a card that is either an ace or a spade. You concluded, by way of the special rule, that the probability of drawing a card that is either an ace or a spade is 17/52. You would be wrong. The statements involved here are not mutually exclusive: there is one card which is both an ace and a spade. So here we would use the general disjunction rule, which would tell us:

Pr(an ace or a spade) = [Pr(ace) + Pr(spade)] - Pr(ace and spade)

which is:

Pr(ace or spade) = [4/52 + 13/52] - 1/52 = 16/52.

We are in effect throwing out duplications. We may see this by looking at a complete list of aces and of spades:

Aces:	**Ace of spades,** ace of hearts, ace of diamonds, ace of clubs	**Spades:**	**Ace of spades, king of spades, queen, jack, 10, 9, 8, 7, 6, 5, 4, 3, 2 of spades**

Notice that one card, the ace of spades, occurs on both lists. If we incorrectly use the special disjunction rule, we count that card as having two distinct chances of being drawn. The outcomes are not mutually exclusive, so we would be misapplying the special rule. Our general rule tells us how to avoid this double-counting. We have a 1/52 chance of drawing the card that is on both our lists, the card that is both an ace and a spade. Note that, given the definition of mutual exclusivity, the special rule is simply a specific case of the general rule.

Suppose I tell you simply that the chance that Amil will come to a party is 1/2 and that the chance that Karim will come to a party is 1/2. Can you compute the probability that one or the other will be at the next party? The answer is that you cannot do so unless you obtain further information, namely the probability that both will be there. This point should, upon reflection, be obvious: our initial information is compatible with a situation in which the two never attend the same party but each goes to half the parties. It is also compatible with both going together to half the parties (and a number of situations in between). You need additional information in order to reach a conclusion, information that typically can only be obtained by looking at the world.

We now turn to negations. The negation of the claim that John will come is the claim that it is not the case that John will come. (Note that English contains various means of expressing negations.) Recall that we use the symbol "~" as our negation sign. Thus "~*p*" is simply the claim that it is not the case that *p*. We can now state the following, intuitively obvious, rule:

Rule 3: Negation

R3: Pr(~*p*) = 1 - Pr(*p*)

If there is a 30% chance that something will happen, there is a 70% chance that it won't. This is another rule that should cause no difficulty.

It is now time to discuss what we shall call *conditional probability*, the probability that something occurs given the occurrence of something else.

Definition of *Conditional Probability*

Pr(*q* given *p*) = Pr(*p* and *q*)/Pr(*p*)

This formula says that the probability of *q* given *p* is by definition equal to the probability of *p* and *q* divided by the probability of *p*. (You may remember from arithmetic that division by zero is impermissible; hence, if the probability of *p* is equal to 0 then Pr(*q* given *p*) is undefined.)

Let us look at a few examples. Suppose a couple is expecting a child. Here it would be plausible to say that there is roughly a 50% chance that the child will be female. However, imagine that this will be their third child, and that the previous two were female. The likelihood that the third child will be female given that the previous two were female is in fact greater than 50%. Again, a standard die has six sides, one side with one spot, another with two spots, and so on. Suppose our die is fair. What is the probability that we will throw a five on our first toss? Given only this information, we can say 1/6. But now suppose I tell you that an odd number was thrown. What is the probability that a five was thrown given that an odd number was thrown? The answer here is 1/3: there is only one outcome that is both an odd number and a five; there are three outcomes that are odd numbers.

We have not yet spoken of how to compute the probability of conjunctions. Here we need to exercise a bit of care. We shall first state a special case and then proceed to the general case.

First, note that certain statements are what we shall speak of as independent. Intuitively, a statement q is independent of a statement p just in case the fact that p is true does not affect the probability of q.

Definition of *Independent*

p and q are *independent* if and only if $Pr(q) = Pr(q$ given $p)$

Notice that we here appeal to the conditional probabilities we discussed a moment ago. Let us consider some examples of independence. Coin tosses are generally thought to be independent events. Suppose that the probability of throwing a head is 1/2. I throw the coin and it comes up tails. I then throw it again. If the tosses are independent, the probability of getting a head on the second toss remains 50%: the probability that I throw a tail on the second toss is the same as the probability that I throw a tail on the second toss given that I throw a tail on the first.

We can now state a special rule for conjunction:

Rule 4.1: Special Conjunction

R4.1: Where p and q are independent, $Pr(p$ and $q) = Pr(p) \times Pr(q)$

Where statements are independent, we obtain the probability of the conjunction by multiplying. This rule is sometimes called the *special conjunction rule*. In the coin-tossing case, the chance of getting two heads if you throw twice is 1/4.

We cannot simply assume that statements are independent. Typically, we have to look at the world to see if they are. Consider the following situation: There is a deck of cards before you. You can draw twice; the question is, what is the probability that you will draw two spades? That is, what is the probability of drawing a spade on draw 1 and a spade on draw 2? But we are missing a vital piece of information. Are we going to replace the card that you draw first, or will it stay out of the deck once drawn? If the draw involves replacement and reshuffling, then the events may plausibly be supposed to be independent. If, however, I do not replace the card you draw first, the chance of getting a spade on the second draw is clearly affected. The statements are not independent.

The rule governing any conjunction, sometimes called the *general conjunction rule*, is:

Rule 4: General Conjunction

R4: Pr(*p* and *q*) = Pr(*p*) × Pr(*q* given *p*)

This says that you multiply the probability of *p* by the probability that (*q* given that *p*) in order to obtain the probability of the conjunction (*p* and *q*). Consider the case of drawing two spades where there was no replacement, where we do not put the card we have drawn back in the deck. On the first draw the chance of drawing a spade is 13/52. But the probability of drawing a spade on the second given that you have drawn a spade on the first is only 12/51. So our rule says that in this case:

Pr(two spades) = 13/52 × 12/51.

Remember that to say that *q* is independent of *p* is to say that:

Pr(q) = Pr(q given p).

This, of course, is why the special conjunction rule is just a special case of the general conjunction rule.

Let us illustrate the application of these rules by considering some problems. First, imagine that an urn contains the following five objects: three globes, two of which are red and one green, and two cubes, one red and one yellow. We will suppose that at any point, any given object has an equal chance of being drawn. The probability of drawing a cube is, of course, 2/5, the probability of drawing a globe 3/5, and so on. Now suppose we ask what the chance is of drawing an object that is either red or yellow. No object is both red and yellow, so drawing a red object and drawing a yellow object are mutually exclusive. Given this, we know that:

Pr(drawing a red object or drawing a yellow object) = Pr(drawing a red object) + Pr(drawing a yellow object) = 3/5 + 1/5 = 4/5.

What is the chance of drawing an object that is either red or a cube? These are not mutually exclusive, so:

Pr(either drawing a red object or a cube) = Pr(drawing a red object) + Pr(drawing a cube) - Pr(drawing a red cube) = (3/5 + 2/5) - 1/5 = 4/5.

Let us move to a different problem. Suppose there are two doors to a building. Two people are entering the building; their entries are independent. Let us further suppose that the chance of entering via a given door is 1/2. What is the chance that both will enter the same door? Quite frequently, people answer 1/4, but this is wrong. Call the people *a* and *b* and the doors 1 and 2. We want to know the probability that:

_a_ and _b_ will enter door 1 or _a_ and _b_ will enter door 2.

As you will see if you utilize the rules to compute this probability, the answer is 1/2 rather than 1/4.

Suppose there are three houses each belonging to different individuals; call the individuals *a*, *b*, and *c*. Now let us suppose that there is a 1/3 chance of an individual entering a house, but that only one person will enter a given house. What is the probability that each will end up in her own house? Note that we can view this as the question of what the probability is that:

((_a_ will enter _a_'s house and _b_ will enter _b_'s house) and _c_ will enter _c_'s house).

The probability that *a* will enter her house is 1/3. However, the three statements are not independent. The chance that *b* will enter her house given that *a* has entered hers is 1/2: try to see why. And the likelihood that *c* will enter her house given that *a* and *b* have each entered their own house is 1.

So our overall result is that the probability of all three entering their own home is 1/6. Let us label the houses the *a* house, the *b* house, and the *c* house. Here are the possible outcomes:

a in *a* house	*b* in *b* house	*c* in *c* house
a in *a* house	*b* in *c* house	*c* in *b* house
a in *b* house	*b* in *a* house	*c* in *c* house
a in *b* house	*b* in *c* house	*c* in *a* house
a in *c* house	*b* in *a* house	*c* in *b* house
a in *c* house	*b* in *b* house	*c* in *a* house

In one out of the six cases they are each at home.

1.3 / Some Tricks and Common Mistakes

In a more advanced study, we would now proceed to study a variety of mathematical techniques that would enable us to compute probabilities rather more quickly than we can by following our rules. But our rules as they stand enable us to compute probabilities for the cases with which we are concerned. We will, however, look at some tricks that will speed the computational process a bit.

We shall look at one common trick in connection with the following case. Suppose I allow you four coin tosses. What is your chance of throwing at least one head? To throw at least one head is to throw a head on either the first, the second, the third, or the fourth toss. We could work out the answer to our question in the following, very tedious fashion:

Step 1: You throw a head on either the first or the second toss. The probability of this is 3/4, as you should be able to see.

Step 2: You throw either (a head on the first or second) or a head on the third. Here "(a head on the first or second)" functions as *p* and "a head on the third" functions as *q*. So the overall probability is equal to (the probability of *p* + the probability of *q*) - (the probability of *p* and *q*). You should be able to see that this is:

(3/4 + 1/2) - (3/4 × 1/2) = 7/8

Step 3: You throw either (a head on the first or second or third) or a head on the fourth. Proceeding as in step 2, we obtain:

(7/8 + 1/2) - (7/8 × 1/2) = 15/16

There is nothing wrong with doing the problem this way, but the following trick would make the calculations less laborious. You could note that throwing at least one head is logically equivalent to not throwing all tails. It is easy to see that the probability of throwing all tails is 1/16. So, by using our rule for negations, we know that the probability of not throwing all tails is 15/16. Hence that is the probability of the logical equivalent, throwing at least one head.

Suppose you were told that an urn contained 15 pink balls and 10 green balls. You will draw from the urn twice without replacing the ball you draw. What is the chance that you will draw exactly one green ball? In order to solve this sort of problem, you must think of a good way of describing the situation. What does drawing exactly one green ball amount to? You should be able to see that it is equivalent to either drawing a green on the first and a pink on the second, or a pink on the first and a green on the second. Once you have described the situation in this way, the computation is straightforward. The probability of a green on the first and a pink on the second = (10/25 × 15/24). The probability of a pink on the first and a green on the second = (15/25 × 10/24). Since these two outcomes are mutually exclusive, we obtain the probability of one or the other simply by adding the two.

One of the kinds of mistake people frequently make arises out of a type of problem we looked at before. Suppose three people are heading toward a building that has three doors. Let us also suppose the actions of the three are independent and random — that there is a 1/3 chance of a person entering any given door. What is the chance that they all enter the same door? Many people will say 1/27, but this is incorrect. There are three doors; call them 1, 2, and 3. There is indeed a 1/27 chance of entering, say, door 1. But the three people may enter the same door by entering either door 1, 2, or 3, so the correct answer is 3/27.

This failure to notice that there is more than one way in which the favorable outcome could be realized no doubt underlies the following typical underestimate. Suppose there is a class of 30 people. There is nothing special about the class — it is merely a random sample of the population. Off the top of your head would you judge it very likely, likely, about 50-50, unlikely, or very unlikely that at least two of those people were born on the same day? Many people judge this to be either unlikely or very unlikely. The correct answer is, however, about 50-50, indeed slightly more likely than not.

We looked above at some questions involving the likelihood that exactly *n* things would happen (for example, that three people would enter a building by the same door). The underestimates of which we are speaking occur in this kind of case too, and are often accompanied by another kind of error. Let us return to a case of the three persons — call them *a*, *b*, and *c* — heading toward doors 1, 2, and 3. Throughout, we assume the actions of *a*, *b*, and *c* are independent and random. At each point below, try to figure out your own answer before reading further.

What is the chance that only *a* and *b* will enter, let us say, door 1? The response is often 1/9. The person who gives this answer is clearly just using our special conjunction rule. Unfortunately, that rule yields the correct answer to a different question: what is the probability that at least *a* and *b* will enter through door 1. Our question was, what is the probability that *a* and *b* enter while *c* does not? This is $1/3 \times 1/3 \times 2/3$. What is the probability that exactly two will enter through door 1?

It is, of course, not 1/9, but it is not $1/3 \times 1/3 \times 2/3$ either. For in this case there are the following favorable outcomes:

> **_a_ and _b_ do; _c_ doesn't.**
> **_a_ does, _b_ doesn't, and _c_ does.**
> **_a_ doesn't, _b_ and _c_ do.**

Each of these favorable outcomes has a probability of 2/27. Since there are three of them, the answer to our question is 2/9. (Note that the above three are mutually exclusive, so we added to obtain our result.)

Finally: what is the probability that exactly two will enter through the same door? Given what we have done above, the answer to this is easy enough to find. They can enter through either 1, 2, or 3, so the answer, again because the outcomes are mutually exclusive, is 2/3.

Let us suppose that there are two people in the room, that their birthdays are independent, and that there is a 1/12 chance that a person is born in a given month. What is the chance that both people were born in April? Well, this is straightforward enough: the answer is $1/12 \times 1/12$. Of course, the probability that the two were born in the same month is $12 \times 1/12 \times 1/12$, but that is not the question that was asked.

Now let us change the evidential situation somewhat. I, who was born in April, look at a person I do not know and ask: What is the chance that that person and I were both born in April? The answer to this question is simply 1/12. The events are independent, but the probability that I was born in April is 1, so the correct calculation is not $1/12 \times 1/12$, but $1 \times 1/12$. What has changed is our evidence, or information regarding the situation.

Suppose a draw of two cards has been made, with replacement, from a group of 10 cards that consists of two queens and a three through a ten. What is the chance that two queens were drawn? This is quite straightforward. Given that there was replacement, the probability is that of a queen being drawn on the first multiplied by the probability of a queen being drawn on the second, that is, $2/10 \times 2/10$. Now suppose we are told that the second card drawn was a queen. We now want to know what the chance is that two queens were drawn. Here the answer is clearly 2/10. We know that the second card drawn was a queen, and there is a 2/10 chance that the other card was a queen. But now suppose we are told that either the first or the second card drawn is a queen. What is the chance that two queens were drawn? It is tempting to think it is still 2/10, but this is incorrect. Let us try to see why. Out of the 100 overall possible outcomes, there are 36 in which at least one queen is drawn. But of that 36 only 4 are cases where 2 queens have been drawn. Recall that our definition of conditional probability was that the probability of q given p is equal to the probability of p and q divided by the probability of p. Let us work this through. p is here the statement that either the first card drawn is a queen or the second card drawn is a queen. q is the statement that both are queens. The probability that p and q is 4/100, while the probability that p is 36/100. From this we obtain our 4/36, which illustrates that our intuitions regarding conditional probabilities must be taken with a grain of salt.

Here is a final example of a kind of problem that does on occasion pose problems. Suppose you are playing a card game (you do not need to understand the game in order to do the problem, which can be solved on the basis of the information supplied). You have five cards, three of which are hearts. Let us suppose that they are the ace, king, and queen. You have, as well, a ten of spades and a nine of clubs. You will throw away those two cards (they do not return to the deck). There are 47 cards remaining in the deck, from which you will randomly pick two to replace the two you discarded. Your hand will be improved if you draw from the 47 remaining cards any of the following:

- **two hearts**
- **one ace or king or queen and one of any non-ace, non-king, and non-queen**
- **an ace and a king, an ace and a queen, or a king and a queen**
- **a pair of anything (a pair is, for example, two kings or two tens)**

The question is, what is your chance of improving your hand? Note that since these alternatives are mutually exclusive, we may compute them individually and add the probabilities to obtain our result.

A 4-Step Example

Step 1:
Two hearts:
$(10/47 \times 9/46) = 90/(47 \times 46)$

Step 2:
An ace and a card other than an ace, king, or queen. Note that here you can get an ace on the first and the other on the second or vice versa. There are 38 cards other than aces, kings, and queens among the 47. So, we have:
$[(3/47 \times 38/46) + (38/47 \times 3/46)] = 228/(47 \times 46)$
The probability is the same for a king or queen and something else, so for this step our result is:
$3 \times [(3/47 \times 38/46) + (38/47 \times 3/46)] = 684/(47 \times 46)$

Step 3:
An ace and king, ace and queen, or king and queen. You can get an ace on the first and a king on the second or vice versa. So, recalling that there are only three aces and three kings left, the chance of getting an ace and a king is:
$[(3/47 \times 3/46) + (3/47 \times 3/46)] = 18/(47 \times 46)$
Since there are three cases like this, our result is:
$3 \times [(3/47 \times 3/46) + (3/47 \times 3/46)] = 54/(47 \times 46)$

Step 4:
A pair. Here we must recall that there are only three each of aces, kings, queens, tens, and nines remaining — we have an ace, king, and queen in our hand and have thrown away one ten and one nine. There are four each of the other eight kinds of cards. Let us do the groups of three first, say, the aces. In the case of the aces, we have:
$(3/47 \times 2/46) = 6/(47 \times 46)$

There are five cases like this, so our result is:
$$5 \times (3/47 \times 2/46) = 30/(47 \times 46)$$
For each case where there are four remaining, we get:
$$(4/47 \times 3/46) = 12/(47 \times 46)$$
Since there are eight such cases, our result is:
$$8 \times (4/47 \times 3/46) = 96/(47 \times 46)$$
We have broken our problem down into mutually exclusive cases, and so we obtain as our final result:
$$(90 + 684 + 54 + 30 + 96)/(47 \times 46) = 954/2162$$

We have, then, approximately a 44% chance of improving our hand. Note that while this problem took rather a long time to go through, it was not difficult; we simply had to think through the various kinds of cases.

We will now indulge in a bit of mathematics that will come in handy for quickly computing certain probabilities if you remember factorials. 5! (we use as is standard ! as our sign for factorials) is 5x4x3x2x1. 0! is taken to be equal to 1. Using our techniques, it is rather tedious to compute the chances of, for example, getting 3 heads on 5 flips of a fair coin. Here is a formula we can use in a situation where we have only two jointly exhaustive and mutually exclusive outcomes. We assume that the tosses are independent and that, if we are using a sample of any size from any given number of tosses, the sample is randomly selected. We will call this a ***binomial probability***.

Binomial Probability

Let **s** be the number of successes, **N** be the number of events and **r** be the probability of a success. $Pr(s) = [N!/(s! \times (N - s)!] \times r^s \times (1 - r)^{N-s}$

We then have:

$$[(5 \times 4 \times 3 \times 2 \times 1 / 3 \times 2 \times 1 \times 2 \times 1) \times .5^3 \times .5^2$$

which is:

$$10 \times .125 \times .25$$

The probability of this is .3125. Our formula is a bit messy, but it does facilitate calculation.

2 / Bayes' Theorem

2.1 / The Basics

Having looked at conditional probabilities, we might wonder whether there is any systematic relation between the probability of *q* given *p* and the probability of *p* given *q*. If there is, it is not a simple one. The probability that a spade was drawn given that a two was drawn is 1/4, whereas the probability that a two was drawn given that a spade was drawn is 1/13. The probability that a pet is warm-blooded given that it is a bird is no doubt 1, but I do not know the probability that a pet is a bird given that it is warm-blooded; it cannot be very high.

There is a systematic relation between these probabilities that can be computed by the use of what has come to be known as Bayes' theorem. In order to facilitate our presentation of these relations we will introduce a new notational convention.

Notational Convention

Pr(*p* given *q*) is abbreviated as "Pr(*p* | *q*)"

We shall develop the full version of this theorem in steps. As a first step, note the preliminary to the theorem:

Bayes' Theorem: Simple Preliminary

$$\Pr(p \mid q) = \Pr(p) \times \Pr(q \mid p) / \Pr(q)$$

We can also see how it is that this preliminary is a straightforward consequence of our definition of conditional probabilities and our rules. The definition, you will recall, was:

Pr(*q* given *p*) = Pr(*p* and *q*)/Pr(*p*)

So:

Pr(*p* given q) = Pr(*q* and p)/Pr(*q*)

Note that by our logical equivalence rule, rule 1.3, Pr(*q* and *p*)= Pr(*p* and *q*), so we know that:

Pr(*p* given q) = Pr(*p* and q)/Pr(*q*)

Using general conjunction, rule 4, and introducing our abbreviation we get:

Pr(*p* | *q*) = Pr(*p*) x Pr(*q* | *p*)/Pr(*q*)

This is just our simple preliminary. After doing all this work let us see what we can do with what we have.

Here is one example. Suppose that an urn contains 40 cubes and 60 spheres. There are 10 pink cubes and 30 green cubes, 40 pink spheres and 20 green spheres. Let us assume that a pink object has been drawn. What we wish to know is the probability that a sphere was drawn given that a pink object was drawn. The probability that a pink object was drawn given that a sphere is drawn was 2/3. Using our preliminary formula:

Pr(sphere | pink) = Pr(sphere) × Pr (pink | sphere) / Pr(pink)

We then obtain:

Pr(sphere | pink) = (60/100 × 40/60)/(50/100) = 24/30

This should fit in with your intuition. You found out that a pink object was drawn. You know that the percentage of pinks among spheres is higher than the percentage of pinks among cubes. So your new information should give you better reason than you had at the start to believe that the object drawn was a sphere.

We have not yet developed a full version of Bayes' theorem. We need first to introduce *total probability*:

Total Probability

$$\text{Pr}(q) = [\{\text{Pr}(p) \times \text{Pr}(q \mid p)\} + \{\text{Pr}(\sim p) \times \text{Pr}(q \mid \sim p)\}]$$

This may look forbidding, but the idea is really quite straightforward. For example, the chance that I will go to a certain party is the sum of (1) the chance that you will go and that I will go given that you do go, and (2) the chance that you won't go and that I will go given that you don't go. You may recall that q is logically equivalent to [(p and q) or ($\sim p$ and q)]. Our total probability is then obtained via an application of general conjunction. Try working this out for yourself.

We are now in a position to state a version of Bayes' theorem:

Bayes' Theorem: Fuller Version

Where $\Pr(q)$ is not equal to 0,
$$\Pr(p \mid q) = \Pr(p) \times \Pr(q \mid p) /$$
$$[\Pr(p) \times \Pr(q \mid p)] + [\Pr(\sim p) \times \Pr(q \mid \sim p)]$$

In the simple preliminary we came to see the following:

$$\Pr(p \mid q) = \Pr(p) \times \Pr(q \mid p) / \Pr(q)$$

Note that our fuller version is obtained immediately via total probability. Again we might wonder what all of this will enable us to do.

In our discussion of our simple preliminary we were faced with only one urn. Let us now suppose there are two urns. Urn A contains 40 balls, 10 of which are yellow and 30 of which are red. Urn B contains 20 balls; of these 8 are yellow and 12 are red. There is, in advance, a 40% chance that urn A is drawn from and a 60% chance that urn B is drawn from. This much, we suppose, you know. You then find out that a yellow ball has been drawn. We can now ask what the probability is that urn A was the one drawn from. We are, in effect, asking for the probability that urn A was drawn from given that a yellow ball was drawn. We do need to know what the probability is that a yellow ball was drawn. You should see that this probability is the probability that either urn A is drawn from and a yellow ball is drawn or urn B is drawn from and a yellow ball is drawn. You can, of course, compute this probability. It is:

$$(40/100 \times 10/40) + (60/100 \times 8/20)$$

In this case we have only two urns, and one or the other will be drawn from, so the probability that urn B is drawn from is just the probability that urn A is not drawn from. Given this we will now use our fuller version of Bayes' theorem to answer our question. In the numerator we have:

Pr(urn A is drawn from) × Pr(a yellow ball was drawn given that urn A is drawn from).

The probability that urn A is drawn from is often spoken of as a *prior probability*. In this case, we specified that this probability was 4/10. If you look back to the contents of urn A, you will see that the chance that a yellow ball is drawn given that urn A is drawn from is 1/4. So our numerator is:

(4/10 × 1/4) = 4/40 = 1/10

In the denominator we have what we just called the total probability of *q*, in this case the probability of a yellow ball being drawn regardless of which urn is drawn from. Given that drawing from urn B is the only alternative to drawing from urn A, the denominator is:

[Pr(urn A is drawn from) × Pr(a yellow was drawn | urn A is drawn from)] + [Pr(urn B is drawn from) × Pr(a yellow was drawn | urn B was drawn from)]

Note that this is a use of the fuller version, since we are taking advantage of the fact that the probability that urn A is not drawn from is the probability that B is drawn from. The probability that urn B is drawn from is 6/10, while the probability that a yellow ball was drawn given that urn B was drawn from is 8/20. And 6/10 × 8/20 = 48/200. So our denominator is:

1/10 + 48/200 = 68/200

We now have:

1/10 / 68/200 = 200/680 = 5/17

The prior probability that urn A was drawn from is, you will recall, 40%. The fraction 5/17 is often called the ***posterior probability***, that which we obtain after taking account of the fact that a yellow ball was drawn. Since 5/17 is approximately 30%, your new information renders it less likely that urn A was drawn from.

We will soon turn away from urns to more concrete applications of Bayes' theorem. However, we will first introduce a fully general version of it. After all, right now we cannot, it would seem, treat of situations in which we have more than two urns. Notice that in

p or ~p

the disjuncts are mutually exclusive. They are further *jointly exhaustive*. That is, all the alternatives are covered in that at least one of the disjuncts must be true. Suppose now that

$p_1, p_2 \cdots p_n$

are mutually exclusive and jointly exhaustive:

Bayes' Theorem: Full Version

Where $\Pr(q)$ is not equal to 0,
and $p_1 \ldots p_n$ are mutually exclusive and jointly exhaustive
$\Pr(p_1 \mid q) = \Pr(p_1) \times \Pr(q \mid p_1) / [\Pr(p_1) \times \Pr(q \mid p_1)] +$
$[\Pr(p_2) \times \Pr(q \mid p_2)] \ldots + [\Pr(p_n) \times \Pr(q \mid p_n)]$

Notice that our fuller version is a special case of this full version. It is difficult to understand theorems like this in the 'abstract', so let us turn to some applications.

2.2 / Applications of Bayes' Theorem

When we find new evidence, whether we are engaging in some scientific study or trying to solve a practical problem, we may find that Bayes' theorem gives us some help. In order to see this, we need to look at some more examples.

Consider the following situation. There has been an armed robbery. Let **R** be the hypothesis that **r** committed the crime and **S** be the hypothesis that **s** committed the crime. We know that **R** and **S** are mutually exclusive and jointly exhaustive; that is, we know that one but not both of **r** and **s** committed the crime. Let us suppose that the prior probability of **R** is 20% and the prior probability of **S** is 80%. We also know that **r** uses a gun rather than a knife only 80% of the time, while the probability that **s** uses a gun is 10%. We discover that **G**, a gun was used. Who is now, given this information, the best suspect? That is, what are the posterior probabilities of **R** and **S**? Using Bayes' theorem we need to compute:

$$[Pr(R) \times Pr(\ G\ |\ R\ )]\ /\{[Pr(R) \times Pr(\ G\ |\ R\ )] + [Pr(S) \times Pr(\ G\ |\ S)]\}$$

The numerator of our equation is then:

$$2/10 \times 8/10 = 16/100$$

and the denominator is:

$$16/100 + (8/10 \times 1/10) = 24/100$$

The posterior probability that **R,** that **r** did it, is thus 2/3. Let us now check the posterior probability of **S**.

$$[Pr(S) \times Pr(\ G\ |\ S\ )]\ /\{[Pr(S) \times Pr(\ G\ |\ S\ )] + [Pr(R) \times Pr(\ G\ |\ R)]\}$$

This numerator is:

$$8/10 \times 1/10 = 8/100$$

while the denominator is:

$$16/100 + (8/10 \times 1/10) = 24/100$$

which is 1/3. Note that in this case **S** is equivalent to ~**R** so we could have used R3 to obtain this answer.

Suppose we know that **a** is ill. We have currently narrowed the possibilities as to the kind of disease to the mutually exclusive and jointly exhaustive set of diseases d_1, d_2, and d_3. We also know that among the people who have this kind of disease 50% have d_1, 30% have d_2, and 20% have d_3. If the appropriate treatments for the diseases were all the same it might not matter which one **a** had. It sometimes, for example, does not particularly matter which strain of flu we have. In such a case we might not bother obtaining further information. But in other cases different treatments might be appropriate for the different diseases. Suppose we have a test for d_2, which is not infallible but which will be positive in 60% of the cases in which d_2 is present. We give **a** the test, and he tests positive. Notice that it would be a mistake, a very common kind of mistake, to say that there is now a 60% chance that he has d_2 or even that it is more likely than not that he has it.

We are *not* taking into account an important question — namely, how probable is it that he would test positive given that he did not have d_2 but instead either had d_1 or had d_3. Let us suppose our studies indicate that there is a 20% chance of testing positive if one has d_1 and a 50% chance of testing positive if one has d_3. Here our test clearly does not 'discriminate' well between d_2 and d_3. However, our information is sufficient to enable us to use Bayes' theorem.

We will ask ourselves initially how likely it is, given the new information, that he has d_2. We will use D_1 for the statement that he has d_1, D_2 for d_2, and D_3 for d_3. We will use T for the statement that the test came out positive. So, initially, we are asking for $\Pr(D_2$ given $T)$. This is:

$$\Pr(D_2) \times \Pr(T \mid D_2) \, / \\ [\Pr(D_2) \times \Pr(T \mid D_2)] + [\Pr(D_1) \times \Pr(T \mid D_1)] + [\Pr(D_3) \times \Pr(T \mid D_3)]$$

Recall that the prior probability of D_2 was 30%. That is, 30/100 or .3, while the $\Pr(D_1$ given $T)$ was 60%, that is, 60/100 or .6. So we have now:

$$.3 \times .6 \, / \\ [.3 \times .6] + [\Pr(D_1) \times \Pr(T \mid D_1)] + [\Pr(D_3) \times \Pr(T \mid D_3)]$$

Using our other information we can move to:

$$.3 \times .6 \, / \\ [.3 \times .6] + [.5 \times .2] + [.2 \times .5]$$

If you compute this you will see that we can conclude, given our new information that there is about a 47% probability that our person has d_2. But what is the chance that he has d_1? We cannot simply assume that its probability given our new information is the same as its prior probability of 50%.

$$\Pr(D_1) \times \Pr(T \mid D_1) \, / \\ [\Pr(D_1) \times \Pr(T \mid D_1)] + [\Pr(D_2) \times \Pr(T \mid D_2)] + [\Pr(D_3) \times \Pr(T \mid D_3)]$$

This is:

$$.5 \times .2 \, / \\ [.5 \times .2] + [.3 \times .6] + [.2 \times .5]$$

We can now conclude that the posterior probability of his having d_1 is about 26%, which is also, as you should see, the posterior probability of his having d_3. In one sense we are not in a better position. That is, our test was not sufficiently discriminating to enable us to decide with any degree of certainty which disease he has. In a situation in which the particular identity of the disease was important, we might seek new tests. Notice that we would take the posterior probabilities from the first tests as the prior probabilities we would use to assess the significance of those new tests.

Chapter Summary

In Section 1 we introduced the primary system. In 1.1 we discussed various concepts of probability. The first which we introduced was the concept of probability as ***mathematical odds***. We here typically take it that each of the outcomes has an equal chance of being selected. Here then our probabilities are ratios of favorable to possible outcomes. We then noted that we are often concerned with probability as ***relative frequency***. Relative frequencies indicate the proportion of the members of one class or group that are members of another class or group. Finally we spoke of ***credibility***, the degree to which it is rational to believe something. Often credibility statements will not be expressed numerically.

We then, in 1.2, turned to the probability calculus. This consists primarily of definitions and a set of rules:

Definitions

Definition of *Mutually Exclusive*

p and *q* are ***mutually exclusive*** if and only if $\Pr(p \text{ and } q) = 0$

Definition of *Conditional Probability*

$\Pr(q \text{ given } p) = \Pr(p \text{ and } q)/\Pr(p)$

Definition of *Independent*

p and *q* are ***independent*** if and only if $\Pr(q) = \Pr(q \text{ given } p)$

Rules of the Probability Calculus

Rules 1.1 - 1.3

R1.1: Where *p* is a logically true statement, $\Pr(p) = 1$
R1.2: Where *p* is a logically false statement, $\Pr(p) = 0$
R1.3: Where *p* and *q* are logically equivalent, $\Pr(p) = \Pr(q)$

Rule 2: General Disjunction

R2: $\Pr(p \text{ or } q) = [\Pr(p) + \Pr(q)] - \Pr(p \text{ and } q)$

Rule 2.1: Special Disjunction

R2.1: Where *p* and *q* are mutually exclusive
$\Pr(p \text{ or } q) = [\Pr(p) + \Pr(q)]$

Rule 3: Negation

R3: $\Pr(\sim p) = 1 - \Pr(p)$

Rule 4: General Conjunction

R4: $\Pr(p \text{ and } q) = \Pr(p) \times \Pr(q \text{ given } p)$

Rule 4.1: Special Conjunction

R4.1: Where *p* and q are independent,
$\Pr(p \text{ and } q) = \Pr(p) \times \Pr(q)$

Notice that we generally need information regarding the probabilities in order to apply our calculus.

In 1.3 we turned to a discussion of some tricks and some common mistakes. Here we also introduced a quick means of calculating certain probabilities:

Binomial Probability

Let *s* be the number of successes, **N** be the number of events and *r* be the probability of a success.
$$\Pr(s) = [N!/(s! \times (N - s)!] \times r^{s} \times (1 - r)^{N - s}$$

In Section 2 we introduced Bayes' theorem. This enables us to see the relation between Pr(*p* given *q*) and Pr(*q* given *p*). We also saw how we can take into account new information which we might obtain. In 2.1 we introduced the basics. We utilized a notational convention:

Notational Convention

Pr(*p* given *q*) is abbrieviated as "Pr(*p* | *q*)"

---

and a simple preliminary:

Bayes' Theorem: Simple Preliminary

Pr(*p* | *q*) = Pr(*p*) × Pr(*q* | *p*) / Pr(*q*)

We then introduced *total probability*:

Total Probability

Pr(*q*) = [{Pr(*p*) × Pr(*q* | *p*)} + {Pr(~*p*) × Pr(*q* | ~*p*)}]

This led to a fuller version of Bayes's theorem:

Bayes' Theorem: Fuller Version

Where Pr(*q*) is not equal to 0,
Pr(*p* | *q*) = Pr(*p*) × Pr(*q* | *p*) /
[Pr(*p*) × Pr(*q* | *p*)] + [Pr(~*p*) × Pr(*q* | ~*p*)]

We then closed 2.1 with a full statement of the theorem:

Bayes' Theorem: Full Version

Where $\Pr(q)$ is not equal to 0,
and $p_1 \dots p_n$ are mutually exclusive and jointly exhaustive
$\Pr(p_1 \mid q) = \Pr(p_1) \times \Pr(q \mid p_1) / [\Pr(p_1) \times \Pr(q \mid p_1)] + [\Pr(p_2) \times \Pr(q \mid p_2)] \dots + [\Pr(p_n) \times \Pr(q \mid p_n)]$

By the use of Bayes' theorem we were able to move from ***prior probabilities*** to ***posterior probabilities*** that took into account information which we might have obtained.

In 2.2 we turned to applications of Bayes' Theorem. These involve computation, but did illustrate taking new information into account.

CHAPTER 12

Inductive Generalizations

In this chapter we will be primarily concerned with a kind of argument that we will speak of as *inductive generalization*. This kind of argument is very familiar to us from, for example, reports of the results of polls. We are inundated with reports, based upon samples, of the popularity of our governments, our politicians, and public policies. For good or ill, decisions that concern us are often based upon such reports. We shall also briefly consider arguments concerned with averages.

However, we should recognize that the kind of argument with which we are now concerned is not restricted to contexts such as political polling. Inductive generalization is common in scientific research and in ordinary life. For example, it is of concern to commercial fishermen and those who set limits upon their catches to know how many fish there are and whether the fish are mature enough to reproduce. We are not in a position to examine each and every portion of the ocean, so what we do is to draw conclusions based upon samples. In the case of fisheries this may involve netting at particular points. Based on the results of our sampling, we may conclude that there is an abundance of fish or that they are scarce. The reliability of our conclusions is, of course, important, as people's livelihoods depend upon the policy decisions based on those conclusions. Again, how many people are HIV-positive? Here as well, because of both cost and concern for individual rights, we are not in a position to examine each and every person in our society. So again we draw conclusions based upon samples of the total population. The conclusions we draw may well affect the direction of our social policies; consequently they should be well-founded.

Do not think that the situations in which we use inductive generalization need be ones that are socially significant. As I look at my watch I realize it is time for my bus to come. It will take me three minutes to walk to my bus stop, but I walk out anyway. I have taken this bus many times before, and I know that it is usually late. This knowledge is, as in the preceding cases, based upon a sample.

1 / Inductive Generalization

1.1 / Appealing to Samples: An Initial Approach

One of the most common forms of inductive reasoning can initially be characterized as follows:

Elementary *Inductive Generalization*

X% of observed *F* (the sample) are *G*.
Therefore, *X*% of *F* (the population) are *G*.

We shall call this sort of argument *inductive generalization*. Recall that in Chapter 3 we introduced the terms *statistical generalization* and *universal generalization*. Those terms were utilized to classify certain kinds of sentences or statements. An *inductive generalization* is *not* a kind of statement, but, as we said, a kind of argument. As you can see, in such arguments we are appealing to a sample. The sample, that is to say, the *F* that we observe, is some (often unknown) percentage of the total number of *F*, the total population. Our conclusion will be either a statistical or a universal generalization, depending upon the results obtained from our sample. If, for example, our sample yields either 0% or 100% we might (though, as we shall see, we need not) conclude that either no or all *F* are *G*.

How shall we assess such arguments? The first rough point to note is that the size of our sample, or more precisely the size of our sample in relation to the size of the overall population, is of some importance. If we know little or nothing about the characteristics of the population, that is the population of all the *F* there are, then typically the larger the size of the sample the better off we are. In some cases we may attempt to generalize from a sample that is "too small". In such a case we shall say that the argument in question commits the *fallacy of hasty generalization*. Typically, a sample of one gives us too small a sample. Suppose, for example, you meet a person for the first time. The person is in a bad mood. You conclude that the person is typically in a bad mood. Your argument is indeed a bad one, and it illustrates the sort of mistake that we have labelled hasty generalization. Here it is obvious that the argument is a bad one. But please note that we cannot make any absolute judgment regarding how large a sample need be. In some particular cases we may know antecedently that the population is, with respect to the feature we are investigating, quite uniform. Suppose we are investigating the composition of water. We have antecedent reason to believe that water is reasonably uniform with respect to its composition: there is little variation. Here, if we find that our sample of water is H_2O, we do have good reason to believe that that is what water is like. In the case of the person in the bad mood, we did not have any particular reason to judge that his moods remained much the same over time. There might, for all we know, be considerable variation. Given that we had no evidence for uniformity in that case, we counted the argument as a fallacious one.

There is another way of identifying the problem with too small a sample. Suppose we are interested in what typical students think about some issue. We pick one student at random and question her; she says that she thinks **Y**. We would not conclude on the basis of this sample of one, at least given that we do not know that the attitudes of students are uniform, that virtually all students think **Y**. Were we to make a new survey, to sample the students again, the student we grab might well say that he thinks **X**. This would not improve our position. The problem here might be characterized as one of impreciseness. If we continued to use the method of sampling one student at a time and drawing a conclusion on the basis of that sample, the conclusion we reached on the basis of each sample could vary from one sample to the next. Choosing a large enough sample would be more likely to achieve similar results, and hence lead us to a similar conclusion, each time.

Detailed study of this claim would require more of an excursion into mathematics than is possible here and now. But think about the point in this way. Suppose we have a population of twenty children in a room. Five of the children are named Smith, five are named Alomar, five are named Carter, and five are named Kazmi. You do not know that this is the distribution of the names. You are allowed to sample either one or two of the children. Clearly, you would think it better to sample two of them: one seems too small a sample. Two might be too small a sample as well, but it is clearly a bit better. Suppose that you are very busy and choose to look at only one child. In the context, if you select again you have only a 25% chance of getting the same result. Suppose, however, that we sample two of the children. The likelihood that any other sample of two children would be the same as or at least overlap with your first sample is higher. Overlapping may be illustrated in this way. Suppose the first time you get a Carter and a Kazmi. If you drew a Carter and a Smith the second time, we would say that the samples overlap. If we take large enough samples, we are likely to obtain the same sort of sample or one that overlaps to a high degree. In this sense, the method of choosing large enough samples is more precise, and using a method that gives us too small a sample is imprecise: it is a method that would likely give us different results, different samples, were we to resample.

Our worry regarding the precision of a sample is related to a more fundamental concern. Is our sample genuinely representative of the larger population? Is the variation in it with respect to the question at hand like the variation in the population at large? If a sample is not representative, we shall speak of the sample as a non-representative sample. Clearly our hope, when we utilize inductive generalization, is that the sample to which we appeal is a representative one. However, the best we can typically do is to adopt a method of obtaining samples that is likely to give us a representative sample. A method that involves taking too small a sample is a method that is not likely to lead to a representative sample.

There is another factor to consider, a factor distinct from the size of the sample that our method tells us to take. Suppose I want to determine whether university students approve of a complete ban on smoking on campus. I walk over to the smoking area and ask the people who are puffing away what they think about a complete ban on smoking. Suppose 80% indicate that they are opposed to such a ban. It should be apparent that I would be presenting a bad argument if I now concluded that a large majority of students are opposed to a ban on smoking. But we must be careful in our statement of the mistake. The sample might in fact be a representative one; but the method I have used to obtain the sample is not one that is likely to yield a representative sample. The problem here is not, as it was with taking too small a sample, that resampling would yield divergent, conflicting results. The problem is that I am likely, given my method of looking only in smoking areas, to get a distribution of views that is not representative. I am considering, in effect, only the views of smokers. The method I utilized to obtain the sample was one that, with respect to the question at hand, was likely to give me a non-representative sample. We will characterize a method of obtaining a sample as *biased* when it is one that is likely to lead to non-representative samples that systematically over-represent or under-represent some portion of the population. And we shall say that any argument constructed by the use of a biased method commits the *fallacy of biased statistics*.

Keep in mind that samples may be chosen by precise methods but nonetheless be biased. Suppose you sample each day the opinion of a large number of people outside of a fundamentalist church; you ask them whether or not they approve of allowing the sale of mildly pornographic literature. You might always get the result that almost all of them disapprove of the sale of such material. It would be rash to draw any conclusion regarding the country's population at large on the basis of this method of sampling. The problem here is the bias rather than the imprecision of the method. Similarly, you would not wish to base a general claim about the incidence of a given disease on its incidence within people currently resident in a hospital.

We also have a tendency to be overimpressed by the sheer size of certain samples. Perhaps thousands and thousands of people daily phone in to talk shows to express their opposition to gun control. Arguments based upon samples consisting of those who make an effort to respond typically commit the fallacy of biased statistics. Opponents of gun control are, for example, often well-organized and active in expressing their views. Those in favor of gun control are, as matters stand, less likely to make the effort to express their views.

1.2 / A More Detailed Approach

It is not my intent to provide a thorough account of sampling methods; to do so we would have to indulge in a bit more mathematics than is here appropriate. Nonetheless I shall attempt to provide a distant glimpse of the technical material.

One of the most common ways of attempting to avoid biased samples is by using the unbiased method of *random sampling*. This method is particularly useful if either the population is quite varied or we simply lack information about how varied the population is. We use random sampling so that each member of the population at large has an equal chance of being selected for the sample. So, if you wish to obtain information about Calgarians, you will not be randomly selecting if you throw darts at the pages of a phone book and call the numbers that the darts hit, for many reasons, including the obvious one that not everyone has a phone. And even if we use random sampling and thereby avoid the fallacy of biased statistics, we must also take care to avoid the fallacy of hasty generalization.

However, that a sample is not strictly speaking a random one need not mean that we should draw no conclusion from that sample. Suppose we did the following. At ten in the morning we go into the student union building. We know that students of all sorts go to this building from time to time. We ask thirty or so students who are sitting around whether they found their high school education satisfactory. Let us suppose that twenty say they did not. This sample is not a randomly selected one, but here we do not have any particular reason to believe that these students are unrepresentative of the general student population. Our survey does give us some evidence in favor of the claim that a majority of students, or at least something near that, believe their high school eduction was not satisfactory.

On occasion, our larger population may be broken into groups. Consider a division of eligible student voters by faculty. Let us suppose that students in a given faculty tend to vote the same way. Suppose further that we know what percentage of the total voting population is in each faculty. We could in this case stick with a random sample of the student population. Such a sample would normally need to be somewhat large, but we can here get by with a smaller sample, which will often be better. What we are doing is called *stratified random sampling*. The core of the idea is simple enough: We sample a few randomly selected students from each faculty. We now have good information about each faculty. And given this information and the information we have about each faculty's percentage of the total student population, we are in a position to make a tolerably decent claim about the results of an election. Here is a quite trivial example. Suppose there are four faculties; that students are voting "yes" or "no" to some proposition; and that faculty A contains 40% of the total population, faculty B 25%, faculty C 20%, and faculty D 15%. Suppose further that everyone in each faculty tends to act in the same way. We sample a student in faculty A and that student will vote "yes"; a student in B will vote "no"; a student in C will boycott the vote; and a student in D will vote "yes". We conclude the following: somewhere around 80% of the students will vote, and the measure will receive roughly 69% of the votes cast. (Note that this conclusion is a bit too specific: we would be on safer ground if we concluded that the measure would pass.)

You may have noted that polls are often based upon an extremely small sample. A good part of the reason for this is that stratified random samples are being used. However, further discussion of the particular techniques used by pollsters lies beyond the scope of this text.

How do we decide how to stratify? This decision is typically based upon inductive evidence. We find out in some way that, for example, most students in a given faculty vote the same way. There might be different ways of stratifying that are equally good or are better in particular cases. We could split between male and female students or by years. We do not have any general way to know in advance that characteristics will be highly correlated with whatever it is that we are interested in; but in many practical situations we do have some information and do engage in informal stratification. If you were interested in the general view of citizens toward the police you would, even if you did not take steps to ensure that your sample is random, take a sample that included males and females of diverse ages. If you wanted to know how well retailers are doing, you would check with various sorts of retailers.

Often when we are presented with statistical claims we are given something more than a bare statistical generalization. The additional information usually concerns one of the following:

1. ***margin of error*** **(or confidence interval)**
2. ***confidence level*** **(or degree of confidence)**

Both of these relate to what we have hitherto spoken of as making your conclusion proportionate to the evidence you have. Consider the following. Suppose we have a decent sample and we find that 86% of our sample favor a certain policy. It would be a bit rash to conclude that exactly 86% of the population favored the policy. We more typically conclude that around 86%, or 86% + or - some percent (the margin of error), favor the policy. (Recall that while we are here using numerical versions, there are non-numerical versions of this type of argument as well.) The confidence level is a statement of how likely it is that the actual distribution in the population will fall within that range. The confidence level of a claim that exactly 86% of people favor the policy would often be quite low (though of course it depends on sample size and the like). So a more full-fledged version of this kind of argument can be characterized as follows:

More Complex *Inductive Generalization*

X% of observed ***F*** are ***G***.
Therefore (with a confidence level of Y%),
X% of ***F*** (+ or - n%) are ***G***.

If you consider this carefully, you should see that with a fixed sample size the confidence level typically increases as we increase the margin of error. And you should also see that what we spoke of as the proportionality of the conclusion to the evidence at hand is what we are here characterizing in terms of margin of error and of confidence level. In the above example of polling students sitting in the student union building, our claim that a majority or something near a majority found their high school education unsatisfactory was one that introduced a fairly large margin of error. (The claim that exactly two-thirds of the student body consider their high school education unsatisfactory allows for no margin of error and is not justified by the evidence we have.)

We will say more about margins of error and confidence levels later in this chapter. But we may note the following: the results of such a further study can sometimes be quite surprising. In particular, we tend to underestimate the value of samples that strike us as 'very small' in relation to the size of a population. Suppose you have a population of 20 million voters. We utilize a random sample of 500 persons. Here, with a level of confidence of 99% we obtain a margin of error of approximately 7%. That is, 99 times out of 100 the result we obtain will be within approximately 7% of the actual distribution. If we were to sample 2000 people the margin of error would be halved. What is equally surprising and counter-intuitive is that even if the population is 200,000 or 100 million the levels of confidence and margins of error are the same as in the 20 million case. These facts indicate that we should be excedingly careful in judging an argument to be a hasty generalization. Because we are often not in a position to take a random sample, taking measures to eliminate bias is in practice of much more signficance than sample size.

There are a number of other problems, particularly in the polling of people, that we have hitherto ignored. For example, those sampled may simply lie. In a recent election in the United States something like this seems to have happened. One candidate was white, one was black, and the election was to take place in a state in which there was good reason to believe that racism was still a significant factor in determining how some people voted. The black candidate seemed, in the pre-election polls, to have an excellent lead. Yet he lost the election. In this case the best explanation seems to be that many of the people who said they would vote for the black candidate actually had no intention of doing so, but considered it socially unacceptable to say they would vote for the white candidate (who was running a campaign that seemed to be covertly racist). There are, however, other kinds of explanations. Polls are, of course, taken at a particular time, and people may thereafter change their minds. And in elections in particular, a certain portion of the population may not vote. Another problem is that people, while not lying, may simply make mistakes. Suppose, for example, you are interested in income levels. You ask people how much they made last year. It is not in the least unusual for them to provide an incorrect answer. Nor is it unusual in endless other cases. Suppose you ask people how many drinks they had last week or how many eggs they ate last week. Few of us can give an answer that is exactly right. In careful polling these kinds of problems are taken into account, but, again, a more careful study is beyond the scope of this book.

We have talked much of polling, but we should not forget that the use of inductive generalization extends far beyond polling. We are often given figures regarding the cost of living, figures usually based on the cost of a bundle of selected goods in a number of standard retail outlets. The results are then used to ground a claim about the general cost of living. If you get sick, you might ask the doctor how long it will be before you can expect to get well. Her answer will usually be based upon a sample taken by someone of the population of people with your illness.

1.3 / Inductive Generalization and Analogy Arguments

We noted in Chapter 2 that there is an intimate relation between analogy arguments and inductive generalizations. What we want to do here is to spell out that relation.

Let us first try to clarify some differences. The conclusion of an analogy argument will be a statement that some object or objects will have some characteristic. The conclusion of an inductive generalization (recall this is our label for the kind of argument discussed above) will be either a statistical or a universal generalization (remember that these are kinds of statements). In an analogy argument we appeal explicitly or implicitly (a premise may not be stated or may be incompletely stated) to similarities. We do not use such a premise in an inductive generalization. Our argumentative move is from the sample to, as we noted, a statistical or universal generalization regarding the population with which we are concerned. What we do sometimes do is to utilize inductive generalization to determine whether or not the presence of some feature F is positively relevant to the presence of a feature Z.

As we said, an important aspect of the strength of an analogy argument is whether or not the cited similarities (say, *F* and *G*) are positively relevant to the presence of a certain characteristic *Z*. If they are positively relevant then, typically, it will be true that most objects that are *F* and *G* are *Z*. Recall also that some analogy arguments are more completely evidenced than others, that is, more evidence is provided for the positive relevance. This evidence consists of additional samples. We might well have moved from this evidence to the conclusion that most *F* are *G*. But if we do not do so, we are not presenting an argument of the sort that we are calling an inductive generalization. We are simply presenting what we have spoken of as a well-evidenced analogy argument. Finally, note that if a sample is a representative one it will in fact be similar to the population at large. But this is not to say that we are presenting an analogy argument when we utilize inductive generalization. The two kinds of argument have different structures.

When we encountered an analogy argument we typically counted the addition of further reference objects that had the target feature *Z* as making the argument that *X* was also *Z* more completely evidenced rather than stronger. Thus, we counted:

> **The first cockatiel I owned was a young male cockatiel and he learned to speak easily. So this one, which is young and a male, will learn to speak easily.**

and:

> **The first and second cockatiels that I owned ...**

as equally strong arguments. We of course labelled the second argument a more completely evidenced one. However, we have, other things being equal, counted inductive generalizations as stronger when the sample is more extensive. Wherein lies the difference? The answer was provided in the preceding discussion. An analogy argument rests upon the claim of similarity and lack of relevant dissimilarity. By citing additional examples we are supporting the claim that the cited similarities are relevant. However, in an inductive generalization the argument involves a direct move from a claim about the characteristics of the sample to a generalization. If we have a different (say larger) sample, we have (other things being equal) an argument that is stronger. We have a different premise that, all else being equal, will make it more likely that the conclusion is true. (For example, the margin of error may be decreased.)

It may well be difficult or impossible to say whether particular passages incorporate an analogy argument or something else: all one can do here is to use one's best judgment on how to reconstruct the argument. Suppose, for example, that one said the following:

> **a, b, c, and d are all Fs that are G. So I suppose those other F will also be G.**

One might take this as a well-evidenced analogy argument in which F is taken as the point of similarity between objects X, in this case a, b, c, and d, and objects Y; or one might take a, b, c, and d as a sample, in which case one will take the conclusion to be that F are probably all G. Given the absence of any further context, there seems no basis for a decision between these two interpretations. But we could nonetheless adopt one or both of the interpretations and proceed to assess the argument.

1.4 / Anecdotal Evidence

You may have heard people speak of some evidence as only anecdotal. In some contexts what this amounts to is that one has conducted a poll, but only in an informal kind of way. For example, suppose you are interested in whether an instructor is an easy marker. You talk to a friend who has taken a course from that instructor, who says her grade was a very good one even though she didn't work too hard. You conclude that the instructor in question typically marks easily. There are, of course, various problems with this argument. But note that at least three of the problems were raised in our previous discussion: Is your generalization a hasty one? Is your sample biased? And, of course, is the person to whom you are talking telling the truth? Clearly, in these sorts of cases one's evidence is rather slender, but one should not assume that in any such case one is arguing fallaciously. The question, again, is whether one draws a conclusion proportionate to the evidence one has. Here one has the sort of evidence that supports the claim that if you are only interested in easy marks then you would be better off taking a course from this instructor than from one about whom you knew nothing.

There are a variety of situations in which many of us, presumably owing to our psychological makeup, find it very difficult to keep our conclusions proportionate to the evidence at hand. Sometimes what is concluded is something the person drawing the conclusion wants to believe. I have heard people (in this case smokers) say the following:

Oh, smoking isn't all that dangerous. Wilson smoked like a fiend, and he lived until he was 90.

That Wilson lived until he was 90 is clearly not good evidence for the claim that smoking isn't dangerous. In other cases, fear can be involved. At some point my grandmother heard that a few people had been afflicted from eating undercooked pork. Even though I presented her with overwhelming evidence that only a certain internal temperature was needed to ensure one's safety, her belief in the extreme danger remained. Eating pork chops at her house was something to be dreaded unless, of course, you happened to like rock-hard, dry pork. You should ask yourself how many of your beliefs are based upon anecdotal evidence that does not in fact justify them; we all have some.

2 / Some Statistics and Their Uses

2.1 / Averages and Arguments

Some other kinds of statements involve statistics with which we are all quite familiar — those referring to *modes*, *means*, and *medians*. Each of these can be called an *average*. Though there are other kinds of averages, we shall confine ourselves to a discussion of these three. We shall introduce these in a context wherein we have complete information with respect to distributions.

Perhaps the simplest form of average is what is known as a *mode*. We have some overall population in which some feature is distributed: in a class we might have a distribution of marks or of heights, or in a bag of candy-coated chocolates we might have a distribution of colors. The mode of a distribution is simply the most common value in the distribution. Let's look at a few examples.

Red Candy	20
Green Candy	15
Orange Candy	18
Purple Candy	21
Yellow Candy	17

Here the mode color is purple — that is, purple is the most common color in this particular group. Note that it makes sense to speak of the mode even if we cannot speak of any order in our group, or cannot speak of more or less, higher or lower. In this example there is no "order" among the colors. Consider now the following table summarizing the marks on a test:

A	8
B	12
C	14
D	3
F	2

The mode here is C. Now, it may well make sense to speak of marks as having an order — of an A being a better mark than a B. But in speaking of the mode we are not appealing to that order; we are merely taking note of the most common mark. Note that mention of the mode leaves out, in this case, a fact in which we might be interested — the fact that far more people received a mark above C than below it.

That modes do not give us much information allows them to be used in a misleading way. Consider the following set of marks:

A+	1
A	2
A-	4
B+	6
B	10
B-	5
C+	5
C	4
C-	6
D+	8
D	6
D-	7
F	7

You come up to me and ask how people did on the test. I say that B was the most common mark — that is, the mode. This is of course true, but it is misleading. Students did not do very well on this test: almost half received a C- or less.

Suppose you read in an ad that more people prefer brand *B* than any other brand (think of the letters now as representing the number of people who have expressed a preference for the brand identified by that letter).

A	8
B	9
C	8
D	7
E	5

Clearly the statement that more people prefer brand *B* than any other brand does not inform us that the overwhelming majority of people prefer some other brand. If you look around at ads, reports, and the like, you should be able to find numerous examples of this particular ploy.

Another kind of average is the *median*, that value in a distribution below and above which there is an equal number of values. Let us look at another listing of marks:

A+	0
A	2
A-	1
B+	3
B	7
B-	1
C+	4
C	4
C-	5
D+	6
D	5
D-	6
F	6

This class has 50 students. Note that there are 22 students with a mark higher than C-, whereas there are 23 with a mark lower than C-. The median mark is then C-. The mode, of course, is still B. But notice that the median is, in this particular case, less misleading. If you ask me how well the class did and I tell you that the median mark was C-, you will clearly have a much better idea of how the test went than if I replied that the mode was a B.

But medians, like modes, can be used in a misleading fashion. Let us look at some cases to see how this is so, beginning with house prices in two neighborhoods:

Neighborhood 1		Neighborhood 2	
House 1	$50,000	House 1	$75,000
House 2	$60,000	House 2	$80,000
House 3	$61,000	House 3	$81,000
House 4	$82,000	House 4	$82,000
House 5	$84,000	House 5	$84,000
House 6	$86,000	House 6	$86,000
House 7	$90,000	House 7	$200,000
House 8	$91,000	House 8	$400,000

In *both* these cases we can identify the median house price as $83,000. Suppose you are interested in how similar the neighborhoods are. Clearly, it would be a mistake to conclude that they are much the same because the median house price in both is the same. A similar point may be made by looking at two grade distributions:

Class 1		Class 2	
A	20	A	1
B	1	B	1
C	1	C	40
D	1	D	1
F	20	F	1

The median mark in both classes is the same, but it is apparent that the classes are very different.

While modes and medians are often used, we are probably most familiar with the **mean,** which is calculated by adding up the values and dividing by the number of cases. To compute a mean we need to have available some underlying quantitative scale. Many schools, for example, use letter grades in which an A is associated with 4, a B with 3, and so on. Once this association is fixed, student averages — the mean — can then be computed. Means sometimes are more useful than medians. Let us look back at our two neighborhoods:

	Neighborhood 1		Neighborhood 2
House 1	$50,000	House 1	$75,000
House 2	$60,000	House 2	$80,000
House 3	$61,000	House 3	$81,000
House 4	$82,000	House 4	$82,000
House 5	$84,000	House 5	$84,000
House 6	$86,000	House 6	$86,000
House 7	$90,000	House 7	$200,000
House 8	$91,000	House 8	$400,000

The mean house price in the first is $82,638.89 and in the second the mean is $176,166.67. Here the mean is very useful, but it often does not give us that much help. Let us compute class averages — means — using the four-point scale:

	Class 1		Class 2
A	20	A	1
B	1	B	1
C	1	C	40
D	1	D	1
F	20	F	1

Here the mean for Class 1 is 2 while that for class 2 is approximately 2.05. Here the mean does not help us much more than the median did.

Means also can often obscure facts that might be of interest. Suppose one noted that the average family income in a society had gone up, and from this concluded that people are better off than they were. But let us look at the initial incomes for five families:

Family 1	$25,000
Family 2	$30,000
Family 3	$35,000
Family 4	$40,000
Family 5	$45,000

Here both the median and mean income is $35,000. Suppose now we look at the later incomes, those upon which the claim that people are better off than they were is, in this case, based.

Family 1	$25,000
Family 2	$30,000
Family 3	$35,000
Family 4	$40,000
Family 5	$200,000

The median income has remained the same, but the 'average' income could now be reported as being a staggering $66,000. Someone might shout that the average income has now almost doubled. Well, that is true, but it is hardly of any consolation to our first four families. Suppose that the later incomes were instead these:

Family 1	$10,000
Family 2	$20,000
Family 3	$21,000
Family 4	$22,000
Family 5	$200,000

The mean income is now $54,600, again a dramatic increase. But here it would seem obvious that most people are worse off than they were. Note that in this case looking at the median income would be at least a bit more informative.

People often say that you can use statistics to prove anything. This is, as far as these examples go, a misleading claim, although one that does have a point. Our claims are accurate, at least presuming we have done our number-crunching correctly. But the question is what sorts of claims are supported by the particular statistic we have. We have just seen that claims that 'averages' have gone up (or down) do not yield conclusions about what happens to most of the individuals.

There are various other ways of describing data that may on occasion give us information not provided by any of the averages we have looked at. We might for instance look at what is called the **range**, which simply tells us the distance between the highest and lowest values. Thus, in the initial stage of the above income distribution the range was $20,000, whereas in the later stage the range was $190,000. Clearly, it can sometimes be helpful to know the range. But the primary problem about a range is that it focuses upon the extremes. It tells us nothing at all about what happens in between those two extremes. And many of you will be familiar with **quartiles**. In a median we found a midpoint; in a quartile we divide into quarters. Thus, the first quartile is the one in which one-quarter are lower and three-quarters are higher, the second is the median, and the third the one in which three-quarters are lower and one-quarter is higher. And more familiar yet, at least with those who have encountered aptitude tests and the like, is the notion of a *percentile*. Suppose you receive an A- on a test. Your percentile rank would only be 50 if 50% of the students received an A- or less and 50% received a better mark.

There is another kind of average used in certain situations. It is often called a *weighted average*. Typically at sports events seats in different sections are priced differently. Suppose the arena seats 10,000 people. 1000 seats are priced at $100, 1000 at $75, 5,000 seats at $50, and 3,000 seats at $10. We might obtain the average ticket price by adding these and dividing by 4. So the average ticket price is $58.75. But what this does not take account of is that there are different numbers of tickets available at each price level. Taking this into account involves taking into account what percentage of the tickets have each price. So in this case it is [(.1 x 100) + (.1 x 75) + (.5 x 50) + (.3 x 10)]. So the weighted average ticket price is $45.50.

You should be able to think of cases where the weighted average is a more useful statistic than the average. For example, the average age of death of a Russian male is considerably less than the age of Boris Yeltsin. We might vividly say that he is 'living on borrowed time'. However, this is very misleading. To compute his life expectancy we would need to use a weighted average. What percentage of people his age live one more year, two more years, and so on? Suppose 10% die after one year, 10% after two years, and so on. The weighted average here is 5 years. So we would say that his life expectancy is 5 years. Generally you do not compute your life expectancy by subtracting your age from the average life span of people in your society. Instead you use the life expectancy of a person of your age. (If you are already older than the average life span, the result of the subtraction is of course a negative number. We could speculate that this is the origin of the metaphor of 'living on borrowed time'. Regardless of whether this is so you should make sure you use the statistic appropriate to the particular case in question.)

In the next section we will examine in more detail different ways of encoding and presenting information about the spread of the data, but those that we have are sufficient for some purposes. We have already seen that statistics may be misleading; even the more sophisticated measures that we shall not examine can be misleading. But we should not conclude that statistical claims are all lies. Rather, we should attempt to understand them, and determine precisely what sorts of conclusions any given statistical statement supports.

In the cases we have been examining, we based our computations of averages upon a complete survey of the data. However, we often do not have such a complete survey. In these cases we initially use inductive generalization to obtain our data.

2.2 / Margins of Error and Confidence Levels Revisited

Let us concern ourselves with situations where we are concerned with a binomial distribution of probabilities (see Chapter 11). In the case of a jar containing some red candies we would distinguish red and non-red. We could of course extend our treatment to include situations in which there are more than two jointly exhaustive and mutually exclusive alternatives but we will not do that now. We will always take for granted that we are doing random sampling with replacement, though of course with huge populations the difference between sampling with and without replacement is minimal.

Suppose we fix some margin of error that we are willing to tolerate. Let us call this ε. It can be shown, where **p** is the actual probability (in the case of our red candies, this would be the actual percentage of the candies that are red), that our confidence level increases for this ε as our sample size increases. (In statistics we might say "as we make more trials" rather than "our sample size increases".)

Normal distributions are those that we standardly see represented by bell-shaped curves, sometimes called *normal* curves. Here is one such:

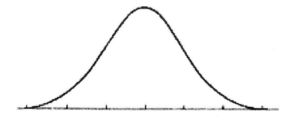

The mean of such a curve is its peak. The standard deviation indicates how steep the curve is. All of this leads, via some mathematics that we will ignore, to the following result that we will present in the abstract now and fill in later. (We will now use μ as our standard symbol for a mean and σ as our standard symbol for a standard deviation.) Let **s** be our sample:

Standard Deviation Theorem

Pr[(μ - σ) $\leq$ s $\leq$ (μ + σ)] is approximately .67
Pr[(μ - 2σ) $\leq$ s $\leq$ (μ + 2σ)] is approximately .95
Pr[(μ - 3σ) $\leq$ s $\leq$ (μ + 3σ)] is approximately .99

Before we can gain any grip on these we need to know a bit more about means and standard deviations. After all we did not define the notion of a mean for colored candies in a jar. And we have said little about standard deviations.

Normal distributions (bell curves) can, when we have a reasonably large sample, be used to approximate the binomial distribution. We will always in fact suppose that we have a sample of at least 100, though as it happens 30 would be sufficiently large. The result that justifies this is typically called, in statistics, the "central limit theorem". But we will suppose a normal distribution. Where **p** is the actual percent of items in the population with the feature in which we are interested and **N** is the sample size we utilize:

Mean	**Standard Deviation**
$\mu = N \times p$	$\sqrt{N \times p \times (1 - p)}$

So much for our abstract presentation for now. Let us look at some simple examples. We know that an urn contains 50% red balls. We draw a sample of 100 balls. The mean here is 50. The standard deviation is 5. What is the probability that we will get between, say, 40 and 60 red balls on this draw? Notice that such a result is exactly 2 standard deviations away from the mean. So by what we called the standard deviation theorem there is a 95% probability that we will obtain such a result. Suppose instead we draw a sample of 50 balls. What is the probability that we will draw between 20 and 30 red balls? The mean here is 25. The standard deviation is around 3.5, which is between 1 and 2 standard deviations from the mean. So the likelihood of this happening falls between 67% and 95%.

You may be able to begin to see why larger samples are rather more valuable than smaller. But we need to say much more if we are to establish this. For example, we have supposed that we know the actual distribution. If we are polling, that is, of course, what we want to find out. You may have noticed that none of the concepts we are utilizing make any reference to the actual population size. This may seem strange at the outset but it makes sense if you think of it. If you have a bag filled with marbles, 50% of which are red, you have, on one draw, a .5 chance of getting a red one regardless of the number of marbles in the bag. Notice that by the techniques of Chapter 11 you can compute the chance of getting 1 red ball and 1 non-red ball when drawing two without knowing anything about the size of the actual population. This obtains for any sample size (remember we are using replacement). Now recall that we are approximating such situations by normal distributions with the mean and standard deviations mentioned in the chart above. We do this primarily to avoid having too many calculations requiring the use of the probability calculus. Let us suppose that we are interested in a confidence level of .95. By our standand deviation theorem we know that:

$$\Pr[(\mu - 2\sigma) \leq s \leq (\mu + 2\sigma)] \text{ is (close enough to) .95}$$

Now let us suppose again that **p** (the actual value in the population) is .5. Our margin of error for a .95 confidence level is always, for a sample of **N**:

$$2 \times \sigma/N$$

We could always compute this, but because these kinds of maneuvers are utterly common there are always tables available to use. Further, we could compute this for any actual distribution. When we do this an interesting fact emerges. The margin of error is always greatest for an actual value of .5. Here is a little chart that gives us some of those values for some common sample sizes.

N (Sample Size)	Margin of Error (p=.5) (95% Confidence Level)
100	±.1
500	±.045
1,000	±.032
2,000	±.022
10,000	±.01

So for any size population we know that, whatever the actual distribution, for a sample of 100 with a confidence level of at worst .95, our sample will be within .1 of the actual distribution. We then report the result of a sampling using this worst case. Notice also that this chart clearly indicates the value of larger samples. With this fixed confidence level, larger samples dramatically reduce our margin of error.

Let us look at some cases. Now that we have the chart we no longer need to worry about doing any math. We ask a random sample of 100 people a yes-no question. 50% say yes. We can then report with a confidence level of .95 that 50% of the population hold the 'yes-view' ± 10%. Alternatively we might say that at a 95% confidence level between 40% and 60% of the population hold the 'yes-view'. Or we might say that, at the 95% confidence level, our **confidence interval** is 40% to 60%. Notice that if we were interested in whether a given measure would pass by a majority vote we could not say anything about the likely election result. Suppose instead that only 30% said yes. Here we could say that at a 95% confidence level between 20% and 40% hold the yes-view. We might here say that it is likely that the given measure would fail.

2.3 / Variance and Standard Deviation in General

One of the problems that we noted regarding averages was that they could be misleading with respect to the dispersion of values. For this and other reasons statisticians typically introduce other ways of summarizing the data at hand. Suppose we have a population of 4 in which hourly wages are as follows:

Person 1	$5
Person 2	$7
Person 3	$10
Person 4	$18

The mean income is here $10. The range is $13. Let us now introduce a statistic called the **variance**. First let us find a way to 'add up' various distances from the mean as follows:

$$(5 - 10)^2 + (7 - 10)^2 + (10 - 10)^2 + (18 - 10)^2$$

We are squaring in order to avoid having to play with negative numbers. Using X_i for the values, μ (μ_x when there is a potential for ambiguity) for the mean, and Σ for summation the formula we are using is:

$$\Sigma(X_i - \mu)^2$$

Notice that were the mean 10 and one value 7 and another 13, this squaring technique would identify their 'distance' from the mean as the same, namely 9. The total that we obtain is 98. But we want instead an average so we divide by N, that is, the number of cases. We thus obtain 24.5, which is the variance in this case. Our formula for variance is then:

Variance

$$\Sigma(X_i - \mu)^2 / N$$

Variances are typically used as a basis for the ***standard deviation***. This restores the original units by way of being the square root of the variance.

Standard Deviation (population)

$$\sqrt{ \Sigma(X_i - \mu)^2 / N }$$

So the standard deviation is, in the case of our example, roughly 5.

Intuitively, the larger the standard deviation the more dispersion there is in the population. So in some cases the standard deviation will give us a better summary statistic than will the mean. Let us look at another hourly wage example.

Person 1	$4
Person 2	$6
Person 3	$10
Person 4	$20

The mean hourly wage is here, as it was in the preceding case, $10. Let us compute the standard deviation. The variance here is 38. So the standard deviation is approximately 6.2.

If you earned $6 per hour you could of course say that you earned $4 less an hour than the mean. On some occasions this is what you might want to know. But in other circumstances it might be more informative to express the difference in terms of *standard deviation units*, or, as they are sometimes called, *standard deviations*. Recall that we use σ (σ_x if there is a potential for ambiguity) as shorthand for the standard deviation as defined above. Recall that $X_i - \mu$ gives us the simple numeric distance from the mean. To change this distance to a measure in standard deviation units, simply divide it by the standard deviation. We will, to avoid overuse of the term "standard deviation", speak of this as a use of a *z score*. So if you earn $6 your *z score* is -4/5.

Our presentation so far has been based upon complete information with respect to a population. More often than not, though, what we are working with is a sample from the populations. For reasons that involve more mathematics than we can manage here, the standard deviation is, where we are using a sample, computed by the use of the following:

Standard Deviation (sample)

$$\sqrt{\Sigma(X_i - \mu)^2 / N - 1}$$

Typically statistical software and calculators utilize this formula. Let us look back at our two neighborhoods, supposing that our chart gives us the result of a sampling:

Neighborhood 1		Neighborhood 2	
House 1	$50,000	House 1	$75,000
House 2	$60,000	House 2	$80,000
House 3	$61,000	House 3	$81,000
House 4	$82,000	House 4	$82,000
House 5	$84,000	House 5	$84,000
House 6	$86,000	House 6	$86,000
House 7	$90,000	House 7	$200,000
House 8	$91,000	House 8	$400,000

The median, you will recall, is $83,000 in both cases. The mean in neighborhood 1 is $75,550, in the other $136,000. But the standard deviation is around $16,000 in the first, while it is around $115,000 in the second.

Let us look back at our income examples, supposing that we now have a sample. The initial incomes were:

Family 1	$25,000
Family 2	$30,000
Family 3	$35,000
Family 4	$40,000
Family 5	$45,000

while the later incomes were:

Family 1	$25,000
Family 2	$30,000
Family 3	$35,000
Family 4	$40,000
Family 5	$200,000

We noted that the mean income shifts from $35,000 to $66,000. But the standard deviation shifts from approximately $7,905 to $75,117. This illustrates again that increases in the standard deviation do sometimes 'tell' us that there has been an increase in dispersion. The extension of what we have done here to include some of the additional points made in the preceding section is not too difficult, but we will not now undertake that extension.

Chapter Summary

In Section 1 we were primarily concerned with a kind of argument that we will speak of as *inductive generalization*. In 1.1 we discussed these appeals to samples, introducing:

Elementary *Inductive Generalization*

X% of observed F (the sample) are G.
Therefore, X% of F (the population) are G.

We also discussed the *fallacy of hasty generalization* and the *fallacy of biased statistics*. In the former case we appeal to a sample that is 'too small'. In the latter case we collect a sample in a way that is likely to make it *biased*, that is, unrepresentative.

In 1.2 we discussed this kind of argument in more detail. We noted that to avoid bias we often use *random sampling* or *stratified random sampling*. We sample randomly when each member of the population in question has an equal chance of being picked. When we stratify we break the population down into subgroups and sample members of those subgroups. We introduced the concept of a *margin of error*. We do not expect that our sample will yield the exact real percentage, but will be in the vicinity of it. The *confidence level* specifies the likelihood that our results are, within the margin of error, correct. These led to:

More Complex *Inductive Generalization*

X% of observed F are G.
Therefore (with a confidence level of Y%),
X% of F (+ or - n%) are G.

In 1.3 we turned to a consideration of the relation between inductive generalizations and analogy arguments. And in 1.4 we took a quick look at *anecdotal evidence*.

We then turned in Section 2 to some statistical claims. In 2.1 we discussed *averages*. We distinguished the *mode*, the *median*, and the *mean*. The mode is simply the most common. The median is the point at which there are as many 'above' as 'below'. The mean is a numerical average obtained by dividing a total (say of incomes) by the number of individuals in the population. We noted that it is sometimes useful to know the *range*, the distance between the highest and lowest values. But the range tells us little about what happens in between. *Quartiles* may be more informative than the median. The first quartile is such that 1/4 are below and 3/4 above. We saw that averages, although they are sometimes quite useful, may nonetheless be used in very misleading ways.

In 2.2 we revisited margins of errors and levels of confidence. We specified the conditions under which we would use *normal curves* to represent the data we have. (We used μ as our standard symbol for a mean and *s* as our standard symbol for standard deviation.) Let **s** be our sample. We noted the following important theorem:

Standard Deviation Theorem

$\Pr[(\mu - \sigma) \leq \mathbf{s} \leq (\mu + \sigma)]$ is approximately .67
$\Pr[(\mu - 2\sigma) \leq \mathbf{s} \leq (\mu + 2\sigma)]$ is approximately .95
$\Pr[(\mu - 3\sigma) \leq \mathbf{s} \leq (\mu + 3\sigma)]$ is approximately .99

We then introduced (where **p** is the actual percent of items in the population with the feature in which we are interested and **N** is the sample size):

Mean	Standard Deviation
$\mu = N \times p$	$\sqrt{N \times p \times (1 - p)}$

We then saw that we could utilize the following chart to estimate **p** on the basis of a sample:

N (Sample Size)	Margin of Error (p=.5) (95% Confidence Level)
100	±.1
500	±.045
1,000	±.032
2,000	±.022
10,000	±.01

So, for example, if a sample of 100 got .5 'yes' responses we could say that at a confidence level of 95% we obtain a *confidence interval* of 40% to 60%. We noted that none of these facts depends upon our knowing the actual population *size*.

In 2.3 we introduced *variances* and *standard deviations* in contexts where we had numerical data.

Variance

$$\Sigma(X_i - \mu)^2 / N$$

Here we are using X_i for the values in the population, μ for the mean in the population, and Σ for summation. N is the population size. The standard deviation is simply the square root of the variance.

Standard Deviation (population)

$$\sqrt{\Sigma(X_i - \mu)^2 / N}$$

We noted that more typically one finds standard deviations for a sample. Here the formula is:

Standard Deviation (sample)

$$\sqrt{\Sigma(X_i - \mu)^2 / N - 1}$$

CHAPTER 13

Hypotheses

We are often interested in finding out why what happens has happened, in finding an explanation or in finding the cause or causes of certain phenomena. We cannot hope to provide a method or methods that will always ensure that we can answer the questions we have, but we can investigate some of the techniques that we use. As we shall see, we typically put forward and investigate *hypotheses*, proposed explanations or proposed identifications of causal factors.

1 / Mill's Methods

Quite recently the following occurred. A website for which I was responsible was in need of an online store (a store on the Internet where one can purchase goods). Establishing such a store typically involves the installation of certain software. The author of the software installed it on the computer hosting the website. The store was tested, and it was discovered that a certain function (so-called secure online ordering) did not work when one utilized a certain browser (a browser is software used to view pages on the Internet). Why did this happen? Well, browsers are temperamental and frequently have "bugs". Perhaps that was the problem. However, this seemed to me an implausible answer. I had purchased the software using secure online ordering and the very browser in question. Well, then, perhaps the store software had been misinstalled. The author of the software had himself done the installation, and recognized that this was a possibility. So he downloaded the software as it had been installed and put it on his own website. It worked there as it was meant to work. Throughout this time, the technical support personnel responsible for the server on which the website was located insisted that there was no problem with their computer. But I was persuaded that the evidence I had accumulated suggested there *was* a problem with their computer. I presented this evidence, accompanied by a threat to move the website, and they undertook a new investigation. After some effort they discovered that the new version of certain very standard security software (which was not yet installed on the other computers) had a "bug". Once they replaced this new version with the previous version, all was well.

In the course of this investigation some of the techniques that have come to be known as Mill's Methods were utilized. We will now turn to a very informal and incomplete sketch of those methods. The core ideas that we find will then be more rigorously examined in the subsequent sections of this chapter.

1.1 / The Method of Agreement

In some cases we are faced with a number of occurrences of a phenomenon that we wish to explain. Our interest might be in hypotheses that identify causally necessary conditions. Events or features G will, as you may recall, be said to be necessary conditions for events or features F if and only if whenever F is present, G is present. Not all necessary conditions are ones that we would take as causally necessary conditions. For example, being about 93 million miles from the sun is, I suppose, a necessary condition of catching a cold from your classmates. But I doubt that we would take it as a causally necessary condition. We shall consider this sort of problem a bit later on, but for now we can proceed while keeping in mind that causally necessary conditions are at least necessary conditions. We will take the method of agreement to be primarily a means of excluding hypotheses that claim such-and-so to be a causally necessary condition.

One often-mentioned kind of application of the ***method of agreement*** occurs in connection with, for example, outbreaks of food poisoning among persons who have been eating at a local fast-food outlet. Typically investigators look to see if there was some particular item that was eaten by all of those who became ill. If there is, that item is viewed, at least initially, as a prime candidate for being the culprit.

We will utilize the following notational conventions. We will use capital letters **A**, **B**, **C** ... for the candidate explanatory factors, typically called the ***antecedent circumstances.*** We will use lower case letters p, q, r ... to indicate the presence of the ***phenomena*** in which we are interested. We will utilize $\sim p$, $\sim q$, $\sim r$ ... to indicate the absence of those phenomena. We can now exhibit the structure of applications of this method as follows:

Case	Circumstances	Phenomena
1	A C D	*p, q*
.	B C F	*p, r*
.	A C E	*p, r*
.	C F G	*p, q*
n	A C E	*p, s*

Here we would take **C** as our initial suspect with regard to *p*, our specific interest in this case. But note that we can do little more than say **C** is a suspect. As we noted in our example of being 93 million miles from the sun, the phenomena always have any number of circumstances in common. Most of those will be irrelevant from the standpoint of providing any part of the account of why the phenomenon in question occurred. The method does not give us an account of which circumstances to attend to — that must come from elsewhere. That is, we begin with a list of circumstances that have in our judgment a chance of being relevant. Even if we do this we have no guarantee that **C**, for example, is in fact a causally relevant factor.

There is another sort of problem as well. Note that either **A** or **F** is present in all the cases. To stick with a food example, let us suppose that **C** is a salad and is in fact irrelevant. Finding out that it is irrelevant will typically involve other kinds of investigation. But both **A** and **F** are meat dishes served with a mushroom sauce. As it happens, this sauce is the culprit. Had we started with a different list of circumstances we might have identified it as a suspect. The method does not itself provide us with a list; it is something that we bring to the situation. And of course we might not have enough cases to apply this method at all.

1.2 / The Method of Difference.

When we apply the ***method of difference*** we are, as the name suggests, looking for what made the difference. Typically we utilize this method when we are looking for causally sufficient conditions. Events or features *F* will be said to be sufficient conditions for events or features *G* if and only if whenever *F* is present, *G* is present. But again not every sufficient condition need be a causal condition. The structure of this method is:

Case	Circumstances	Phenomena
1	A B C	*p, r*
.	A B C	*p, s*
.	A B C	*p, q*
.	B C	*~p, r*
n	B C	*~p, s*

Notice here that the phenomenon *p* in which we are interested is absent when A is absent. Here we might suspect that A is, at least in such circumstances, causally sufficient.

If you look back to my investigation of the website problem, part of that which was described was in fact an application of the method of difference. One circumstance was the presence of the installed software. Another was its installation on my website's server. We can chart the situation as follows:

Case	Circumstances	Phenomena
1	Installed software Running on my server	Malfunction
2	Installed software Running elsewhere	No malfunction

This, of course, is part of what made me suspect the server. But notice one feature. These circumstances are rather vague. At best they served to identify something that should be examined more carefully.

Problems aside, uses of the method of difference abound both in everyday life and in science.

1.3 / The Joint Method

The joint method is not 'new'. Rather it is simply that in the course of an investigation we use both the method of agreement and the method of difference. If you look back to the website example you should note that in fact it involved a use of the method of agreement that came up with a negative result. That is, the presence of the software as such was not the problem, as it was present where the malfunction was not present. Similarly, it was not the particular setup of the software that was responsible. That is why the author of the software copied that particular setup to his own website. Had that particular setup malfunctioned on his website we would have had:

Case	Circumstances	Phenomena
1	Particular setup	Malfunction
2	Particular setup	Malfunction

But this did not happen. As noted, the method of difference was then appealed to.

1.4 / The Method of Concomitant Variation

The preceding methods were limited to phenomena that were either present or absent. However as often as not we are interested in phenomena that vary in certain ways. The variations may be among individuals in a population. Some persons are taller than others, and some dogs are more responsive to training than others. In other cases we might notice variations among populations. Smokers, as we know, are more liable to lung cancer than are non-smokers. Suicides are more common at some times than others, more frequent in some populations than others. The *method of concomitant variation* enables us to say something about some of these claims.

Let us briefly look at smoking. Suppose we divide a population of similar persons into subpopulations of smokers and non-smokers. We note that the incidence of lung cancer is high in the subpopulation of smokers, at least by comparison with the subpopulation of non-smokers. We might represent this as follows.

Case	Circumstances	Phenomena
1	Ordinary people Smokers	High rate of lung cancer
2	Ordinary people Non-smokers	Low rate of lung cancer

If we proceed in this way we are simply applying the method of difference. But suppose we investigate a bit more and discover that a higher incidence of lung cancer is correlated with heavier smoking. Notice that we could equally have described this situation as one in which a lower incidence of lung cancer is correlated with less smoking. When we do something like this and conclude that smoking may be causally related to lung cancer we are using the method of concomitant variation.

We will not at this point introduce any chart to exhibit the general structure of this method. At this point we will simply note that where we find either that an increase in one factor is correlated with an increase in another or that a decrease in one factor is correlated with an increase in another, we suspect the presence of a causal relation. In the next section we will turn to a more rigorous study of correlations and their significance.

2 / Correlations and Studies

Some studies of which we hear or in which we indulge are simply designed to find something out. How many citizens are overweight? How many teenagers smoke? The techniques we characterized in the preceding chapter are typically used to answer these questions. But often, if not incessantly, we are inundated with reports that tell us, for example, that consumption of a particular food is found to be related to a decrease in heart attacks. Many persons take astrology seriously to at least some degree. This involves the belief that there is some sort of correlation between astronomical phenomena at the time of our birth and what befalls us or what character we have. So let's turn to a study of correlations.

2.1 / The Basics of Correlations

In some cases phenomena vary together in a very direct way. Consider, for example, atmospheric pressure and altitude. But more often we find only what might be characterized as a tendency for phenomena to vary together. Weight and caloric intake are related, but we cannot simply say that the more you eat the more you will weigh.

We noted above that, at least in some cases, when we find correlations we suspect that there is a causal relation. But it is important to recognize that the notion of a correlation is a general one. A correlation is not in and of itself a causal relation. Let us look at a simple case to see exactly what correlations are. Suppose we are looking at a population that consists of round objects and square objects. The objects are either yellow or green. Here is the distribution in our population of 100 objects:

> 40 round and yellow
> 20 round and green
> 15 square and yellow
> 25 square and green

In this population being round is positively correlated with being yellow. This is *not* the claim that there are more round yellows than there are square yellows. It is rather the claim that the percentage of rounds that are yellow is greater than the percentage of squares that are yellow. Notice that we could equally have said that being green is positively correlated with being square. The correlation relation is symmetric (see chapter 9). And here there is a negative correlation between being round and being green. Given the structure here where we have two alternatives, this is equivalent to our statement that there is a positive correlation between being round and being yellow.

Be very careful, in thinking about correlations, to make sure you understand what kinds of evidence do not at all support any claim about correlations. Suppose, for example, you are told that 70% of those who use cocaine have previously smoked marijuana. Does this show that there is a positive correlation between smoking marijuana and using cocaine? The answer is no. To show that there was such a correlation we would need to know that the percentage of those who have smoked marijuana and use cocaine is higher than the percentage of cocaine users who have not smoked marijuana. Here is one population that illustrates that there need not be a correlation.

> 85 marijuana, no cocaine
> 7 marijuana, cocaine
> 2 no marijuana, no cocaine
> 3 no marijuana, cocaine

Note that 70% of the cocaine users have smoked marijuana. But here there is a positive correlation between not having smoked marijuana and using cocaine. Of those who have not smoked, 3/5 are cocaine users while only 7/92 of those who have smoked are cocaine users. Notice that the above distribution might well be reported by the claim that more than twice as many cocaine users have smoked marijuana as cocaine users who have not. These kinds of claims do not support any claim that there is a correlation. For all I know there might be a correlation between pot and cocaine, but statistics such as those cited have not the slightest tendency to show this.

We now need some way of specifying the *strength* of a correlation. The strength is typically reported as falling in the interval $-1 \leq 0 \leq 1$. One simple idea, not normally used in practice, is to subtract the one from the other. In the example we looked at above, 2/3 of the rounds were yellow and 1/3 were green. We would, utilizing this measure, say that the strength of the correlation is +.333. There is a negative correlation between being round and being green. The strength of the negative correlation between round and green is - .333.

Of course we are typically looking at evidence based on a sample. Let us just take a quick look at some possible situations. We will utilize a .95 confidence level and start with a sample size of 1,000. Recall our quick chart from the preceding chapter.

N (Sample Size)	Margin of Error (p=.5) (95% Confidence Level)
100	±.1
500	±.045
1,000	±.032
2,000	±.022
10,000	±.01

Out of our sample we find that 500 have used marijuana and 500 have not. Out of these, 100 use cocaine and 400 do not. (Notice that obtaining a reliable sample would be difficult. Perhaps people might be honest with respect to the question as to whether they have used marijuana. But it is not very plausible to suppose that they will be honest with respect to whether they use cocaine. We shall ignore this problem. One way in which people attempt to sidestep it is to guarantee anonymity, presuming that this will make people more honest.) In doing this sampling we have examined a sample of 500 marijuana smokers. In this sample 100 — that is, 20% — are cocaine users. The margin of error at this confidence level is 4.5%. So between 15.5% and 24.5% of the marijuana smokers are cocaine users. To decide whether or not there is a correlation we need to know how many cocaine users have not smoked marijana. Let us suppose that there are 50, that is to say 10%. So we can say that between 5.5% and 14.5% of the cocaine users have not smoked marijuana. Here there is a positive correlation. We cannot say precisely what it is but we do know that it is quite weak. With our .95 confidence level it could be as small as .01 (the difference between 15.5% and 14.5%) but only as high as .19. Suppose we had found 100 cocaine users in each of the smoking and non-smoking groups. Notice that here we could have no correlation, a weak positive correlation or a weak negative correlation. That is, our data are compatible with 20% of both smokers and non-smokers being cocaine users in which case there would be no correlation. Or there could be a positive correlation if 24.5% of the smokers, for example, are cocaine users and only 19.5% in the non-smoking population. Or there could be a negative correlation were those numbers reversed. But the evidence we have does not allow us to make any of these particular judgments.

2.2 / More on Correlations

More commonly a rather more complex means of identifying the strength of a correlation is used. We will now turn to contexts in which the data we have are quantitative (height and weight, for example) so that we can utilize our old friends — the mean and the standard deviation — and one new concept, that of covariance. We introduced the notion of variance in a situation where we were concerned with only one feature. We now need to introduce the concept of *covariance*. We now have two variables X_i (height, for example) and Y_i (weight, for example). Covariance is then:

Covariance

$$\text{Covariance }(X,Y) = \sum [(X_i - \mu_x) \times (Y_i - \mu_y)]/N$$

Let's use r_{XY} for "the correlation or relation between X and Y". Now we can introduce the *correlation coefficient*:

Correlation Coefficient (a computational formula)

$$r_{XY} = \text{Covariance } (X,Y)/ \sigma_X \times \sigma_Y$$

That is, we divide the covariance by the product of the standard deviations. This is a pretty dreadful formula. Another very common way to compute the correlation coefficient is to do the following. We spoke of standard deviation units, which we ended up calling **z scores**, in the preceding chapter. When we use those we always have a mean of 0 and a standard deviation of 1. Our two variables are then measured in those units. Given this, we can use the following overtly simpler formula:

Correlation Coefficient (a computational formula)

$$r_{XY} = \sum (Z_{Xi} \times Z_{Yi})/N$$

Here Z_{Xi} is the distance of X_i from the mean expressed as a **z score**. The computations are still complex if done by hand.

Here is one simple example. Suppose we have given a standardized test to the 10 students in our class. Our interest is in whether there is any correlation between age and test performance. We will present the data using z scores.

Student	Age	Mark
1	-1	-.5
2	-.5	+1
3	-.5	-1.5
4	0	+1
5	0	-1
6	+.5	+.5
7	+.5	-.5
8	+1	+1
9	+1.5	+2
10	+2	+1

Recall that we are using z scores. So student 1's age is one standard deviation younger than the mean student age. Student 10's mark is one standard deviation above the mean student mark. Our formula tells us to calculate (I have omitted the ones that are 0):

$$(-1\times-.5)+(-.5\times1)+(-.5\times-1.5)+(.5\times.5)+(.5\times-.5)+(1\times1)+(1.5\times2)+(2\times1)$$

and divide by the number of cases, in this case 10. The result is .675. But of course this bare number, although it does indicate a positive correlation, is not self-interpreting. This is, for example, a very small class. We will later look at some of the ways of assessing the significance of such results.

2.3 / Correlations and Causality

Tobacco companies conceded quite early on that there was a correlation between smoking and lung cancer. But they denied that there was a causal relation. We have already conceded that they could have been right. There was a correlation between shape and color in our earlier example but, presumably, there was no causal or explanatory relation between those two features. That would remain true even if the correlation had been 1.

There are a number of points to keep in mind. Correlations are indifferent to temporal order. The shape does not come before the color. Under our standard way of thinking, causes come before their effects. But do not make the mistake of thinking that where we have two correlated phenomena, one of which precedes the other, we can automatically conclude that the earlier phenomenon is the cause of the later phenomenon. To proceed in such a fashion is to argue fallaciously.

Fallacy of *Post Hoc ergo Propter Hoc*

Arguing that phenomena are causally related simply on the basis that they are correlated and that one precedes the other.

What is sometimes taken as a particularly striking example of this occurred on a radio talk show quite recently. One of the topics under discussion had been the use of fluoride. A caller announced, with some distress, that her mother had used a fluoride mouthwash and then had died four days later.

The clear suggestion, though it was not made explicitly, was that there was some causal connection. Clearly the caller had taken notice that one unusual event was followed by another unusual event. However, nothing was said that indicated that the caller had any beliefs as to whether there is any correlation between fluoride treatments and deaths. So we will not take this as a case of this fallacy. It would be better viewed as a fallacious application of the method of difference.

Case	Circumstances	Phenomena
1	Ordinary routine, save fluoride taken	Death
2	Ordinary routine	Life

We are not in a position to assert for sure that the fluoride treatment played no role. But I would count this as a fallacious application of the method of difference because here we are in a situation where there are a number of alternate techniques available for investigating the death and a number of standard causes of death that we need to consider. There seems no reason initially even to consider the fluorides. This is particularly true as there is no (known) correlation between the treatment and deaths. Eclipses of the sun are quite rare events. Suppose the caller had said that there had been a solar eclipse and that her mother had died four days after seeing it.

Let us grant that there is a correlation between smoking marijuana and then using cocaine. If we were, on that basis alone, to assert that smoking marijuana causes cocaine use, we would be committing the fallacy that we have labelled *post hoc ergo propter hoc*. This has nothing to do with the character of this particular example. It simply reflects the fact that there are far more correlations than there are causal relationships. The only legitimate conclusion we can draw on the basis of this kind of correlational evidence is that there *may* be a causal relationship.

The way in which this example was stated reveals another problem. The temporal relation between phenomena is not always clear. (One might call this a chicken-egg problem.) Suppose that 'behaving badly' (**b** in the chart below) is correlated with physical punishment (**p** in the chart below). Of course it might well be true that a first punishment might follow a first bit of bad behavior. But that does not really help us at all. During any given time period they both may occur. Which is 'first' will depend simply on our choice of these periods. Look at the following sequence:

b, p, b, p, b, p, b, p, b

There is another possibility with respect to such sequences. **b** might be causally related to **p**, and **p** to **b**. For example eating more might cause one to weigh more, and weighing more — if, for example, one ceased to care about one's weight — might contribute to one's eating more. The presence of such sequences does not, of course, guarantee that there is any causal relation.

In some cases there may be an extraordinarily high correlation but no causal relationship. One not uncommon circumstance in which this might happen is when the phenomena that are correlated have a ***common cause***. Storms and falling barometers are correlated. But neither causes the other. There is an underlying atmospheric condition responsible for both. One of the early claims of tobacco companies, after they had conceded the presence of a correlation, was that there might well be some underlying causal condition that disposed people both toward smoking and toward lung cancer. In the absence of any other evidence or any other kind of evidence this claim is correct. What later happened was that various studies were undertaken that indicated there was no such underlying condition.

And we may discover correlations that are to be explained in a way other than what we initially think. Suppose we find that women typically pay more than men for any particular kind of car repair. There is a positive correlation between being a woman and paying more. We might then be inclined to believe that repair shops are more inclined to rip off women than they are men, or that men are better bargainers. But if we were to investigate further we might find the following. There is one group of repair shops, which are expensive, and another group which are 'reasonable'. For whatever reason, women go more often to the more expensive shops. But at each shop men and women are treated equally. So our speculative explanation regarding repair shops being more inclined to rip off women is simply misguided. It is perhaps true, and I will suppose true, that the number of churches in any given area is correlated with the number of murders in that area. Cities have more murders and more churches. Both of these examples are examples of what are often called ***spurious correlations***. But this term is very misleading. It is not that the correlation is spurious in the sense of not being there.

It is that we draw inappropriate conclusions from the correlations. Or that the correlation in question is irrelevant to the hypothesis that we are considering.

What happens if we find that there is no correlation? Should we conclude that there is no causal relation? We should not do this. Our correlations capture only what we might call linear relations. But consider the following situation (presented using **z scores**):

Case	X	Y
1	-2	+2
2	-1	0
3	0	0
4	+1	0
5	+2	+2

Here the correlation is 0. But there are situations like this where there is nonetheless a causal relation. Think of a measuring device that responds to a very light weight and a very heavy weight but does not respond to an intermediate weight. The weight is causally relevant but the relation between weights and responses is not a linear one. Plants might die with too little sunlight or too much sunlight but grow much the same with intermediate amounts of sunlight. A somewhat different case is one in which the ingestion of small amounts of a substance is only minimally related to an increase in the rate of incidence of a certain disease, but in which large amounts are dramatically related. This would not be a strong correlation from our current point of view either, but clearly there might be a causal relation. The primary moral of all this is that the absence of the sort of correlation obtained with our measures does not show the absence of causal relationships.

We have talked much of problems regarding the relation of correlations and causes. But it must be emphasized that we are not denying that the presence of the correlation gives us reason to suspect that there might be a causal relation. Nor are we are denying that we might have sufficient reason to investigate further. All we are saying is that such evidence does not in and of itself justify us in claiming that there is a causal relationship. Again we must ensure that our conclusion is proportionate to the evidence at hand.

And we should go on to look at some of the other techniques available that will enable us to provide good evidence for our hypotheses.

3 / Experiments and Tests

We often think of experimentation and testing as central features of the pursuit of science. That is certainly true. But it is also true that experimentation, at least at a simple level, occurs on a day-to-day basis. Let us turn to a brief examination of experimentation.

3.1 / Experimental Studies

Many experimental studies are undertaken in the following circumstances. We have found a correlation between *F* and *G*, and want to find out whether there is a causal relation. Or we might suspect that there is a correlation, but not yet know.

We have seen that we are rarely in a position to examine whole populations. So we have relied upon sampling. Ideally, when we undertake an experimental study we proceed as follows. We randomly select a test group from the population with which we are concerned. What population we are concerned with depends, of course, on the question we have. If we are interested in whether a particular vaccine is effective against a childhood disease our population would be children who do not have and have not had the disease. If we are interested in the efficacy of a particular treatment we would choose from a population of those who suffered from the illness or condition that the treatment was intended to address. How large a sample we choose depends upon on all sorts of considerations, not all of which are related to such factors as a desired margin of error. (We might have very limited funding, for example.) Our sample is then divided randomly into two groups. One group is called the control group, the other the experimental group. One might wonder why it is important to get a random sample. Suppose that we are testing a vaccine. There might well be some characteristic **I** such that those with that characteristic are immune to the disease in question. Let us suppose that there is such a factor but that we have no feasible way of distinguishing those with and those without **I**. By randomly choosing the study group and then randomly putting subjects into the experimental and control groups we ensure, insofar as we can, that it will not be the case that more people in the experimental group will have **I** than will people in the control group.

Particularly if our population consists of humans, a number of additional techniques are frequently utilized. We often would not want our subjects to know which of the two groups, control or experimental, they were in. We call a study ***blind*** if the subjects do not know which group they are in. If a treatment involves, for example, taking a pill three times a day, it could not be blind if we simply gave nothing to the people in the control group. So often something known to be irrelevant, a ***placebo***, is given to those in the control group. A placebo is sufficiently similar to what is given to the subjects in the experimental group to prevent the subjects in the control group from telling that they are not members of the experimenal group. There are many kinds of cases in which it is important to use a blind study. For example, the study may rely upon reports from the subjects. Clearly a subject might, even quite unintentionally, give one report if she believed she was a member of the experimental group, another if she believed that she was not. You most likely have noticed placebo effects in children. Sometimes they say they feel bad. You give them something, almost anything, emphasizing that it will make them feel better. Often they will report that it has made them feel better. And in certain other kinds of cases it is important that one use not just a blind study but what is called a ***double-blind study***. Here the experimenters who are assessing the results are also kept uninformed as to which group the subjects are in. This is particularly important where assessment involves a judgment call. For example, the experimenter might have to judge whether a subject is 'more responsive'. Even the most conscientious of researchers can suffer from unconscious biases.

Here are some aspects of a typical study, one now known as the Breast Cancer Prevention Trial (BCPT). As you know, breast cancer is a very serious problem for women. For some time the drug tamoxifen has been used to treat some cases of breast cancer. (Indeed, it is one of the most widely used treatments). What tamoxifen does is to some extent known: it interferes with the activity of estrogen, a female hormone which promotes the growth of cancer cells. It was thought that the drug might also be effective in preventing breast cancer, because it seemed to inhibit the development of cancer in the other breast of women receiving the treatment. As you can imagine, the question of whether it inhibits the development of breast cancer is not something that can be determined by any quick glance.

Here is a brief account of the way in which the study proceeded. (More complete information is available from the National Cancer Institute in the United States.) The population to be studied was that of women at high risk for breast cancer. Previous studies and computer modeling were used in order to identify "high risk". Of course, it is not possible to simply go out to the population and randomly grab people and start experimenting. Persons must enter such trials willingly after being fully informed of exactly how the study will proceed. That is, ***informed consent*** is required. Some 13,000 women were involved in the study. Three age groups were involved: 40% of the women were in the 35–49 age group, and 30% in each of the 50–59 and 60+ age groups. This was necessary as age is a factor in determining risk. All the participants were identified as having a risk of getting breast cancer in the next five years equal to or greater than that of a woman aged 60+. In this group 17 out of 1,000 can be expected to develop breast cancer within the next five years. The study was to last five years, and most participants were tracked for four years. The study was a double-blind study; that is, approximately half of the women received a placebo, and the women's physicians did not know whether their patients were in the experimental or the control group. The participants were placed in the groups via a random procedure.

The preliminary results indicated the following. In the control group 154 women developed invasive breast cancer, whereas 85 women in the experimental group developed it. Notice that the absolute numbers here are very small. This, of course, is one reason why such a large-scale study was required. But the result is nonetheless a significant one. (Simply to report that there was a 45% decrease does not show this. Such a percentage decrease is not always significant though in this case it is. We will look at some of the ways in which significance is measured in 4.1.) The study results do not 'prove' that the drug is effective, but we now have very good reason to believe that it is. Should women now rush out and start taking the drug? Not necessarily, for there are some other considerations. For example, there are, as is not uncommon in such cases, side effects that have to be taken into account. Drugs like tamoxifen were antecedently known to increase the risk of endometrial cancer. As was expected, the study indicated that this risk was still there where the drug was used for prevention rather than cure. And there was as well an increased risk of blood clots. So at the very least those who contemplate using the drug have to weigh the benefits and risks. Further, this study only focused on the high-risk population. We do not know, on the basis of the study, whether similar results would be obtained in other populations. The results obtained were sufficiently impressive for the experimenters to make the study 'unblind'. So now all participants can decide for themselves whether to use the drug.

One further point has to be mentioned. If an experiment is to be of any value, care has to be taken (insofar as it is possible) to ensure that the members of the group are not treated differently. Oral contraceptives have certain kinds of effects that could have affected the results of the study. So steps were taken to ensure that none of the women were using these contraceptives. This is, of course, an aspect of experimentation in general. Experimenters try to ensure that there are no other variables present in the groups that might make a difference. In many cases the only way to do this is by way of using random procedures. That we have tried to ensure that there are no other differences is one of the reasons we take the results of experimental studies to indicate that we have causal relations.

The BCPT is an example of a randomized experimental design. A slightly different kind of design is known as a *prospective study*. Here we start off with a population, one portion of which has the feature that we suspect might be a causal factor. For example, we might look at police officers and non-police officers who have not yet had heart attacks. We then track them and see what the incidence of heart attacks is in the future. Notice one difference between this study and the BCPT. Here the subjects are initially different, that is, some are police officers and some are not. In the BCPT the women were all the same in the sense of being in the high-risk population. So the prospective study has the problem that it will not identify any factor that might dispose people both for becoming a police officer and for heart attacks. That we initially find it implausible to suppose that there is a factor that disposes us toward both becoming a police officer and having a heart attack is not itself evidence that there is no such factor. So a good study will try to ensure that those we study are as similar as possible precisely so as to guard against this problem. But this is very difficult to do. It should be clear that the randomized design would be preferable. But we are not in a position to randomly select, say, a group of 18-year-olds and divide them into experimental and control groups. We would of course have to get the members of the experimental group to become police officers. This is neither feasible nor morally permissible. And consider replacing a prospective study of the health effects of smoking. Here we would, for example, obtain a sample of 12-year-olds and get the members of the experimental group to become heavy smokers. Even if this were feasible, it would be morally unacceptable.

Prospective studies may be contrasted with *retrospective studies*. Here we look into the past, at a population at a given point. For example, we look at the population of persons who have lung cancer. We then attempt to determine how many of these were smokers and how many were not. Let us suppose that 60% of the patients were smokers. Note that at this point we cannot even draw a conclusion regarding a correlation. (We saw this when we considered the claim that a huge percentage of cocaine users had been marijuana smokers.) What is typically done is to sample those who do not have lung cancer and determine how many of them have smoked and how many not. (Note that we would typically try to make them as similar as possible in terms of such factors as age, weight, and lifestyle.) If only 10% of those who do not have lung cancer have smoked we would have some evidence for the dangers of smoking. But as you can see, this approach has problems similar to those in prospective studies.

In some cases animal experimentation is used. For example, animal experiments are typically used to determine whether or not a given substance is a carcinogen (a cancer-causing agent). One of the reasons that it is now taken for granted that smoking is causally related to lung cancer is that it was found, via animal experimentation, that 'tar' contained carcinogens. And tar is taken into the lungs when smoking. Animals are not, of course, humans, and what happens to animals is not necessarily the same as what would happen to humans. So how to decide when such studies are justified and how to assess the results of such studies raise difficult issues that we cannot here undertake to resolve. Nonetheless, animal experiments have sometimes provided us with useful information that would have been difficult, if possible at all, to obtain in any other way. This is not to say that animal experimentation is always legitimate. Deciding whether it is depends upon moral considerations, upon the value of finding out whatever it is the study is meant to find out and numerous other considerations as well.

3.2 / Some Experiments

Most of us think of experimentation, testing, and careful observation as premier characteristics of science. They are, but it should not be forgotten that they play a role in ordinary life as well.

Clearly in any experiment we attempt (insofar as it is possible) to ensure that there are no variables that make a difference, other than the ones in which we are interested. Suppose we are interested in whether a particular fertilizer enhances the growth of grass. We plant our grass and carefully fertilize one area while not fertilizing another area. Sure enough, the grass in the fertilized area grows well. We have a lush, well-rooted lawn. The grass in the other area is not nearly so nice. Is this a good experiment? Well, given the information we have, we cannot tell. For example, did we ensure that the soil in both areas is much the same? Did both receive the same amount of sunlight and water? What one typically attempts to do, as we in effect noted in the preceding section, is to **control for** these other variables that might be expected to have an effect. So one might use areas that are all sunny or areas that are all shady. Or one might break down the experiment into sunny and shady areas for both the fertilized and unfertilized plots. (Note that this might give us additional information.) Clearly it is difficult to assess a bare report of the result of an experiment if we do not know which, if any, potentially relevant variables were controlled for by the experimenters.

This experiment was devised in order to test the hypothesis that the fertilizer was effective. But in many cases it might be more apt to characterize an experiment as oriented toward collecting data or toward finding something out rather than being oriented toward the testing of a hypothesis. Suppose we noticed the following. Grass tends not to grow well under the pine trees in our yard. The rest of our yard has no pine trees and is rather sunny. We suspect that either the shade or the soil might be the cause of the problem, and we might devise an experiment to find out. As an initial crude stab we could remove some of the soil from each portion of the yard, put it in containers and plant some grass in the containers. Some containers might be placed under the pine trees, some in the sunny portion of our yard. This experiment is not a particularly good one. But it should indicate that most of us do use experimental techniques when we are curious about something.

Notice that there is no significant difference between experiments that test hypotheses and experiments that collect data. The primary difference is that we tend to speak of testing hypotheses when someone or another has put forward a claim. (Suppose I had been told that the soil under pine trees is very bad. I might then characterize what I described in the preceding paragraph as testing the hypothesis that the soil is bad.) If no one has put forward a claim we tend to speak of ourselves as collecting data.

Let us follow the history of one classic episode in the history of science. If you pull a piston up in a tube filled with water, the water will 'follow' for around 33 feet. If you use this sort of pump you can only pump around 33 feet. One question is simply, why does this happen at all? During the seventeenth century the theory was that 'nature abhors a vacuum'. Given this the water will rush upward to fill the vacuum created by pulling up the piston. This might not be the sort of explanation with which we are familiar, but it is an explanation nonetheless. The scientist Evangelista Torricelli (a friend of Galileo in his later life) contemplated another explanation. Given that air has weight and that we live in, as it were, a sea of air, the weight of the air 'pushing down' would equal the weight of the liquid 'going up'. Note that here we also have a potential explanation of the particular heights we could expect. Torricelli proposed the following experiment. Take a glass tube closed at one end. Fill it with mercury. In some way close the end of the tube (for example, hold your finger over the end), invert it, and stand it vertically in a bowl of mercury. The mercury level in the tube should fall if Torricelli is right. Torricelli did not himself perform this experiment, but the device was soon used in further experiments. Blaise Pascal (after whom the programming language was named) proposed the following experiment. If there is a sea of air, then the weight should decrease with altitude. If nature abhors a vacuum, then altitude should not matter. Our experiment will simply consist of carrying a barometer up a mountain. If there is such a thing as atmospheric pressure, the level of the mercury should decrease as we go upward. If nature abhors a vacuum, the level should not change. As it happens the height does change: the level goes down. The device we have described is of course the first barometer, a device used to measure atmospheric pressure. Notice one additional feature of the experiment we have described: the inversion of the tube would seem to create a vacuum. If nature abhors a vacuum, why does the mercury fall at the outset?

In some cases what are typically called *crucial experiments* are devised. Typically we speak of crucial experiments when there are two important hypotheses or two general theories between which scientists wish to decide. The task is then to devise an experiment that will have one result if one theory is correct, another if the other was correct. There need not be anything 'special' about the structure of a crucial experiment. We speak of it as crucial given the context in which it is carried out. The barometer experiment that we just discussed could well be described as a crucial experiment. But we have neglected one point. Did our experiment show conclusively that the atmospheric pressure hypothesis was correct? Not really; after all, perhaps nature's abhorrence of a vacuum is a function of altitude. This suggestion was made. It is an example of what is typically called an *ad hoc hypothesis*. We shall discuss these more in 4.2.

We are not in a position to enter into any extended discussion of what makes for good experimental design. But before we turn from the subject, there is one final point that should be made. In most areas of science it is very important that experiments be replicable. That is, if the same experiment is carried out in another place it should yield the same results. This is in effect a means of guarding against errors that can creep in by accident or by design. Some time ago some scientists announced the discovery of what is called cold fusion. Fusion, one way of producing energy, is a thermonuclear reaction that is normally supposed to require very high temperatures to take place. The experiment involved placing an electrode into heavy water. It was said that excess energy (in the form of heat) was produced. This report quickly received vast press attention. If there is such a thing as cold fusion, we might well have a source of virtually cost- and pollution-free energy. The problem that arose was that the results did not, initially at any rate, seem to be replicable. That is, when performed in other laboratories the experiment did not yield the excess energy. Of course, the fact that the initial results were not replicated does not resolve the question. Perhaps the further experiments involved some kind of mistake. But the consequence, after further investigation, was that mainstream scientists decided that there was no such thing as cold fusion. The controversy has not ended. A quick visit to the Internet will provide anyone with numerous reports regarding cold fusion and its immense promise. But it is not our task to decide. What we should note is that if there is such a thing as cold fusion then anyone who follows the same procedures should get the same result. That is the primary force of the demand for replication. If the phenomenon is there, it should be found by anyone who does the same thing in the same way in the same circumstances. Note that anyone who carried a barometer up the mountain would obtain much the same result.

4 / Evaluating Hypotheses

In this section we will consider some additional questions regarding the evaluation of hypotheses.

4.1 / Significance Tests

You find a coin from an unknown country. You identify one side of it as heads, the other side as tails. Out of curiosity you start flipping it. You flip it 10 times and it comes up heads 8 times. Did this happen by chance or is the coin biased, that is, not fair? How good is your evidence one way or another? Significance tests are one way in which we try to answer such questions.

We have here a situation in which we have two hypotheses that are mutually exclusive and jointly exhaustive. With respect to any hypothesis — or so far as that goes, any claim at all — we can either accept the claim (believe it to be true), reject the claim (believe it to be false), or neither accept nor reject it. Let us represent this situation by the following chart:

	H	**~H**
Accept H	Correct	Incorrect
Accept ~H	Incorrect	Correct
Accept neither H nor ~H	No false belief Missing accepting	No false belief Missing rejection

In performing significance tests we make use of what is commonly known as a **null hypothesis**. The null hypothesis is typically the hypothesis that the results we obtain have occurred by chance. Or in cases where we wonder if a treatment is effective, the null hypothesis would typically be that the treatment has no effect. If our coin is fair it should (in some sense) come up heads approximately 50% of the time. We might decide to compute the likelihood of our results given that the coin is fair. In this case this is simply an application of probability theory. Using the formula to compute the binomial probability (see Chapter 11), this comes out as approximately .044. That is to say, given the null hypothesis it will happen around 4.4% of the time. But should one then argue that the coin must be biased because this outcome is so unlikely? We should not proceed so quickly. Standard statistical techniques require calculating what we shall call the **probability value** in this kind of situation. To obtain this value we calculate the probabilities of all outcomes that are the same as or more extreme than this one and then total these. These outcomes are 8 heads, 9 heads, 10 heads and 2 heads, 1 head, and 0 heads. What we are asking is the probability of getting any particular result that is at least that unlikely. These total approximately .11. If the coin is fair, there is an 11% chance of getting the result we did or an even more deviant one. Suppose we obtain the same proportion in a larger number of tosses, such as 16 out of 20 heads. The probability value of this is considerably less. In effect this would be to say that we have better evidence that the coin is unfair.

It is traditional to call the rejection of a true null hypothesis (in this case the hypothesis that the coin is a fair one) a *Type I* error. This is typically construed to mean that one accepts the claim that the null hypothesis is false. On our chart this is the case where we have accepted ~H where H is true. But there is some divergence with respect to the characterization of a *Type II* error. Many authors speak of it as the failure to reject a false null hypothesis. Some authors take this as the case wherein we accept H when ~H is true. Others take this as the case where we accept neither H nor ~H in the situation where H is true. Yet others take it to cover the disjunction of these two alternatives. It is typical in a given situation to decide in advance upon some probability value that we will deem as sufficient to reject the null hypothesis. This value is typically called the *significance level*. If we obtain a probability level equal to or less than the significance level, we speak of our result as *statistically significant*. The most commonly used levels are the .05 level and the .01 level. The lower the level the more the sample would have to diverge before we would reject the null hypothesis.

It is important to note several points. The probability value varies with sample size in the way that we would expect. That notwithstanding, we cannot conclude that our null hypothesis, whatever it is, has been shown to be false. In this particular case that amounts to saying that we have not conclusively established that our coin is biased. In the case that we examined, the null hypothesis would not normally be rejected. (It is not significant at either the .05 or the .01 level.) So it is doubtful that we would bother to investigate further. But if we got 16 heads out of 20 we might well decide to investigate further. (Or we might not use that coin when we make a decision by flipping a coin.) Typically, further investigation would involve looking for some source of bias, for example, establishing whether one side of the coin was heavier than the other. In the case of dice this has been done. Some dice are manufactured by drilling holes of equal depth in the various sides. Consequently the 6 face weighs slightly less than the 1 face. Such dice have a slight bias. Often this would not matter, but in other cases we might wish to have dice that are minimally biased. So some dice are manufactured by drilling holes of different depths on the various sides: the hole on the 1 face would be deeper than the holes on the 6 face.

We must also keep in mind the following. We are not in a situation wherein we can declare that we have conclusively established some claim. Even if the null hypothesis is false, that is, our coin is biased, this may not show up in any feasible number of trials if this bias is slight. And of course the extraordinarily unlikely can happen: a fair coin can land heads up 20 times out of 20.

Well, what should we believe and what should we do? There is no general answer. If the question is important (we need, for some strange reason, an unbiased coin), then we might flip the coin 100 more times and see what happens. If avoidance of a Type I error is very important, then we will perhaps set our significance level at .01 and, in the case in question, stick with the null hypothesis. These further considerations become clearer if we consider other kinds of cases in which significance testing is used.

We have what we think is a treatment that will cure some disease, will lead patients to recover. Does it actually do anything? Or is its apparent success merely due to 'chance'? We all use certain measuring devices, such as thermometers, scales, or police radar. Given the readings, is the device still functioning or is it malfunctioning? Serious testing in these kinds of cases requires the introduction of statistical methods far beyond the scope of this text. For example, we do not automatically have a null hypothesis. Few measuring devices are perfect. But what sort of variation should we expect by chance? In the case of the coin tosses we had a clear-cut null hypothesis that the coin was fair. This led immediately to a .5 value. In these other cases we have to decide what to use as our null hypothesis. And more advanced statistical techniques than we have presented are often used as well.

What to do with any results we obtain depends a lot upon the kind of case we are considering. Suppose, for example, we are concerned with a treatment for cancer. We don't know whether it is effective, but we do have good reason to suppose that it has virtually no bad side effects. Here we might well decide that the treatment should be used if there is even a minimal chance that it does something. But suppose instead we were using measuring devices that are exceedingly costly to recalibrate. If it were police radar we might argue that minor malfunctions, which we might suggest aren't very important, should be ignored. We would here demand much stronger evidence that the null hypothesis should be rejected. Of course those who get speeding tickets might disagree. But this is just to say that there are various considerations that we take account of before deciding how to proceed.

4.2 / More on Science and Evaluation

We will not attempt to provide any thorough account of 'what science is'. Presumably we all have some idea of what science is that should at least enable us to identify certain kinds of questions that we should raise regarding certain kinds of claims. In the course of considering these questions, we will as well be in a better position to see how to evaluate various kinds of claims.

Many beliefs are based upon anecdotal evidence. A considerable number of persons, ranging from cab drivers to hospital personnel, believe in what is often called the moon effect. The hypothesis is that, in some way or another, the full moon brings about increases in violent crime, accidents, strange behavior, and countless other phenomena. But the evidence here is typically anecdotal. That is, cab drivers, police officers, and hospital personnel report striking incidents occurring at the time of the full moon. Those who have tried to study the supposed phenomena have been unable to find any evidence suggesting that there is any correlation between phases of the moon and the exciting phenomena.

That prayer contributes to healing is typically based on anecdotal evidence. There is no reason to believe that it could not be helpful; indeed there are some reasons to believe it might be helpful. There is also good reason to believe that it could not be harmful. In a circumstance such as this we might well encourage people to pray. But note that this is not based upon our belief that it is helpful, but upon a belief that it *might* be combined with the belief that it is not harmful. The critical point is that anecdotal evidence does *not* provide one with more than a reason to believe that something might be true or with more than a reason to investigate further. Whether or not there is even a correlation is something we could only discover via further study. No general claims can reasonably be accepted solely on the basis of anecdotal evidence.

We are often inundated with testimonials, that is, claims from people that something helped them, was enjoyed by them, solved their problems, and so on. Let us simply assume (which we cannot do in practice) that all the testimonials are sincere reflections of the beliefs of the persons in question. How we should respond depends a lot on what is claimed. If you want to go see a movie and you hear people saying that they enjoyed it a lot, then you might want to go see that movie. This is essentially a use of analogy argumentation. In other cases testimonials are used as a means of presenting some sort of argument from authority. In either case one should approach them using the criteria for assessment that pertain to those kinds of arguments. But, as often as not, testimonials are simply a means of providing us with anecdotal evidence. They should then be treated in the same way as any anecdotal evidence.

The general moral here is that we should be wary of claims supported by anecdotal evidence or testimonials. Remember that our task as critical thinkers is not to reject claims wholesale. Our task is rather to develop the ability to draw such conclusions as are proportionate to the evidence we have.

Scientists design their experiments. But it has become fashionable, particularly in areas which are at best 'fringe science', to place a heavy emphasis upon the claim that the researcher has used a 'protocol' or 'scientific protocol'. *Protocols* are simply detailed plans or specifications of the experiment, procedures, or treatment. It is often desirable to have a detailed protocol, not just for scientific reasons but because we must make financial decisions about who to fund and ethical decisions about the acceptability of research projects. The critical point, though, so far as the question of whether experimentation will give us reason to accept or reject a hypothesis, is not whether or not there is a detailed protocol, but whether or not the experiment will show anything. That there is a protocol does not in and of itself tell us this. Of course, if we have a detailed protocol and know that it was carried out, we may be in a better position to make some judgment. But it does not decide the question.

During the eighteenth century many scientists believed in phlogiston theory. Phlogiston was an ingredient in, for example, combustible metals. Burning results in a release of the phlogiston into the air. Similarly, rusting involves the release of phlogiston. Charcoal clearly has a very large percentage of phlogiston since it leaves so little behind. Various observations and discoveries had been made that posed difficulties for the phlogiston theory, but it remained to Lavoisier (often held to be the founder of chemistry in a form similar to that in which we know it) to undermine the theory. Via careful experimentation and measurement he showed that the products of combustion weighed more than the original material. (I gather that a rusty nail weighs more than a similar nail which is not rusty.) What is instructive from our point of view is the response of the phlogiston theorists. Originally it had been held that phlogiston had a positive weight. But one response to Lavoisier's findings was to say that in at least some instances phlogiston has a negative weight. This is an example of an ad hoc hypothesis, that is, one put forward to save a hypothesis in circumstances that would otherwise lead us to believe that it is false. No other independent evidence is introduced, such as evidence that would have supported the ad hoc hypothesis in the absence of the particular experiments that cast doubt on the original hypothesis. We cannot say that ad hoc hypotheses are always wrong or unacceptable. But the introduction of them, particularly the continued introduction of them, indicates that the original hypothesis is in serious trouble. And in some cases introducing enough of them may even make it difficult to decide what, if anything, remains of the original hypothesis.

In 3.2 we noted that one might have responded to the findings produced by carrying a barometer up a mountain by asserting that nature's abhorrence of a vacuum might vary with altitude. This is an ad hoc hypothesis in the sense that it was a claim introduced only to protect the initial claim from refutation. Suppose we take it seriously, though. If we do, we should predict that if we remain at the same altitude the level of the mercury should not change. Unfortunately it does. No doubt we could, with sufficient ingenuity, come up with another ad hoc hypothesis to account for this. But, as we noted, it is becoming increasingly unclear not only as to what remains of the original hypothesis, but increasingly unclear as to what predictions the hypothesis yields.

One well-known example of the introduction of ad hoc hypotheses occurred in connection with an individual who claimed to be able to bend spoons through the use of psychic power. When, via filming, cheating was discovered, some diehard supporters said that the cheating was a consequence of the observation or a consequence of being tired. It would seem instead that, pending some sort of evidence for this, we should conclude that the person was in fact a fraud. Regardless, you should be particularly wary in circumstances where responses to the criticism of a hypothesis seem systematically to involve the introduction of ad hoc hypotheses.

Perhaps the most important point was introduced in one form in the previous section on significance levels. We often cannot really assess hypotheses save by way of comparison with alternatives when there are alternatives available. Let us see how this point works in general.

Any legitimate hypothesis tells us something about what is to be expected given that the hypothesis was true. It enables certain predictions. We saw that the phlogiston hypothesis, wherein it was supposed that phlogiston had a positive weight, led us to expect that what remains after combustion weighs less. This hypothesis was not absurd, it was simply wrong. But suppose we have a hypothesis that is not wrong in this sense. That is, suppose that it does yield correct predictions. This might seem automatically to give us reason to accept the hypothesis but, as we have claimed, it does not.

Suppose I decide to impress you with my psychic powers. Here is my first set of predictions that I provide to you just prior to your first year in university. You will encounter a person in the next week who will seem to you very weird. You will find some of your professors boring. I continue in the same vein with many more predictions. Most come true. I doubt that you will, on the basis of this, credit me with psychic powers. But why not? After all if I do have psychic powers most of my predictions should come true. And they did. Certainly I am not simply guessing. The reason you do not believe I have psychic powers is quite obvious. We all have what might be called 'normal' predictive powers based upon our common knowledge of the world. That most of these predictions would come true is something we would expect given that I have and use my normal predictive powers.

This kind of problem occasionally occurs in the case of those who do claim to have genuine psychic powers. But other sorts of problems occur as well. One is vagueness. If one speaks vaguely enough, what one says can be taken so as to count as true regardless of what happens. That something you will view as important will happen to you in the next week is vague in this sense. A high success rate with vague predictions is of course not evidence of psychic powers. But let us suppose that vagueness is not a problem. Let us further suppose that the predictions are not ones that would be made by using what we called our normal predictive powers. Here the problem is that, so far as I know, no psychics have more than an occasional success with predictions of this sort. If this is so, what we called the null hypothesis will explain the success.

But suppose now the psychic has astounding success. At this point a term like "psychic power" is only a means of indicating that it is likely that something other than chance is responsible for the success. The result does not in and of itself tell us what that something is.

Discussions of 'strange phenomena' or 'the unexplained' often suffer from problems mentioned above. The claim that there are such phenomena is often, upon further investigation, shown to be incorrect. But even where it is not, there is a strong tendency to speak as if some particular hypothesis is thereby shown to be well-founded. Suppose that there are a significant number of UFO sightings that we are unable to explain in any standard kind of way. One particular explanatory hypothesis is, of course, that these are alien spaceships. But there are other such hypotheses. Perhaps they are natural phenomena that we do not yet understand. Perhaps they are secret experimental craft. Perhaps they are some mix of both. The point is that this sort of evidence on its own does not single out any one of these.

What we want of a hypothesis is not just that it gives us correct predictions but that those predictions would not be true, or would not likely be true, unless that hypothesis was true. If there are equally plausible alternative hypotheses that make the very same predictions, then the fact that the predictions come true does not favor any one hypothesis over another.

One kind of case in which these considerations are particularly important is when we are considering questions regarding common causes and origins. Such questions arise frequently in such varied contexts as biology, anthropology, linguistics, intellectual history, and plagiarism cases. Consider a typical plagiarism case. A student submits a paper discussing critical thinking. You encounter the following paragraph:

> **I might decide to impress you with my psychic powers. Here is the first set of predictions I provide to you your first week in university. You will encounter a person in the next couple of weeks who will seem to you very weird. You will find some of your professors boring. I continue in the same vein with many more predictions. Most come true. I doubt that you will, on the basis of this, say that I have psychic powers. But why don't you? After all if I do have psychic powers most of my predictions should come true. And they did. Certainly I am not simply guessing. The reason you do not is quite obvious. We all have what might be called 'normal' predictive powers based upon our common knowledge of the world. That most of these predictions would come true is something you would expect given that I have and use my normal predictive powers.**

The paragraph strikes you as one that you have heard before. So you look around in sources in which you think you might have read this. (In this case simply look a few paragraphs above.) The passages you find are the same save for some differences in pronouns and the like. You call the student in and accuse her of plagiarism. What you rely on is not simply the fact that this is what you would expect if it had been lifted from this text. It relies on the fact that it is quite unlikely that just this wording would have been used had the student not used this text. Not just any similarity will do, though. Suppose the passage had instead been one regarding Lavoisier and his achievements. Now it is utterly unlikely that this just magically popped into the student's head. That she read it in this book is one hypothesis, of course. But there are any number of other books in which much the same information is presented. At most the student is guilty of failing to footnote. And even that would not hold to the extent to which this is simply 'common knowledge', at least common to a vast number of reasonably well-educated persons. Some historical reconstruction proceeds in much the same way as do our plagiarism cases.

An often-cited example was presented by Stephen Jay Gould, a noted paleontologist, evolutionary theorist, and writer on natural science. The example is that of the panda's thumb. (The article "The Panda's Thumb" is reprinted in his *The Panda's Thumb: More Reflections in Natural History* published by Norton in 1982). This thumb is actually not really a thumb. It is rather an enlargement (there are other changes as well) of a bone that is normally a component of the wrist, and is used by the pandas to grasp the bamboo which is a staple of their diet. It is clumsy, but with it they can make do and survive. What we are considering are two hypotheses. The first is that pandas evolved. The other is that they were brought into existence by an ideal designer. If they evolved we would expect just the "remodelling" of antecedent structures which we find. But on the other hypothesis we would expect a 'thumb' that did not have some of the drawbacks that the one of the panda does. So here we have some confirmation of evolutionary theory. There of course is more to the description of this case than I have provided, but Gould's article is quite accessible.

We have by no means exhausted the topics we have considered in this chapter. But we hope we have provided clues as to how to investigate further should we wish or need do so.

Chapter Summary

In this chapter we turned to a discussion of hypotheses. In Section 1 we introduced Mill's Methods.

In 1.1 we introduced the ***method of agreement***. Schematically its structure is:

Case	Circumstances	Phenomena
1	A C D	*p, q*
.	B C F	*p, r*
.	A C E	*p, r*
.	C F G	*p, q*
n	A C E	*p, s*

We look for a circumstance that is present in all the cases in which the phenomenon is present. If there is one, we can conclude that it might be causally related to the phenomenon in question.

In 1.2 we introduced the *method of difference*. Its schematic structure is:

Case	Circumstances	Phenomena
1	A B C	*p, r*
.	A B C	*p, s*
.	A B C	*p, q*
.	B C	*~p, r*
n	B C	*~p, s*

Here we look for a circumstance that 'makes a difference' in the sense that we do not find the phenomenon if it is absent.

Very often we use the *joint method of agreement and difference*, discussed in 1.3. As the name might suggest, it is simply the use of both methods at once in a particular investigation.

Next, in 1.4, we briefly looked at the *method of concomitant variation*. Here we look for relations between phenomena. For example, boiling might occur faster as more heat is applied. Basically this method involves identifying *correlations*, which we discuss in Section 2.

In 2.1 we looked at the basics of correlations, introducing one simple way to measure the *strength* of a correlation. We noted that statistical generalizations such as "70% of *F* are *G*" do not support the claim that there is a correlation between *F* and *G*.

In 2.2 we turned to a more technical approach. Various notational devices were used. **N** is the number of cases in our sample, μ is the mean, and σ is the standard deviation. We needed an account of:

Covariance

$$\text{Covariance } (X,Y) = \sum [(X_i - \mu_x) \times (Y_i - \mu_y)]/N$$

We then introduced two ways of calculating the *correlation coefficient*. Here we may read r_{xy} as "the correlation or relation between **X** and **Y**".

Correlation Coefficient (a computational formula)

$$r_{XY} = \text{Covariance } (X,Y)/ \sigma_X \times \sigma_Y$$

Here we divide the covariance by the product of the standard deviations. We then introduced a second formula:

Correlation Coefficient (a computational formula)

$$r_{XY} = \sum (Z_{Xi} \times Z_{Yi})/N$$

This involves the use of z scores, which were introduced in the preceding chapter.

In 2.3 we discussed the relation between correlations and causes. We introduced:

Fallacy of *Post Hoc ergo Propter Hoc*

Arguing that phenomena are causally related simply on the basis that they are correlated and that one precedes the other.

We then noted that the existence of a correlation does not guarantee the existence of a causal relation. For example, there might be a ***common cause*** or a ***spurious correlation***. Nonetheless, correlations often do give us good reason to suppose that there might be some sort of causal relationship.

In Section 3 we looked at experiments and tests, turning in 3.1 to a discussion of ***experimental studies***. We emphasized the importance of using, where possible, random selection both of subjects and of members of the ***experimental group*** and the ***control group***. We noted that it is often necessary, particularly if our study involves persons, to make our study ***blind***. Doing this often involves the use of ***placebos***. Here the subjects do not know whether they are members of the experimental group or the control group. In a ***double-blind*** study certain of the experimenters also do not know which group the subjects are in. We noted that some studies are ***retrospective***, while others are ***prospective***. Both have certain problems arising, for the most part because randomization cannot be fully used.

In 3.2 we discussed some particular experiments, noting the importance of *controlling for* variables other than the ones in which we are interested. We noted that often the phrase ***crucial experiment*** is used in contexts wherein the experiment will enable us to decide between two competing theories. We mentioned ***ad hoc hypotheses***, but these are discussed in more detail in 4.2. We noted that it is important, where possible, that experiments be capable of replication. That is, the same experiment should yield the same results when repeated.

In Section 4 we discussed some aspects of the evaluation of hypotheses. In 4.1 we discussed the rather technical topic of ***significance testing***. We noted that we often make use of what is usually called the ***null hypothesis***. Often this is characterized as specifying what we would expect to obtain by chance. In the case of coins our null hypothesis is that the coin is fair. Using our null hypothesis we can calculate what we called the ***probability value*** in the given situation. If, for example, we obtained 8 out of 10 heads we would calculate and then add the probabilities of all outcomes equally or more extreme than this one. We distinguished ***Type I*** and ***Type II*** errors. The former is typically spoken of as the rejection of a true null hypothesis. The latter is often spoken of as the failure to reject a false null hypothesis. We noted that the latter in particular is understood in different ways by different authors. Typically a researcher decides upon a ***significance level***. This is a specification of a probability value that we will take as sufficient to reject the null hypothesis. If the probability value we obtain is less than or equal to the significance level the results are often spoken of as *statistically significant*. .05 and .01 are two commonly used significance levels.

In 4.2 we considered various aspects of the evaluation of scientific and supposedly scientific claims. We noted that although *anecdotal* and *testimonial evidence* may be suggestive, they have little evidential value. We noted that while *protocols* (detailed specifications of an experimental or testing procedure) are desirable, the mere fact that one uses a protocol does not guarantee that one's procedures are of any value. We considered *ad hoc hypotheses* in more detail. We emphasized that the fact that a hypothesis yields true predictions is not invariably sufficient to justify us in accepting it. It is much more important that it yield predictions that would not likely be correct unless the hypothesis was correct. We illustrated this point in connection with the hypothesis that I have psychic powers. We also warned against the premature adoption of particular hypotheses. For example, if some UFO phenomena are not at this point explicable, this does not in and of itself justify the claim that they are alien spaceships.

CHAPTER 14

Decisions and Games

Each day, and perhaps most moments of each day, we are forced to make decisions. In the first section of this chapter we shall present one account of how one makes reasonable decisions. Our focus will be upon cases where we must consider the probable consequences of our choosing to act one way rather than another. We will then turn, in the second section, to situations in which we are interacting with other persons.

1 / Decisions

1.1 / Making Decisions

The decisions we are called on to make can range from the trivial, as when I decide whether or not I want to add a bit more hot water to my bath, to the significant, as when one decides whether or not to go to university. Our concern here is with what is required for decisions we make to be reasonable ones.

We shall think of ourselves as being in some particular situation. For example, suppose you are at the racetrack and are attempting to decide whether or not to bet on a certain horse. In that particular situation, you have a choice of actions. Let us suppose that if you bet on a horse, you must bet on the horse to win; so your choice is between placing a bet on the horse or not placing any bet. We shall always suppose that our alternatives are mutually exclusive, that is, if you choose one of the options you cannot choose the other(s). In any situation there are certain results of any action, certain ways that the world might turn out; in our case the horse will either win or lose the race. Let us speak of the possible ways that the world might turn out as the "possible states of the world". Your horse's winning and your horse's losing are then the relevant possible states of the world, and because states of the world are, we suppose, mutually exclusive, only one possible state can turn out to be the real state of the world. Finally, we will suppose that the actions at our disposal and the possible states of the world are jointly exhaustive: one of the actions must be performed, and one of the possible states of the world will be the real state of the world.

Each of the proposed alternative actions, in conjunction with a possible state of the world, gives rise to a particular outcome. For example, if you buy a ticket and your horse wins, you will win some money. If you buy a ticket and your horse loses, you will be out the cost of the ticket. We can display this in the following way:

Example 1	*1: Horse wins*	*2: Horse doesn't win*
1: Place bet	A win	Loss of bet
2: Don't place bet	No loss, no gain	No loss, no gain

On the left we have listed the actions open to us, along the top the possible states of the world. We then entered the outcome in the appropriate cell. We shall label the outcome in which we win "$O_{1,1}$", and that in which we lose the amount of the bet as "$O_{1,2}$". In this way we can always provide a unique label for each outcome.

We will represent any decision situation as follows: in the left column we will enter the alternative actions and in the top row we will specify the possible states of the world. Let us look at one more example. Suppose you have invited three people to a small party. You must decide whether you will buy additional supplies for one, for two, or for three guests. (Let us assume the supplies will spoil if not used.) These, let us suppose, are your available alternative actions. The possible states of the world are that one, two, or all three guests show up. Whence we obtain:

Example 2	*1: One comes*	*2: Two come*	*3: Three come*
1: Buy for one	Right amount	Short one	Short two
2: Buy for two	Waste of one	Right amount	Short one
3: Buy for three	Waste of two	Waste of one	Right amount

Before we can make any decision, we must have what we shall call a consistent preference ranking of the outcomes. Let us examine this in connection with our first, racetrack, example; we shall return to our second example at a later point. It is not too implausible to suppose that at the racetrack our preference ranking is directly related to monetary gains and losses. Let us assume that a ticket costs us $2 and that we will receive $10 if the horse wins. We now can now redo our chart:

Example 1′	1: Horse wins	2: Horse doesn't win
1: Place bet	+$8	-$2
2: Don't place bet	No loss, no gain	No loss, no gain

On our assumptions, the best outcome is $O_{1,1}$, in which we gain $8, and the worst outcome is $O_{1,2}$, in which we lose $2. Our preference ranking, from most preferred to least preferred, is:

$$O_{1,1}$$
$$O_{2,1} / O_{2,2}$$
$$O_{1,2}$$

Notice that two outcomes are tied, that is, neither is preferred to the other.

What should we do? Before we can consider this question, we must ask ourselves what kind of decision-making situation we are in.

Types of Decision-Making Situations

1. We know for sure what the state of the world is: ***decision-making under certainty.***
2. We have no idea at all as to what is likely to happen: ***decision-making under uncertainty.***
3. We are in a position to estimate the likelihood of a given state of the world: ***decision-making under risk.***

Situations of the first sort are, one would think, relatively rare. Most of us greet the idea of a sure thing, whether it be in horse racing or almost anything else, with extreme skepticism. But we can say the following: if we were ever certain of all outcomes, there would be little trouble in deciding what to do. We would simply pick the action that had the highest-ranking outcome (or, if more than one action had a highest-ranking outcome, one of those actions). There may, however, be some familiar situations that we are prepared to treat as being cases of decision-making under certainty. Suppose your stereo is on and is distracting you from studying, but nonetheless you are really enjoying the music. You can get up and flip the switch to the off position, or you can stay seated and not flip the switch. Let us look at a chart for this situation:

Example 3	*1: State 1 of world*	*2: State 2 of world*
1: Flip switch	Stereo off: no distraction	Stereo still on: distraction
2: Don't flip switch	Stereo on: distraction	Stereo off: no distraction

Normally, we would take the world as being in state 1; that is, we would treat this as a case of decision-making under certainty. We would not normally consider the possibility that the power might go off or the stereo break down. We would characterize our choice of actions as leaving the stereo on or turning it off. We cannot here decide when, if ever, it is appropriate to treat a situation as a case of decision-making under certainty, but we can say that if it is such a situation, or one it is appropriate to treat as such, then we should choose the action with the highest-ranked outcome.

More commonly, though less often than we might suppose, we are in the situation that we called decision-making under uncertainty. Let us revisit an above example:

Example 1′	*1: Horse wins*	*2: Horse doesn't win*
1: Place bet	+$8	-$2
2: Don't place bet	No loss, no gain	No loss, no gain

We might know absolutely nothing about the chances of the horse; and if we know absolutely nothing, what should we do? If you think there is no single correct answer here, you are right. All we can do is note that there are various policies that might be followed.

We might initially ask how we can find the best choice of action, which we will characterize as the one yielding a state of the world in which one does better than is possible via any other action open to one, but no state of the world in which one would have done better by choosing any other action. Situations in which there is such a best choice are relatively rare. Note that example 1′ is not a case in which there is a best choice. If state 1 of the world obtains, that is the horse wins, we do indeed do better if we choose to bet. But if state 2 of the world obtains, that is the horse doesn't win, we would do better if we choose not to bet.

Here is an example of a case in which there is a best action: Suppose you are giving a dinner party. Some of the people may be vegetarians — you're not sure — but you know that all of the non-vegetarians are happy if served vegetarian food.

Example 4	1: Some are vegetarians	2: None are vegetarians
Serve a vegetarian dinner	All happy	All happy
Serve meat	Some happy, some unhappy	All happy

Here serving a vegetarian meal is the best choice. As noted, however, such situations are rare, so let us examine some policies to cover situations where there is no best choice.

Consider first:

The Pessimist

The pessimist chooses from those actions that have worst outcomes better than or equal to the worst outcomes of any other action.

In example 1', our horse race, the pessimist would choose not to bet. This is often spoken of as involving the **maximin criterion**. The *security level* of an action is simply the value of the lowest payoff for that action. So the maximin criterion tells us to choose the action which maximizes the minimum payoff (whence the name). But let us look at a slightly more complex example (here lower numbers represent better outcomes, so rank 1 is better than rank 2):

Example 5	1: State 1	2: State 2	3: State 3
1: Action A	Rank 2	Rank 4	Rank 4
2: Action B	Rank 3	Rank 4	Rank 4
3: Action C	Rank 1	Rank 5	Rank 5

If you are a pessimist you will choose action A. You might yourself be inclined to choose action C rather than action A on the grounds that it contains the best outcome. If so, you are most likely adhering to the following principle:

The Optimist

The optimist chooses from those actions that have outcomes better than or equal to the outcomes of any other action.

In example 5 an optimist would choose action *C,* as it contains the best outcome. Note that neither the pessimist nor the optimist has any guarantee that the world will be in state 1.

Consider now example 6:

Example 6	1: State 1	2: State 2	3: State 3
1: Action A	Rank 2	Rank 2	Rank 3
2: Action B	Rank 2	Rank 1	Rank 5
3: Action C	Rank 3	Rank 2	Rank 4

Here the optimist would choose action *B* and the pessimist action *A*. We have specified these situations, making decisions under uncertainty, as ones in which we have no idea what is likely to happen. Decision-making under risk, by contrast, involves choosing to act when we do have some idea as to the probabilities of outcomes. Let us now turn to the latter, keeping in mind that we can treat decision-making under uncertainty as like decision-making under risk if we treat the outcomes as equally probable.

1.2 / Decision-Making Under Risk

Hitherto we have ranked only outcomes, that is, we have specified only whether one outcome was better or worse than another. In order to study decision-making under risk, we need a bit more information. Consider the following: I rank eating a rare roast beef sandwich higher than eating a ham sandwich. I rank eating either higher than eating a cheese sandwich. And I rank all three of these higher than eating a peanut butter and banana sandwich. We might exhibit this ranking as follows:

> **Rank 1: Roast Beef**
> **Rank 2: Ham**
> **Rank 3: Cheese**
> **Rank 4: Peanut Butter and Banana**

This, however, fails fully to describe the situation. My preference for roast beef over ham is a slight one, not nearly so great as my preference for either over cheese. And I really consider a peanut butter and banana sandwich a desperation choice, acceptable only if facing imminent starvation. We will not suppose that we can specify this in quantitative terms involving 'units'; I cannot, for example, say that eating a roast beef sandwich gives me 3.5 units of enjoyment whereas eating a peanut butter and banana sandwich gives me only .05 units of enjoyment. But we will suppose that we assign numbers roughly representing the distance between the outcomes (with larger numbers representing higher-ranked alternatives). The preferences must meet certain other conditions if they are to be coherent, but we will not study these in any detail. (One main requirement is that the preferences be transitive.) But it is very important not to be impressed by the size of the numbers we choose. Our sandwich case might be represented as follows:

20:	**Roast Beef**	
19:	**Ham**	
12:	**Cheese**	
1:	**Peanut Butter and Banana**	

But from our standpoint that ranking is exactly the same as this one:

110:	**Roast Beef**	
105:	**Ham**	
70:	**Cheese**	
15:	**Peanut Butter and Banana**	

Our numerical rankings are, as the jargon goes, only unique up to positive linear transformations.

Now suppose that we are going to choose between two sandwich shops. It is late in the day, and we know from past experience that each shop will have only one kind of sandwich left. Let us first enter into a table the numbers we initially used to represent our ranking of the outcomes.

Example 7 Ranking	1: Roast Beef	2: Ham	3: Cheese	4: PBB
1: Go to shop A	20	19	12	1
2: Go to shop B	20	19	12	1

From past experience we are able to estimate, for each shop, the probability that a given kind of sandwich will be the one available.

Example 7 Probability	1: Roast Beef	2: Ham	3: Cheese	4: PBB
1: Go to shop A	30%	20%	40%	10%
2: Go to shop B	40%	10%	10%	40%

In each cell we multiply the number representing the ranking by the probability.

Example 7	1: Roast Beef	2: Ham	3: Cheese	4: PBB
1: Go to shop A	20 × .3 **6**	19 × .2 **3.8**	12 × .4 **4.8**	1 × .1 **.1**
2: Go to shop B	20 × .4 **8**	19 × .1 **1.9**	12 × .1 **1.2**	1 × .4 **.4**

We then add the results in each row, obtaining what we shall call the *expected value* of that action. We can now choose an action guided by the following principle:

Principle for Decision-Making Under Risk (Maximizing Expected Value)

Choose an action with a largest expected value.

We shall also speak of this directive as the policy of *maximizing expected value*. In example 7 the expected value of going to shop A is 14.7 and that of going to shop B is 11.5. Our principle tells us to choose to go to shop A, which decision has the largest expected value. Let us now look back at an earlier example, that of the party.

Example 2	1: One comes	2: Two come	3: Three come
1: Buy for one	Right amount	Short one	Short two
2: Buy for two	Waste of one	Right amount	Short one
3: Buy for three	Waste of two	Waste of one	Right amount

Suppose we rank the three alternatives in which we are exactly right as:

Right amount: **20**

and the other alternatives as:

Short one: **15**
Waste of one: **10**
Waste of two: **5**
Short two: **1**

Note that this is just a sample ranking. Different persons might rank the outcomes in different ways. Suppose that the probability that one comes is .3, that two come .5, and that three come .2. We are now in a position to use our principle to determine what to do.

Example 2	*1: One comes*	*2: Two come*	*3: Three come*
1: Buy for one	20 × .3 6	15 × .5 7.5	1 × ? .2
2: Buy for two	10 × .3 3	20 × .5 10	15 × .2 3
3: Buy for three	5 × .3 1.5	10 × .5 5	20 × .2 4

Adding along each row, we obtain an expected value of 13.7 for buying for one, of 16 for buying for two, and of 10.5 for buying for three. Given these rankings and these probabilities, our principle tells us to buy for two. Suppose that, with exactly the same probabilities, our ranking had instead been the following:

Right amount: **20**
Waste of one: **15**
Waste of two: **10**
Short one: **5**
Short two: **1**

A person who ranks the alternatives in this way will choose to buy for three, since it is the action with the largest expected value.

Let us look at another example of decision-making under risk before going on to explain why our decision principle is indeed a sensible one. Suppose we are trying to decide whether to raise funds for our favorite club. We can either hold a hamburger barbecue on the Student Union patio or sell burritos inside the Student Union building. As our concern is here to raise money, we can use monetary amounts as the basis for our value ranking. Whether the weather is good or bad we can expect to raise $100 from the sale of burritos. If the weather is good we can expect to raise $400 from the outdoor barbecue; if not good, we will barely break even, making only $10. Let us suppose that there is a 6/10 chance of rain.

Example 8	*Weather good*	*Weather not good*
Barbecue	$400 \times .4$ **160**	$10 \times .6$ **6**
Burritos	$100 \times .4$ **40**	$100 \times .6$ **60**

You, being a faithful adherent of maximizing expected value, push through the decision to have a barbecue. The expected value of the barbecue is, after all, 166, whereas the expected value of selling burritos is only 100. The fateful day comes and it rains. An emergency club meeting is held and you, after being subject to extreme criticism, are voted out of the club. Several members comment that the club could have made at least $100 in these circumstances had it opted to sell burritos. There are several points to be made here. First, it should be clear that maximizing expected value — this is what you did — does *not* in any way guarantee that you will do better in any particular case than if you had made some other decision. Here, you would have done better had you held the indoor sale. We shall discuss this kind of criticism below. Second, there is another kind of issue: we cannot invariably assume that monetary values, even in a case like this, give an accurate portrayal of the situation. Suppose the situation of the club was as follows. A profit of less than $30 would not allow the club to continue operating; it would have to shut down. We suppose that shutting down would be a disaster. Rather than ranking this outcome as +10, let us rate it as -100. (Our numbers, which indicate our valuation of the outcomes, need not in any simple way be based upon the amounts of money involved.) Let us suppose that if we raise $100 the club will survive, but just barely; we will rank this outcome as +100. And let us keep our ranking of the $400 as 400. But recall that these rankings are designed only to (roughly) represent the distance between the outcomes. This gives us:

Example 8	Weather good	Weather not good
Barbecue	400 × .4 **160**	-100 × .6 **-60**
Burritos	100 × .4 **40**	100 × .6 **60**

Here we have a tie — our alternatives have equal expected value — and our decision principle says there is nothing to choose between them. Some might still object, pushing for the burritos, but if they do, it is plausible to suppose that they rank the demise of the club as a much greater disaster than we have, as perhaps -1,000. If so, our decision principle would counsel them to choose the burritos.

Let us examine lotteries, keeping in mind the point that monetary value may not provide us with an adequate base for our value rankings. Lotteries of various sorts are very familiar to us, particularly since many governments now use them to raise money. Government involvement in lotteries has come under much criticism, as lotteries are, some claim, in effect a tax on the poor. It is not our task to discuss this issue, but to consider another claim: that it is somehow irrational ever to buy a lottery ticket. Here is one example of the way in which this argument typically proceeds. Suppose that the lottery is a fair one in which 1,000,000 tickets are issued. Each ticket costs $1. The organizers of the lottery take 10% to cover expenses and profits, so the prize is $900,000. Now let us suppose that we can represent the value rankings involved by the monetary amounts involved. (Note that "ticket A" is just a label for a ticket you do buy or would have bought.)

Example 9	Ticket A drawn	Ticket A not drawn
Buy ticket A	(900,000 -1) × .000001 **.899999**	-1 × .999999 **-.999999**
Do not buy	**0**	**0**

(Here we computed the expected monetary value by subtracting the cost of the ticket in each cell. Notice that this is equivalent to doing the following: Do not enter the cost of the ticket in the cell. Instead, enter the amount of the prize and subtract the cost of the ticket after adding the results in each cell. We would have had [900,000 × .000001] + [0 × .999999]. This is, of course, the same result, but doing it this way sometimes simplifies computations.)

Since 0 is greater than -.1, you should not buy a ticket. Any lottery of this sort will, if expected monetary value is a measure of expected value, be one in which you should not buy a ticket. The conclusion that some reach is that it is always irrational to buy a lottery ticket.

But that conclusion is based upon the mistaken supposition that expected monetary value is always the same as expected value. As we saw above in the case of the club, this is not so. I sometimes buy lottery tickets, and I am, or so I argue, not at all irrational in doing so. A lottery ticket costs $1. Having or not having that dollar in my wallet makes no difference to my life, so for me the outcomes of having a ticket that does not win and not having a ticket at all are for practical purposes the same. By contrast, having a winning ticket would make a vast difference to my life. Think of this as saying that the cost of the ticket is from my point of view no cost, just as the "cost" of not buying a ticket is no cost. In short, from my standpoint I have everything to gain and nothing to lose. This is properly represented in the following way:

Example 9	Ticket A drawn	Ticket A not drawn
Buy ticket A	(900,000 -1) × .000001 **.899999**	0 × .999999 **0**
Do not buy	**0**	**0**

If this is my value ranking, the correct decision for me is to buy a ticket.

Our decision principle is sometimes thought of as being somehow inherently selfish, as encouraging selfish decisions. This is simply a confusion. In any situation in which we find ourselves, we make a decision on the basis of our own value ranking of the outcomes, but our decision principle says nothing at all about *the factors on which these value rankings are based.*

Recall the club case: My interest in the club may arise from my desire to be praised for being a successful president. Or again, perhaps I just think the club is worthwhile. There is, in general, nothing to prevent altruism from influencing or even determining the values that we attach to outcomes. Put another way, the claim that we are selfish in maximizing expected value is a claim about the origin of our values; it is, perhaps, the claim that all values, all rankings of alternative outcomes, are in some sense based upon a desire for self-gratification. It is true that the rankings upon which we base our decisions are our own rankings, but this leaves it open why we have the values we do. It does not commit us to any particular claim about why we have those values; yet the claim that we are selfish is precisely a claim about why we have the values we do.

We have already noted that adhering to our decision principle need not give us the best result in any particular case. Why, then, do we support this principle? The first point to note is that we cannot act upon information we do not have. Imagine that I am deciding whether to wear my heavy coat when I go cross-country skiing. The forecast is for warm weather; there is only a very small chance that it will turn very cold. I decide not to wear my heavy, uncomfortable coat even though I know I will be very cold if the weather does turn bitter (though only for a short while). Even though I could take off my coat if the day remains warm, carrying it will be quite a burden. Let us suppose this table represents my position:

Example 10	*Weather not cold*	*Weather cold*
Wear coat	-10	20
Don't wear coat	20	-12

Let us suppose there is only a 10% chance of the weather turning cold. You take your coat and I do not. This might be explained by your finding the prospect of being cold much, much more distasteful than I. Let us suppose that the weather does turn cold. As we return from our trip, I shiver and you, basking in the warmth of your coat, adopt a superior smile. I cannot help but think that if only I had brought my coat … Was my decision wrong? If not, how can I show you that it was not wrong?

My decision might have been wrong in that I had forgotten how much I dislike being cold. That is, I might have misrepresented to myself my own attitudes toward being cold. But let us suppose that this is not so. The first point to note is that I can concede that, had I known it would turn cold, I would have worn my coat. But at the point at which we had to decide, neither you nor I knew that. I acted upon the best information I had, and acting upon that information led me not to wear my coat whereas, for some reason, you chose to take your coat. I cannot deny that in this case I would have been better off had I worn my coat but, as noted, I can say that I didn't know it would turn cold, though I did take that possibility into account when I introduced probabilities into my computation. What we can say in my defence is that in the long run, I will be better off following the policy of maximizing expected value than I would be if, for example, I always avoided the worst outcome regardless of its probability.

2 / Games

2.1 / Basic Theory — Zero-Sum Games

We are often in situations where we interact with others. The mathematical study of such situations is what has come to be known as *game theory*. Clearly "game" is being used in a very broad sense and is not to be understood to refer simply or even primarily to games such as Monopoly and poker. Our focus will be on two-person games. We shall typically represent such games with a chart such as the following:

Game 1	B_1	B_2
A_1	$O_{1,1}$	$O_{1,2}$
A_2	$O_{2,1}$	$O_{2,2}$

Here A_1 and A_2 represent the actions open to individual **a**, B_1 and B_2 those open to **b**. There may be any number of actions; we have simply illustrated the case where there are two. The $O_{i,j}$ represent as usual the outcomes, in this case the outcomes that occur given the particular actions chosen by the participants. We suppose that the individuals have preference rankings of the outcomes and are aware of the situation they are in. In particular each knows the other's preference ranking.

The first type of game we will look at is typically called **zero-sum** or **strictly competitive**. The primary characteristic of these games is that if **a** prefers one outcome to another, then **b** has the opposite preference. If **a** ranks two outcomes as the same, then so does **b**. Are there such games? Many games in the ordinary sense are at least meant to be strictly competitive. And, supposing that our preferences are strictly based upon money, many betting games are strictly competitive. Here is one very simple game.

Game 2	B_1	B_2
A_1	+1, -1	0, 0
A_2	0, 0	-1, +1

(The name "zero-sum" arose because in strictly competitive games there is always a numerical representation of the rankings such that the numbers sum to zero.)

But let us turn to another game.

Game 3	B_1	B_2	B_3	B_4
A_1	10	4	0	20
A_2	0	4	3	2
A_3	6	5	5	6
A_4	3	4	7	22

Notice that we have made only one entry for the outcomes. This we stipulate is for **a**. Since this is a zero-sum game the entries of **b** are simply **-n** where **n** is the entry for **a**. Let us speak of the choice of a particular action as a **pure strategy**. Notice that A_3 is the maximin choice for **a**. Let us look at **b**. For **b** B_2 is the choice that has the best security level. In the context of zero-sum games, where as above we enter positive numbers for the first player (taking for granted that the corresponding negative number could be used for the second player) it has become common to call the strategy that yields the best security level for the second player the **minimax** choice. If you look to the above chart you will see why. In picking the column with the lowest positive integers **b** is picking the column with the largest negative integers, that is, the column with the highest security level. The pair A_3, B_2 has a property that game theorists have found of extreme interest. It is a pair that is in **equilibrium**. To say of a pair that it is in equilibrium is to say two things:

(1) **Given that b will choose that action, a has no better choice.**

(2) **Given that a will choose that action, b has no better choice.**

Notice in the above example that, given that **a** is choosing A_3, the best choice for **b** is B_2.

Should we invariably choose an action that is a member of an equilibrium pair? The answer is yes if we know that our opponent is making such a choice. After all, if the opponent's choice is known, we cannot improve our position by making any other choice. But we may be in the situation that we described in the preceding section as uncertainty. If we are inveterately optimistic we might go for the action that has the highest potential reward. (Notice that in our current jargon that would be, for **a**, a maximax strategy.)

So long as we confine ourselves to pure strategies not all zero sum games have an equilibrium pair. Consider:

Game 4	B_1	B_2
A_1	16	32
A_2	24	8

If you check through this you should see that there is no equilibrium pair. For there to be such, there has to be an entry that is the minimum of its column and the maximum of its row. If it were not the minimum of the column, **b** would have reason to switch. If it were not the maximum of its row, then **a** would have reason to switch. But now let us introduce the notion of a **mixed strategy**. Suppose I decided to flip a coin and choose A_1 if it came up heads and A_2 if it came up tails. This is a mixed strategy. Notice that there are — potentially anyway — an infinite number of mixed strategies. But why would one ever choose a mixed strategy?

One reason is simply that in some cases mixed strategies increase our security level. Let us look back to the game that had no equilibrium pair.

Game 4	B_1	B_2
A_1	16	32
A_2	24	8

A_1 is the maximin choice for **a**. But suppose I choose the mixed strategy mentioned above (the 50-50 one). If **b** chooses B_1 I have a .5 chance of 16 and a .5 chance of 24 for a total of 20. If **b** chooses B_2 I have a .5 chance of 32 and a .5 chance of 8 for, again, a total of 20. So it would seem that I should adopt this mixed strategy rather than opting for the pure strategy of choosing A_1. However, at this point many people make the following claim. If I choose A_1 I am guaranteed at least 16. But if I adopt the mixed strategy I may get as little as 8. And surely this is bad.

We cannot here undertake a full defense of this mixed strategy as being better than the pure strategy. The problem is not fundamentally different from one we noticed in the preceding section. There we saw that maximizing *expected* value may leave us in a position whereby we obtain the outcome that we like least. The same is true here.

Now that we have introduced mixed strategies (we can view a pure strategy as a special case of a mixed strategy where the probability is equal to 1) we can go on to state the primary result of games theory. This result, typically known as the **minimax theorem**, is that in any zero-sum game there are always equilibrium pairs. These may be pairs of mixed strategy but they are in equilibrium in the same sense. That is, given the other's choice of a mixed strategy we have no better one.

2.2 / Non-Zero-Sum Games

Many games are not strictly competitive. Let us turn to a study of some of these. Perhaps the most famous of games is one that has come to be known as the prisoners' dilemma. The police have arrested two persons for a major crime. They do not have enough evidence to convict the prisoners of the major crime unless one confesses. But they can fabricate sufficient evidence for a conviction on a lesser charge if neither of the prisoners confesses. Let us suppose that if both confess both will be jailed for five years, as neither is in a 'special' position. If neither confesses they will both spend two years in jail. If one confesses and the other does not, the one who confesses will receive 6 months in jail and the other will receive 10 years in jail. Let us suppose that the preferences of each are directly related to the length of time he or she will spend in jail. So we can represent 10 years in jail as -10 and 6 months in jail as -1/2.

Prisoners' Dilemma	Confess	Don't Confess
Confess	-5, -5	-1/2, -10
Don't Confess	-10, -1/2	-2, -2

Note that this is not a zero-sum game. Each prefers neither confessing to both confessing. What will they do? Suppose I am A, the person on the left. If B confesses, I am clearly better off if I confess. And if B doesn't confess, I am clearly better off if I confess. In a situation such as this we will characterize the strategy of confessing as **dominant**. That is, it is my best response to any of the actions open to my opponent. Notice that B can reason in precisely the same way. So the police are quite confident that the prisoners will confess. If they do, they will each spend 5 years in jail. But clearly they both would prefer the outcome in which neither confesses. One might think that they could simply agree beforehand not to confess.

Prisoners' Dilemma	Break Agreement	Keep Agreement
Break Agreement	-5, -5	-1/2, -10
Keep Agreement	-10, -1/2	-2, -2

Notice that A can see that if B breaks the agreement A is better off to break it. And if B keeps the agreement A is better off to break it. B can reason in the same way. Situations that approximate to the prisoners' dilemma are

not uncommon in real life. OPEC (the Organization of Petroleum Export-
ing Countries) was created with a primary goal of keeping oil prices high
by way of the various countries limiting production. But it has been difficult for OPEC to function. (In part this is because not all oil-producing countries are members, but the problems would remain even if they were.) Here
is a simplified chart.

OPEC	Break Agreement (Unlimited Production)	Keep Agreement (Limited Production)
Break Agreement (Unlimited Production)	10, 10	21, 9
Keep Agreement (Limited Production)	9, 21	20, 20

The idea is as follows. If both break the agreement, the vast production will
lower the price and each will receive some amount of money that we have
labeled 10. If both severely restrict production, the price will rise dramatically and each will receive an amount of money that we have labeled 20. If
one severely restricts but the other doesn't, the one who doesn't will reap
the benefits of the other's production limitation. Even though the price is
higher than it would have been had neither limited production, the country
that is still severely restricting production will not receive as much as it would
receive were it to move to unlimited production. As you can see, this is a
prisoners' dilemma. That the real OPEC situation is somewhat similar may
explain why OPEC has a tendency to destabilize.

Many suggestions have been made to 'resolve' the prisoners' dilemma
and many arguments regarding the 'significance' of it have been presented.
Some have suggested that it shows the need for a mechanism wherein
agreements can be made binding, perhaps via the introduction of sanctions.
Others have suggested that it provides a partial account of why and when
a 'government' is needed. Yet others have suggested that it provides the
basis for an account of what morality is and why it is necessary. The idea
here is that by accepting some sort of moral code we are able to 'escape'
prisoners' dilemmas and thereby gain. We will not here pursue these suggestions further.

Some have suggested that the prisoners' dilemma arises because people are in some important sense 'selfish'. It is true that the examples we gave were ones in which the individuals did consider only themselves. But this is not in general true. These types of situation can arise even among persons who are concerned with others. Suppose I care little about how well I do, but a lot about how well you do. The same is true of you. The following chart abstractly represents the situation:

Altruists' Dilemma	B_1	B_2
A_1	10, 10	21, 9
A_2	9, 21	20, 20

If I do A_1 and you do B_1 we each receive $10. If I do A_2 and you do B_2 we each receive $20. Each of us simply gives the other what we make. If I do A_2 and you do B_1 I receive $9 and you receive $21. Remember that in this situation our preferences are directly related not to how much I make but how much the other makes. So my valuation of this outcome is 9 while yours is 21. If I do A_1 and you do B_2 you will receive $9 and I will receive $21. Notice that this is a prisoners' dilemma. Here we will end up with $O_{1,1}$ even though this is not the best result. Could such a situation arise? Yes, they can. Granted, this particular example is 'unrealistic', but it exhibits the point that a prisoners' dilemma is a certain structure. It does not matter whether the preferences are based upon concern for oneself or concern for others.

When we are involved in a game that is not strictly competitive there are often potential benefits arising from cooperation, in effect from the adoption of some joint strategy, typically a mixed strategy. Whether these can be reached by persons on their own or whether outside enforcement is required is a question that we will not consider. It has also been claimed that the theory of games can shed some light upon bargaining situations and upon questions regarding fair divisions of gains. We will quickly take a look at these claims.

Let us first see how it is that cooperation can introduce the possibility of gains not otherwise available. Consider any chart of the following sort:

Cooperation	B_1	B_2
A_1	10, 5	0, 0
A_2	0, 0	5, 10

Notice that neither player, on her own, can ensure the avoidance of the mutually undesirable outcomes. But by agreeing to a joint strategy of, for example, deciding between A_1 and B_1, and A_2 and B_2 by the flip of a fair coin, both have an expected value greater than that of any individual strategy. Here we might well take it as obvious that this is the 'fair solution'. This is particularly true if we think of the chart as representing the following situation. The alternatives are going to a movie and watching TV. I like movies, you like TV. But both of us like doing things together. However, this may not be as obvious as we think. Suppose the situation is one in which in the outcome $O_{1,1}$ a receives a grand prize which is something he has desired all his life whereas **b** receives the second prize. In the outcome $O_{2,2}$ **b** receives the grand prize and **a** receives the second prize. But, as we might put it, the grand prize does not 'mean' as much to **b** as it does to **a**. Our account does not consider such factors. Our numbers do *not* capture any sort of notions of 'units' of value or pleasure. Nor do they enable us to make any interpersonal comparisons of the sort we had in mind in saying that the grand prize means more to **a** than to **b**. Look at the following chart:

Cooperation	B_1	B_2
A_1	1000, 5	0, 0
A_2	0, 0	500, 10

Do not think that this chart somehow shows that we should favor **a**. As we noted in Section 1, this chart reflects a situation similar to the preceding one. The absolute values of the numbers are simply not significant.

These problems aside, we can examine some claims that might be defensible. If cooperation is to make sense then presumably we must expect to be better off if we cooperate or agree to some kind of arbitration. Why should I cooperate, for example, if I do not attain to a security level at least equal to that which I have on my own? And surely an arbitrated solution is not a good one if there is an available solution preferred by both parties. However, such constraints as these do not uniquely determine a solution. Theorists have gone on to make various suggestions. But a study of these is beyond the scope of this text.

Chapter Summary

In Section 1 we discussed decision-making. In 1.1 we looked at reasonable ways of making decisions. We identified various types of decision-making situations.

Types of Decision-Making Situations

1. We know for sure what the state of the world is: *decision-making under certainty*.
2. We have no idea at all as to what is likely to happen: *decision-making under uncertainty*.
3. We are in a position to estimate the likelihood of a given state of the world: *decision-making under risk*.

In the case of certainty, we simply choose the action with the preferable outcome; in the case of uncertainty, we have two policies to choose from. We can choose between a pessimistic stance:

The Pessimist

The pessimist chooses from those actions that have worst outcomes better than or equal to the worst outcomes of any other action.

We noted that this is sometimes spoken of as involving the use of the *maximin criterion*. An action with a highest *security level* is chosen. We then looked at:

The Optimist

The optimist chooses from those actions that have outcomes better than or equal to the outcomes of any other action.

We then turned, in 1.2, to decision-making under risk, advocating the following principle:

Principle for Decision-Making Under Risk (Maximizing Expected Value)

Choose an action with a largest expected value.

To the various outcomes we assigned numbers representing the values of those outcomes, and the rough distance (in value) between them. We then obtained the expected value of an outcome by, first, multiplying the probability of a given state of the world by the number representing the value of that outcome and, second, adding the results in each row. This gives us the *expected value* of the action in question. We spoke of this principle as expressing a policy of *maximizing expected value*.

In Section 2 we turned to the theory of games. In 2.1 we looked at *zero-sum* or *strictly competitive* games. The primary characteristic of these games is that if **a** prefers one outcome to another then **b** has the opposite preference. We saw that such games could be represented by charts like the following:

Game 4	B_1	B_2
A_1	16	32
A_2	24	8

Here the number represents the result for **a**. Since the game is a zero-sum one, the entries for **b** would simply be the negatives of these. So **a** achieves her best security level with a *maximin* choice, one that maximizes the minimum in a column. **b** achieves his best security level by a *minimax* choice, one that minimizes the maximum in a row. We noted that some zero-sum games have an *equilibrium* pair. This is a pair such that:

(1) Given that b will choose that action, a has no better choice.

(2) Given that a will choose that action, b has no better choice.

We then introduced the notion of a *mixed strategy*. Rather than picking an action directly we utilize a chance device such as a coin and will, for example, choose one action if heads comes up, another if tails comes up. We noted but did not prove that if mixed strategies are admitted every zero-sum game has at least one equilibrium pair.

In 2.2 we examined games that are not strictly competitive. In particular we gave an example of a prisoners' dilemma:

Prisoners' Dilemma	Confess	Don't Confess
Confess	-5, -5	-1/2, -10
Don't Confess	-10, -1/2	-2, -2

We noted that there are some 'real-world' cases that seem at least to approximate to being prisoners' dilemmas. Some theorists have argued that the existence of these shows one role that governments might play.

We then looked at some situations wherein the players could benefit from cooperation. Many theorists have suggested various criteria that would specify a fair way of dividing these benefits, and, what is much the same, a fair way for an arbitrator to determine a solution.

Index